MW00565196

GENDER MAGIC

GENDER MAGIC

LIVE SHAMELESSLY,
RECLAIM YOUR JOY, AND STEP
INTO YOUR MOST AUTHENTIC SELF

RAE McDANIEL, MEd, LCPC, CST

New York Boston

The tools and information presented herein are not intended to replace the services of trained mental health professionals, or be a substitute for medical or mental health advice. You are advised to consult with your health care professional with regard to matters relating to your physical or mental health, and in particular regarding matters that may require diagnosis or medical attention.

Details relating to the author's life are reflected faithfully to the best of their ability, while recognizing that others who were present might recall things differently. Many names and identifying details have been changed to protect the privacy and safety of others, including clients who shared their stories for this book.

Balance
Hachette Book Group
1290 Avenue of the Americas
New York, NY 10104
GCP-Balance.com
Twitter.com/GCPBalance
Instagram.com/GCPBalance

First Edition: May 2023

Balance is an imprint of Grand Central Publishing. The Balance name and logo are trademarks of Hachette Book Group, Inc.

The publisher is not responsible for websites (or their content) that are not owned by the publisher.

The Hachette Speakers Bureau provides a wide range of authors for speaking events. To find out more, go to hachettespeakersbureau.com or email HachetteSpeakers@hbgusa.com.

Balance books may be purchased in bulk for business, educational, or promotional use. For information, please contact your local bookseller or the Hachette Book Group Special Markets Department at special.markets@hbgusa.com.

I Want / I Wonder Dance Party on page 133 adapted from Lucie Fielding, *Trans Sex: Clinical Approaches to Trans Sexualities and Erotic Embodiments* (New York: Routledge, 2021).

Library of Congress Cataloging-in-Publication Data
Names: McDaniel, Rae, author.
Title: Gender magic : live shamelessly, reclaim your joy, and step into your most authentic self / Rae McDaniel, MEd, LCPC, CST.
Description: First edition. | New York, NY : Balance, [2023] |
Identifiers: LCCN 2022057858 | ISBN 9781538724897 (hardcover) | ISBN 9781538724910 (ebook)
Subjects: LCSH: Sexual minorities. | Gender identity. | Self-acceptance.
Classification: LCC HQ73 .M358 2023 | DDC 306.76—dc23/eng/20230111
LC record available at https://lccn.loc.gov/2022057858

ISBNs: 978-1-5387-2489-7 (Hardcover); 978-1-5387-2491-0 (ebook)

Printed in the United States of America

LSC-C

Printing 1, 2023

For Elise Malary (March 29, 1990–March 17, 2022).
We only briefly met, but your loss and your legacy continue to send ripples through the Chicago transgender community and beyond. Thank you for reminding me of my why. You deserved the world, and the world was better with you in it.

I hope this book creates a little magic to make it possible for women like you—unapologetic, joyful, passionate, and kind—to thrive.

Contents

A Note on Language and Client Stories

Language, especially related to gender identity and expression, is dynamic. It changes quickly, and there are often different opinions within the transgender and non-binary communities about what words feel the best and most affirming. I am not the final word on language or definitions. I have done my best in this book to use the most up-to-date, affirming, and inclusive language. However, there might be language used within this book that doesn't resonate with everyone, and as with most books speaking to and about transgender/non-binary folks, the language I use today might be the outdated language of tomorrow.

For example, I've also chosen to use the word "folks" instead of "folx." While some transgender and non-binary individuals feel that "folx" is more intentionally inclusive of diverse gender identities, others prefer using "folks" since it is also a gender-neutral term.

You'll also notice that I refer to those under the trans umbrella as transgender/non-binary in some sentences but separate the identities in other moments. I do this intentionally. In my work with clients, one of the most common things I hear from non-binary folks is that they don't feel "trans enough" based on the cultural emphasis on binary trans identities. Many non-binary people also feel self-conscious and fear being perceived as a fraud when entering explicitly transgender spaces. This is especially true for non-binary individuals who choose not to significantly alter their physical appearance.

By varying my usage of "transgender/non-binary" and "transgender and non-binary," I want to be clear that, while there is a distinction between the identities and often different lived experiences, both binary and non-binary transgender individuals exist under the larger transgender umbrella, whether or not the term "transgender" resonates personally. Both identities may or may not include medical transition.

This book is the beginning of what I believe is a paradigm-shifting conversation, but it is not the end. I'm committed to continuing to learn, grow, and strengthen my work as a clinician, coach, writer, and educator, and I invite you to reach out to me on www.gendermagic.com with any upgrades, and I will do my best to revise future editions of this book.

As a therapist and a coach, I know confidentiality's importance for my clients.

I also know hearing stories about how others have navigated gender exploration, expansion, and transition is powerful and helps you see how to put these ideas into action.

For this reason, I've included stories as I can while still protecting my clients' privacy. These stories often do not represent singular living, breathing individuals I've worked with. Instead, I've taken themes, patterns, and conversations I've had with *many* clients over the years and mashed them up to create a new character. Occasionally, I got explicit permission to use parts of someone's story.

In general, details may be changed and identities protected, but any stories you see in these pages are true.

You can find more resources and information on topics in this book at www.gendermagic.com.

INTRODUCTION

Transition Isn't the Point

When you grow up as the adopted child of fundamentalist Christian traveling puppeteer missionaries from the Deep South, becoming a non-binary, queer gender and sex therapist, coach, and speaker isn't the outcome you expect.

The journey to my non-binary identity was like discovering I'd been walking around in shoes a half size too small. Until I was almost thirty, I didn't notice how uncomfortable and constricted I felt in my assigned gender as a woman, but after decades limping around with blisters, my cramped toes screaming for relief, something had to give. Over the next five years, I started going by a different name, using they/them pronouns, taking low-dose testosterone, and I had top surgery.

Walking in shoes that fit was a revelation, but putting on the right-size shoes isn't the point of this metaphor. The point is this: Instead of hobbling around trying to put Band-Aids on my blisters, I could finally dance and run and climb without pain. My feet weren't distracting me from doing all the things I loved.

Learning to authentically articulate and express our gender in whatever way feels good to us deserves celebration as a fundamental part of personal growth and self-discovery. Throughout my journey and the journeys of hundreds of clients, friends, and community members, I've seen gender exploration and transition be a place of joy, pleasure, and profound intimacy with ourselves and the chosen families we build around us.

Whether you're transgender, non-binary, cisgender, or any other diverse gender identity from across the globe* gender is a powerful force in life, dictating how we experience the world and ourselves. The power of knowing who you are and living as your true self without shame isn't easy, and there's a reason the societal narrative about exploring gender identity is negative, restrictive, and downright scary.

According to the Human Rights Campaign, thirty-three states within the United States passed or proposed over one hundred anti-trans bills in 2021 alone, with over two hundred anti-LGBTQ+ bills still in the works at the end of 2022, often targeting children who want to explore a gender that's different from their sex assigned at birth.[1]

As transgender individuals become more visible in mainstream media and the conversation about transgender and non-binary identity and rights advances in Western culture, there is a backlash from those who feel their sense of reality threatened by a new understanding of gender, those who have objections to the idea of gender identity as a cultural construct rooted in white supremacy and reductive understandings of religious texts, and those who are unwilling to update their understanding of gender because it causes the discomfort that comes with change. The hate that stems from fear and discomfort often, tragically, ends in violence directed toward transgender individuals, especially transgender women of color.[2] While we are making great strides in visibility, this does not always equate to safety.

We contend with systemic barriers and gatekeeping in the medical and mental health fields, housing discrimination, workplace discrimination, microaggressions, and the constant gendering experienced while walking around in the world—all of which are sources of trauma and an exhausting burden on trans folks. Additionally, many transgender/non-binary people live at the intersection of multiple oppressed identities, including but not limited to race, ability and disability, neurodivergence, citizenship, and class, and simply existing becomes an act of resilience.

---

* Including but not limited to indigenous identities such as Two-Spirit, hijra, fa'afafine, and mak nyah.

I am not here to ignore these facts.

And yet. Gender transition does not *have* to center on anxiety, self-doubt, systemic harms, and distress. When suffering is the uniting banner for trans folks, it creates a culture where many transgender support groups, community discussions, forums, and even scientific research center on the experience of suffering. Is it important to help ease suffering for transgender folks? Absolutely yes. But if we focus *only* on easing suffering, we're assuming that relief is the best thing a transgender or non-binary person can hope to achieve in their life. We lose out on the opportunity to connect on experiences like the joy of creative expression, pleasure in all its forms, laughing till we pee, and fiercely celebrating each other.

As a certified gender and sex therapist, I know from working with hundreds of clients that, while the barriers and discrimination we face are impactful and sometimes difficult to navigate, gender transition can be incredibly positive. For the clients I work with, discovering and embodying who they truly are is empowering. Transition can be a time to explore yourself and build community.

More and more, I'm seeing people, both cis and trans, stepping out of the box they were assigned at birth and celebrating who they are. In media, trans and non-binary actors and identities are being positively represented on shows like *Pose*, *Sense8*, and *The Politician*. And—gasp—sometimes the plot isn't even about them being transgender/non-binary! We get to experience the delight gender freedom brings when a Black woman who is transgender writes a *New York Times* bestselling memoir, when a cisgender man wears a dress on the cover of *Vogue* or to the Oscars, or when a non-binary individual clips earrings onto a popular talk show host.[3]

Many folks are hungry to learn more in order to be supportive, both personally and professionally. We are finding new ways to better affirm transgender identities, and many people are beginning to understand that gender is not a binary.

It's a revolution, and it's ongoing.

In the United States, and many other cultures worldwide, society doesn't celebrate the vast diversity of gender identities and expressions. Folks who dare to express their gender in unexpected ways are often ridiculed into compliance with restrictive norms of what we consider masculine or feminine. In many cases, people who are transgender and non-binary experience discrimination, are told their identities are invalid, and experience emotional and physical harm for simply existing.

The typical cultural narrative we hear of a transgender person's journey to actualization doesn't help. It goes something like this:

Once upon a time, there was a child. From a young age, they did things like putting on Mom's heels, which was against the "rules" for their sex assigned at birth. Their parents shamed and punished them, and the child shut down a part of themselves, burying it deep. As the child went through puberty and their body changed, they felt like they were in the wrong body. Something was wrong with them, but they couldn't quite put their finger on what. Anxiety and depression crept in as they struggled to feel comfortable and fit in at school, and they started cutting to try to manage their big feels.

The child grew up and realized what they were experiencing was gender dysphoria. They were transgender. This realization rocked their world, sending them spiraling into intense fear, self-hatred, self-doubt, and debilitating anxiety. Eventually, they medically, legally, and socially transitioned their gender to a binary transgender identity. Every step of the process was overwhelming and confusing.

"Post-transition," the allies of the world called them "brave" and "inspirational." But at the end of the day, they are alone, underemployed, and struggle to feel valid in their identity.

I've heard this story—or something very much like it—from dozens of my clients over the years. I don't want to minimize anyone's story if this is your experience. It's real, and it happens.

But here's the truth: This narrative sucks.

If lifelong struggle with no potential for joy is the only experience we have to look forward to, no wonder exploring and transitioning your gender is so anxiety provoking!

This narrative also assumes (again) that suffering is a cornerstone of transition and that all transgender folks identify with a binary gender and want gender-affirming surgeries, making those who don't see themselves in this story feel not "trans enough."

As a non-binary person and transgender inclusion and diversity speaker, I know the obstacles we face. I have a PowerPoint slide about the disproportionate rates of violence against transgender individuals, Black transgender women, and transgender women of color in particular. Every single year since I started speaking on this topic in 2016, I have updated that slide to say the current year was the highest year on record for violence against transgender people. Suicidal ideation and death by suicide is also disproportionally high in the transgender population. A study by the Williams Institute reports that 98 percent of study respondents expressed suicidal ideation after four or more experiences of discrimination and violence in a year (many transgender people experience four or more microaggressions or aggressions *a week*) and 51 percent of them attempted suicide that year.[4]

Given these stats, it's easy to see why harm-reduction strategies (by which I mean things like STI prevention, suicide prevention, housing, and anti-violence work) become the focus of support for folks exploring and transitioning their gender. These strategies are important and necessary. However, we need something more. We need a new model for gender transition.

Hell, we need a new model for gender.

One that acknowledges the intersecting identities and systemic oppression of marginalized groups and myriad ways that culture and a binary gender system make existence as a transgender or non-binary person difficult AND one that celebrates gender exploration and expansion as an exciting place of growth, individually as well as systemically.

We need a narrative of gender exploration, expansion, and transition that is hopeful and full of ease, curiosity, joy, and pleasure. A narrative that centers on gender freedom and gives transgender/non-binary folks room to thrive.

Exploring gender is a natural, critical part of becoming ourselves fully, wholly, and authentically. And you, reader, deserve space and support to do that exploring and to be celebrated for who you are.

Gender Transition Isn't the Point of This Book

The point of this book is for you, me, all of us, to experience the freedom to identify and express our gender intentionally and genuinely. The world is better when people are walking around as their most lit-up selves, and we are not truly free until we are *all* free to live authentically in the world.

For trans/non-binary folks, gender transition is about focusing on gender intensely for a time so they can go on and live their life as the boldest shame-free, actualized version of themselves possible. In other words, they want to live a life where gender dysphoria, or a sense of incongruence about their gender identity or expression, no longer defines their days.

One client captured this idea best, saying, *Why would I transition my gender and not transition the rest of my life?*

Let's be clear: I'm not here to erase or minimize the painful and challenging aspects of living as a queer and transgender person. I will not "love and light" the way through gender transition, painting a rosy view of what transition can look like. But I do want to imagine a bolder, more audacious future where the narrative of gender transition also includes ease, joy, and curiosity.

My goal is to shift the conversation about gender transition to one of play, pleasure, and possibility.

The Gender Freedom Model

After working for five years as a therapist and chief operating officer at a sizeable LGBTQ+ counseling center in Chicago, I started my private therapy practice, Practical Audacity, focusing on gender and sex therapy work. I had eighteen clients my first week and had a waiting list in under two months. My practice quickly grew to five clinicians, then ten, and in year five, as I write this book, we have twenty-one clinicians with over one thousand new client requests a year, often exceeding our ability to provide services.

As I continued to focus my work on the intersections of gender identity and sexuality, I noticed my transgender/non-binary/gender-questioning clients were all struggling with similar things. In short, gender transition felt like an overwhelming, anxiety-producing process full of confusion and self-doubt. Like a slog through the mud in the middle of a thunderstorm.

So, I started to ask the question differently. Rather than focusing on mitigating the risk factors of not being a cisgender person, I wondered, How do we make gender transition a place of joy, curiosity, self-growth, and pleasure? I researched, looking at studies on how LGBTQ+ and transgender/non-binary folks experience identity exploration, coming out, anxiety, depression, trauma, and sexuality. I explored research in strengths-based positive psychology, adult play, resiliency, effective coping skills, and sex therapy. I pulled from interdisciplinary literature on human-centered design thinking, educational theory, and coaching theory, among many others.

Listening to my clients' struggles helped me notice patterns in how they were thinking about gender transition, taking up space, and navigating being transgender/non-binary people in our world. I read about transgender and non-binary experiences online, reflected on my journey and my friends' journeys, and took lots of notes. And after months of a living room scattered with note cards, sticky notes posted everywhere, and a very annoyed roommate, I distilled everything I was learning into a framework—the Gender Freedom Model—that has become the basis of my work and this book.

The Gender Freedom Model is a framework of key concepts, mindsets, and skills to facilitate gender exploration, grounded in three pillars: play, pleasure, and possibility.[5] Using this model has helped both me and my clients see hope for a better, more authentic future in a practical way, giving folks the tools, resources, and encouragement they need to take up space in the world, knowing the world is a better place when they do.

Most models related to gender transition follow a linear path of identity confusion, exploration, and reflection (including childhood and adolescent gender nonconformity); discovering a transgender/non-binary identity; disclosures to significant others; gender-expression exploration, including social/legal/medical transition; and finally, integrating their trans identity into their life with pride. This is a useful framework for the people who follow this path, but many of my clients and I feel this path is restrictive and doesn't reflect everyone's experience of gender exploration. I'm not looking to replace these more linear models, but I *would* like to expand the conversation.

The goal of the Gender Freedom Model isn't to give you a step-by-step guide to discovering your gender identity. What it will give you are the mindsets, tools, and support you need to follow whatever path gender exploration takes you down.

I often think of it this way: On a solo trip to Lisbon, I wandered through the steep, winding streets in the oldest part of town. Street signs were few, and alleyways led to delicious tiny restaurants and bars seating no more than five or ten people at a time. Around dinnertime, I sat down in one of these hidden gems and ate fresh fish, chatting with hand motions and drawings on napkins to the older French couple sitting beside me. I listened delightedly as the cook, the grumpy old lady glaring at me from the street, and about a dozen other guest singers serenaded us with fado, the melancholy soul music of Portugal. I didn't know where I was, or how to get back to my hotel or what was next. But I didn't care. Because at the moment, I didn't want to be anywhere else in the world.

The Gender Freedom Model is like that experience. It's not Google Maps, directing your way through unfamiliar streets. Rather, it's a travelogue, inviting you to come along on a journey of curiosity, awe, and discovery, where part of the joy is in not knowing exactly where you'll end up. You'll take in the moments of wonder, connection, and ease along the way, knowing that wherever you are, that's where you're supposed to be.

My Story

Everyone starts somewhere.

And sometimes that "somewhere" is a swamp with puppets.

I grew up in a small Louisiana town. Bayous, Spanish moss, nutria rats (think a cross between a beaver and a rat), and cottonmouth snakes. Home of Tim McGraw and *True Blood*.

In an unusual plot twist, when I was nine years old, my dad brought home a puppet and declared God called him to be a missionary. I was an odd and relatively isolated kid, so I joined him in his new hobby. My mom was peer-pressured to join us soon after. While the other kids sang pageant-style renditions of The Chicks' "There's Your Trouble" in the middle school talent show, I walked on stage with a bird puppet. I was about as popular as you might imagine.

Pretty soon, we went on the road full-time to share the gospel of Jesus Christ all over the United States. With puppets. We lived in motels, a race-car trailer with no bathroom, and finally (thankfully), a motor home. We performed four nights a week in churches, schools, and summer camps with crowds ranging from twenty to a thousand, moving every week for five years of my life.

Most people saw my six-foot-two dad as a quirky, goofy guy who made fart jokes and pulled pranks. Appearances were everything to him. He was especially concerned about any hint of "gayness." While casual homophobia is far from unusual in the South, my dad's version scorched the earth behind it.

My high-school boyfriend wore a pair of skinny jeans to a church performance and my dad deemed the pants too gay to function, despite my boyfriend being in a heterosexual (ha!) relationship with me. He loomed over me, whisper-yelling and poking his finger into my chest repeatedly behind the puppet stage curtain minutes before I had to perform, now shaking, in front of hundreds of people. He once threw out a closet full of dress shirts because he discovered the previous owner was gay, making jokes about catching HIV from them.

I went to a tiny Baptist college in the woods of East Texas, where being an out member of the LGBTQ+ community was an offense risking expulsion if the wrong people found out. My best friends became the theater kids who were some of the only out-ish gay men on campus. We had sleepovers in my apartment, just far enough off the main campus that the school didn't bother us. We stayed up late watching Disney movies and *Buffy* with some god-awful, cheap blue liquor. I wasn't yet out as queer (even to myself), but for the first time in my life, I wasn't walking on eggshells.

I watched my friends come out to religious families, get into relationships, and deal with a healthy dose of self-loathing and internalized shame from the homophobic environment we were all stuck in. Between my sophomore and junior years of college, something big shifted in me. Simply living your life shouldn't be as hard as it was for my friends. A supposed god of love who inspired such hatefulness toward other humans, who inspired my friends (and me) to believe we were broken and wrong, no longer made sense to me.

Around this time, my parents visited my tiny college apartment and saw a singular Corona beer in my fridge. Along with my nose ring, tattoos, and apparent drift away from the church, this confirmed their worst fears about me. I was destined for a life of sin—lost. "I failed as a parent," I read on my mom's lips, not quite hearing her through the ringing in my ears and the sobs I was holding my breath to keep in. I turned to stone to get through my dad's tirade with my chin up. They disowned me, cutting me off financially. I had enough financial aid and work to finish college, but it would be a year before I spoke to my mom again, two years before I saw my dad.

Along the way, I fell in love with psychology. People fascinated me, and I wanted my friends to feel less pain while exploring their sexuality and identities. So I began my journey to be a therapist who worked with the LGBTQ+ community. I got accepted into a graduate school in Chicago and ran screaming from the Deep South.

Lumbering along in my U-Haul down Lake Shore Drive in Chicago, I looked at the lake, the closest thing to an ocean I'd ever lived near. I looked at the skyline. And I took the deepest breath I'd taken in my whole life. Something settled in me, and something shifted. Free from an oppressive religious environment for the first time, my latent queerness felt less like a new discovery and more like an obvious inevitability.

Within a few months, my then husband helped me pack yet another U-Haul, this time just for me, and I moved into a tiny apartment on the other side of town with a mutual friend who had just come out as transgender a few months earlier. While painful, our split was amicable as we sent each other on our own journeys, and he remains one of my biggest supporters.

The next few years were full of messy experimentation and messier relationships as I explored my newfound queerness.

When my parents came through for a visit several years after "Coronagate," they refused to set foot in my apartment once they knew my roommate was trans. They've never made it past the entryway of my home in the ten-plus years since. This experience gave me a not-unexpected preview of their feelings about transgender folks.

I dreaded coming out to my parents as queer, so I put it off for a while but finally had The Conversation. As I shared my queer identity with my mom on the phone, my dad snatched the phone away from her to tell me to stay away from his family and his wife and threatened me with a restraining order. My world stopped, but I mopped the snot dripping down my face and sat down in my therapist chair for a full day of sessions helping other people navigate their queer identities.

Just when I thought I had myself all figured out, a little tickle started about my gender. Some people have lightbulb moments about their identity. My journey felt more like a gentle stretch in the morning: an opening up and a gradual awakening. I'm privileged to live in a giant blue dot of a city, and by the time I came out as non-binary, I had a chosen family and queer community, a supportive partner, financial independence, and self-employment. These things allowed me to explore my gender in a way that didn't feel pressured.

I know this kind of ease isn't everyone's story of gender exploration. And I also understand what it's like to experience rejection, pain, and consequences in the journey to my queer and non-binary identities. I see you. And I've got you.

In fact, you're the reason I wrote this book.

Who This Book Is For

If you've changed clothes a thousand times because nothing feels right, worried about being a fraud, sobbed while wondering if you'll be alone forever, felt the outrageous joy of being seen and accepted for who you are, I see you.

Maybe you're transgender/non-binary and tired of gender transition (or simply existing as a trans person) feeling like a never-ending dentist appointment. Perhaps you're questioning your gender and in dire need of some clarity. Maybe you're cisgender, and you feel trapped by the intense gendered expectations of our society. This book is for anyone who feels like society has stuffed them into a tiny box of assigned gender and is gasping for air.

Or maybe you picked up this book because you want to support a child, loved one, employee, client, or colleague on their gender journey.

Whatever brought you here, I invite you to read this book not only to gain empathy and understanding for the transgender/non-binary folks in your life, but to gain a deeper understanding of the ways assigned gender (and all the expectations that go with it) has affected *your* life.

Whether you are transgender, non-binary, or cisgender, this book will help you unlock and experience your gender in fresh ways.

Some Caveats

I am white, queer, thin, androgynous, chronically ill, neurodivergent, highly educated and credentialed, a US citizen, transgender/non-binary, and a survivor of emotional and religious abuse. I'm also a business owner in a liberal city who holds a leadership position. These intersecting identities both help and hinder my work in different ways. I benefit from structures, including whiteness, power, and capitalism, that have caused immense harm, especially to trans folks, BIPOC folks, disabled folks, and many other identities that are not cisgender, straight, white males.

I strive to be aware of my privilege and how it impacts my work and perspective. It is my intention and work to write this book from an intersectional frame. However, I know I still have gaps I am not yet aware of. I also cannot claim any special knowledge on the lived experience of transgender people of color or folks who exist outside of the paradigm of gender diversity within the white, Westernized United States culture, including Indigenous communities that live within the now United States.

The Journey Ahead

I divided this book into three parts based on the pillars of the Gender Freedom Model: play, pleasure, and possibility.

In part 1, I'll show you how adopting an attitude of play during gender exploration can immediately turn down the volume on anxiety, self-doubt, and fear. I'll review some basics of gender to get us all on the same page and introduce some key mindset shifts and tools necessary to explore gender with more ease. We'll dive into how tiny steps and experiments can help you discover more of your authentic self (whether or not that includes social/legal/medical transition), and I'll give you questions to ask yourself, practical advice, and methods for making decisions about things like medical transition, name changes, and coming out.

The second part of the book will delve into pleasure, sex, and relationships. I'll show you how to design intimate relationships of all kinds (including your relationship with yourself!) and create a sex life that lights you up and makes you feel wholly seen. You'll also learn how to find pleasure in your body today, even if you want to change that body in the future, knowing that we don't need to love every part of our body to be kind to it. After all, pleasure is a portal—full of energy and life—that connects us to ourselves and others, giving us fuel to create the world we dream of.

And finally, in part 3, we will imagine the possibility of a future worth having—because gender doesn't exist in a vacuum. From a nourishing chosen family network to intentionally designing a life that lights you up, I'll give you questions to consider and practical tools to help you make that future happen. Pride is our final topic, but not in a rainbow-float kind of way. Rather, pride is actively working to create the world we want to live in, based on pleasure and joy.

Throughout, you'll find prompts for reflection and invitations to take action. Because here's the thing: I want you to feel relief, inspiration, and affirmation, but most of all, I want you to walk away from this book changed. And that can only happen when you start trying new behaviors, new ways of talking to yourself, and new ways of existing in the world.

Exploring your gender identity and expression is a beautiful, generative process that takes time. Remember there is no rush. There is no arrival. There's only becoming.

If you feel confused, anxious, or full of self-doubt related to your gender identity and expression, here's what I want you to know right now:

- You are trans enough.
- You are not a burden.
- You are worthy.
- Your identity is valid.
- You are lovable.
- You are beautiful.
- The world is better with you in it.

I've supported dozens of individual and group therapy and coaching clients through this process, and I've shared these ideas with thousands more through speaking, writing, and social media, as well as applied them in my own life.

And I'm excited to go on this journey with you.

This book is not only about celebrating our gender but also about growing in relationship with ourselves and with others. It's designed as an empowering, insightful read that motivates as much as it educates, honoring action as much as thought. You'll walk away a better-equipped human, in and out of all gender fuckery, after reading this. And on hard days, you'll have the confidence and tools you need to do hard things. Because you *can* do hard things. I promise—it's worth it. *You* are worth it.

PS: I think you're magic.

PART I

PLAY

CHAPTER 1

Back to Basics

My grandfather was a foreman on a ranch in West Texas. He's a proper cowboy of few words and prefers being on a horse to interacting with most humans. Walmart is his idea of hell.

His ranch was one of the few places where I felt grounded. I'd spend as much time as possible at the barn, brushing the horses, touching their velvet noses, running my hands down their necks. Granddaddy and I went on beautiful adventures, barely talking but riding as far out into the rolling hills as we dared before sunset. If we were lucky, we'd find ancient Indigenous drawings on the walls of the steep canyons we rode through.

As soon as it got dark, I would walk out to the barn, sit on the fence, and stare at the Milky Way. I sat awestruck in the crisp stillness, listening to my breath slow with every second, feeling the tension in my body release, and trying to wrap my brain around the infinity of stars above me.

Something about the smell of manure and the sensation of being a part of the infinity of all that space made my problems and big feelings seem more manageable. Sitting there in the face of something vaster than I could comprehend, seeing I am a small part of a much larger story, helped me feel connected to myself, to others, and to the universe.

The importance of feeling grounded and a sense of awe was one of the greatest lessons I learned from my grandfather. Well, that and never lay your cowboy hat brim down. All your luck'll run out that way.

Maybe you've also felt awe as you've taken in a sky full of infinite stars and planets. Or perhaps that feeling came to you when you stood in the waves of an ocean, walked through a forest, marveled over the complexity of something you thought was simple, or experienced a beautiful piece of art.

Whatever it was, experiences of awe do not make us shrink. Then and now, tapping into the feeling of looking up at those stars reminds me to take up the space I need unapologetically and opens up a sense of possibility deep in my bones. Standing in awe of something larger than ourselves is both grounding and expansive, and that's the feeling I hope you will hold on to as we go through this chapter.[1] Stay humble. Stay curious. Stay open.

Because gender is a galaxy.

What We "Know" Is Changing

As much as we understand about bodies, brains, biology, and gender today, we have barely scratched the surface of what we *will* know. The vastness and complexity of gender can be beautiful, grounding, and awe-inspiring—not overwhelming, confusing, or something we need to "solve."

The more we discover, rediscover,* and explore sex/gender,† the more we realize what we don't know—and that's a good thing. It gives us space. It invites us to explore. It also makes it essential for transgender and cisgender folks alike to come to the conversation about sex/gender, gender identity, and gender expression with the same humility, curiosity, and openness as a scientist putting aside preconceived notions when studying galaxies.

I like to educate folks on sex/gender by going back to the "basics"—even though these topics are anything but. Starting from a shared

---

* For people of color, "discovering" knowledge about themselves and their gender identity might mean reconnecting to a culture and heritage lost through colonialism and assimilation.

† I use "sex/gender" to acknowledge the fact that biology and our social constructions of gender are multifaceted and interconnected. Sex and gender are not the same, but we cannot discuss either without recognizing that much of what we consider to be innate traits of biology and our binary system of sex assigned at birth is influenced by intensely gendered cultural norms.

framework gives us all the opportunity to gain more nuanced and expansive understanding of human biology, identity, and experience and to see how truly individual we are, whether you identify as trans, non-binary, cis, or something else entirely.

The Galaxy of Identity

As we dig into our understanding of sex and gender, imagine you are the pilot of a spacecraft. In front of you are three dials. You can turn any dial independently of the others; each has its own spectrum. There's no right or wrong way to turn the dials. Different combinations of these dials get you different results, with none better than the others. Those dials are (1) sex assigned at birth, (2) gender identity, and (3) gender expression.

Dial #1: Sex Assigned at Birth

A doctor turns this first dial the instant you enter the world. They look at your genitals for a hot second (yes, this is the medically accurate term) and declare, "It's a boy!" or "It's a girl!" This is the binary model we're used to, but it's scientifically inaccurate.

Yep. Not accurate. Our Western biomedical sex/gender system hinges on the idea that there are only two genders—male and female—and that these categories are obvious, fundamentally different from each other, biologically determined before birth, unchangeable, and predict psychological traits, interests, and behavior; however, the reality is that the sex system is more of a Venn diagram than two distinct checkboxes.

For a system as complex as sex to be genuinely binary, it must contain internal consistency, meaning *every* system in our understanding of sex must be universal across the categories of "male" and "female." Yet science continues to show us that biology is much more expansive and diverse than we initially thought, mirroring the inherent diversity in nature.[2]

For some folks, this is unsettling, and for others, it feels downright dangerous. This isn't the first time we've needed to adjust how we understand the world and our place in it. For example, in 1632, Galileo wrote a book that pissed off the Catholic Church. In *Dialogue Concerning the Two Chief World Systems*, Galileo endorsed—in direct opposition to church doctrine—the Copernican view that the sun is the center of our solar system. The invention of tools like the telescope changed our understanding of physics and astronomy, and our view of the world needed to change with it.

Not wanting to be tortured or burned at the stake for this "heresy," Galileo recanted his views to the Inquisition and spent his remaining years under house arrest. But legend says Galileo whispered, "And yet, it moves," as he left the Inquisition's chamber, a rebellious last word. Galileo didn't have the tools we have today to prove conclusively that the earth revolves around the sun. Still, he saw the limitations in the current understanding of physics and the universe and wanted to expand our knowledge.

And yet, it moves.

Our understanding of biology and gender diversity is at a similarly critical place of expansion. We are shaking up people's fundamental views about the world with new understandings of gender as a spectrum and not binary boxes. I believe this is one reason we are seeing violence and discrimination against transgender people.

Now, let me be very clear: Even though biological research advancements continue to reinforce the diversity of bodies and gender, we don't need biological research to validate transgender and non-binary identities.

Transgender/non-binary folks exist and are valid. Period.

But for the sake of argument—and who doesn't love shaking up the cisnormative bullshit of the status quo—let's take a quick peek at three systems we assume are fundamentally different between folks assigned male or female at birth: hormones, brains, and chromosomes.

Hormonal Differences

Let me say it straight: There are no male or female hormones. All bodies produce testosterone, estradiol, and progesterone in varying amounts, and there is considerable overlap in typical amounts of testosterone and estradiol/progesterone in folks assigned male or female at birth. We *all* have different amounts of each hormone, and those levels will continue to change over time, based on what's going on in our lives, how old we are, and, crucially, our environment.

While we often assume that our hormones determine our gendered behaviors, research in the burgeoning field of social neuroendocrinology (which is also a great term to whip out at a family dinner when you want to sound smart) has found that it's (shockingly) more nuanced than that. Our *behaviors* impact our hormones just as much, if not more, than our hormones impact our behaviors. Our body chemistry, our actions, and our current context are in constant dialogue with each other, creating our unique hormonal makeup.

For example, researcher Sari van Anders found that having sexual thoughts increases testosterone levels in folks assigned female at birth and that nurturing parenting behaviors decrease testosterone in folks assigned male at birth.[3] Similarly, in contrast to gendered stereotypes, engaging in competitive contests increases estradiol and progesterone in folks assigned female at birth. Van Anders's findings also suggest that testosterone levels respond to gendered norms and socialization, rising and falling in accordance with cultural expectations related to competitive or protective behavior and nurturing behavior.[4] For instance, a baby's cry will increase testosterone in any gender if we feel the baby is in danger, but the same cry will decrease testosterone if the kiddo just needs a hug or a bottle. Our first reactions hormonally are often dependent on the role society has placed on you—nurturer or defender/provider.[5]

In other words, we've made the classic scientific method mistake of assuming correlation equals causation. Research highlights how hormones, thought to be primary biological building blocks of "men" and "women," are pretty malleable across genders and within each of us. While parts of our hormonal makeup are inherited, how much or how little testosterone or estrogen is in our blood is greatly influenced by our choices, gendered expectations, and environment.

Brain Differences

We've likely all heard about "male brains" and "female brains" from pop culture references, including the bestselling book *Men Are from Mars,*

Women Are from Venus. Curious whether this old wives' tale would bear out, researchers at the Tel Aviv University looked at MRIs of more than fourteen hundred human brains. They compared seven to twelve brain systems that typically have the largest difference between folks assigned male or female at birth to determine if there was evidence of internal consistency—two distinct categories of brains.

Spoiler alert: There wasn't.[6]

Mosaicism, or brains having both female-typical and male-typical characteristics, occurred in 23 to 53 percent of brains. Internal consistency (where all seven to twelve systems would be perfectly consistent with what researchers were told to expect given the sex assigned at birth) only occurred in 0.7 to 10 percent of brains.*

In other words, every brain is different but not because of the sex/gender we were assigned at birth. It's impossible to pull apart biological brain differences from gendered socialization impacting our brain's development.[7]

And for the record, all of us are from Earth.

Chromosomal Differences

Folks assigned female at birth typically have XX chromosomes, and folks assigned male typically have XY chromosomes. When discussing sex/gender differences between those with XX and those with XY chromosomes, people often fall into gendered tropes. For example, X is still considered to be the essence of "femaleness," and gendered adjectives such as sexy, motherly, mysterious, contradictory, complicated, unpredictable, and intuitive are regularly used to characterize the gene.[8] But let's be real. An X chromosome is about as sexy, feminine, and motherly as your spleen.

This is not the first time we, and scientists, have mistakenly made assumptions about what someone's genes mean about their sex/gender. One genetic variation is XXY, an extra X, typically seen in those assigned male at birth. This chromosomal difference influences factors like fertility, height, and muscle mass. The XXY genetic syndrome became associated

---

* Percentage variability was dependent on which brain feature(s) and subsets of the participants were being studied.

with sex/gender in the 1950s, characterizing people with XXY as feminine or "genetic females," or alternatively, predictive of someone being gay or "cross-dressing." Today, researchers have widely accepted that having an extra X in your chromosomes doesn't give you a penchant for binging *RuPaul's Drag Race*. Shocking.

Regardless of whether your chromosomes are XX or XY or another variation, there is zero scientific support to connect someone's chromosomes with their gender identity.[9] The human genome is 99.9 percent alike across biological differences, and chromosomes do not determine your destiny.[10]

Differences in Sexual Development

Sometimes, a baby is born and the doctor finds their genitals ambiguous. Here, they pull out a ruler (yes, a literal ruler) and measure the external genitalia. The doctor determines whether to label the child as male, female, or intersex.

If the doctor labels a child intersex, further investigation of other parts of the sex system is used to determine treatment goals, including unnecessary and harmful genital surgeries. However, if there is no ambiguity in the genitalia at birth, it's often not apparent that someone has a difference of sexual development (DSD) until later in life. It may show up during puberty, when trying to have children, or even during an unrelated medical procedure.

The number of babies that are born with some DSD is roughly equal to the number of people in the world who have red hair. Put another way, this is twice the population of Canada. Worth noting, too, is that these numbers are likely to be underrepresented since most doctors assign sex at birth based solely on the appearance of genitalia, checking no other variables in the sex system.*[11]

---

* This argument is not insinuating that intersex people will go on to identify as transgender or are the only "real" transgender people based on biological diversity. Many intersex people go on to identify as a binary gender and others go on to identify as transgender, in the same way as folks assigned male or female do. Rather, this argument is being used to make clear that the binary system of sex is fundamentally flawed as a primary way to categorize human beings.

Now, let's imagine for a second that we created a taxonomy of hair colors and listed blond, brown, and black as options. We decided to leave out people with red hair because there weren't enough of them, and they weren't important enough to count. Furthermore, in this imagined world, leaving out redheads is not only unfair but has violent consequences for anyone with a hint of red in their hair. And people who fall somewhere on the spectrum between blond and brown or between brown and black are assigned to a single group even though they have markers for both.

This is exactly what we've done with the binary system of sex assigned at birth (and the system of gender we've built on top of it). This framework is based on outdated and biased science, influenced by assumptions of two distinct categories, that pathologizes anything outside that binary. Instead of humans existing within the two distinct categories of male and female (and viewing intersex folks as outliers), I invite all of us to see our bodies as a blend of genetics, gonads/hormones, and genitals that appear in a unique mosaic.

THE SEX/GENDER BINARY HURTS ALL OF US

The sex we're assigned at birth has lasting implications for our life outcomes physically, mentally, socially, emotionally, financially, and beyond. And whether you're cisgender, transgender, or exist outside the binary, adhering to a binary system of sex/gender comes with significant societal and personal costs that are completely avoidable.[12]

Life-threatening illnesses are missed for both cisgender and transgender individuals because we have healthcare that makes assumptions based on gender, rather than treating the body parts a person has. For example, heart disease is rarely caught in cisgender women, with sometimes fatal consequences, because symptoms manifest differently than in cisgender men.[13] Likewise, depression is underdiagnosed in cisgender men because it's assumed to be more prevalent among women.

For transmasculine folks, getting medically necessary gynecologic healthcare and fertility support often includes getting turned away at the front desk of a "women's health center" and dealing with insurance issues because a legal man cannot get reimbursed for gynecological care. Similarly, many transgender women do not get appropriate medical screening for prostate cancer because many urologists do not provide a welcoming or safe environment for *everyone* with a prostate.

Another way the sex/gender binary harms is through gender discrimination, expectations of performance based on gender stereotypes, and gender privilege that permeates our legal and social policy. In one notable study, eleven-month-old infants were asked to crawl down varying slope angles. Imagine a dog agility course, but for babies. Mothers were asked to predict how their children would respond to risk (steeper slopes) and their ability to crawl down the slopes. Mothers consistently overestimated the boys' performance and underestimated the girls' performance, but researchers found no gender differences in performance or risk tolerance.[14] Similarly, cisgender men feel intense pressure to conform to toxic norms of masculinity, which damages men's emotional and physical health, increases risk of domestic and gun violence, and is harmful to relationships of all types.

What I want you to know about the spectrum of biological sex is there aren't just two checkboxes. Relying on a five-second external genitalia exam at birth to assign sex and erasing the spectrum of natural variation serves no one. The sex/gender binary impacts the way we see ourselves and others, as well as what we believe people are capable of. It limits the world we dream of creating.

Sex assigned at birth is a label.

And labels are only helpful when we get to apply them to ourselves. By giving less power to an assigned label, we can create space to value all bodies equally and for each person to express themselves authentically as individuals, rather than conforming (or not) to social norms based on their assigned sex/gender.

Dial #2: Gender Identity

Let's get this out of the way early: Gender is a construct. We made it up. Of course, it's more complicated than that, so stick with me for a minute.

As a society, we've decided that clothes and toys for little girls should be pink and for little boys, blue. Y'all, colors are neutral. It's a wavelength of light.

We, and especially people in power, construct gender collectively—as a society. And sometimes in weird ways.

I've come across some strangely gendered things, like these:

pink women's earplugs (for tiny, delicate ears)
"mansize" Kleenex (for men's giant boogers)
Scrub Daddy and Scrub Mommy sponges (for those who like a little sexual innuendo with their cleaning supplies)

When we construct gender, society does more than define what falls into a "male" or "female" category—it determines the relationship between those genders and, most importantly, the power dynamic. Though expectations of gendered behavior differ across time and cultures, when folks step out of line with societal expectations, they're often punished for it.

Spoiler alert: The patriarchy comes out on top here, centering on white, cisgender men to the exclusion of all other genders and racial identities. Black folks, other people of color, and anyone who is not a cisgender man have gotten the raw end of the deal on this one, experiencing systemic oppression and marginalization.*

But even though the concept of gender is a construct, it's also an important part of many people's core identity. Gender identity is self-determined, but many people don't question the default (or the norms that go along with it) they were assigned at birth from a doctor's quick glance at their bits.

Gender identity is a deep, internal sense of your own gender. This may match up with your sex assigned at birth, or it may not. For some people, gender identity is something they understand about themselves at a very

* Transgender women often have histories of being "punished" for displaying behavior that does not conform to stereotypically masculine expectations. Additionally, transgender women experience sexism, misogyny, and transmisogyny over their lifetime. Transmisogyny describes this complex interplay between transphobia and misogyny that trans women are faced with. Similarly, "white femininity" and "white masculinity" are used as the criteria to determine what is right, proper, and acceptable behavior to the exclusion of other cultures.

young age and that stays stable over time, whether they are cisgender or transgender/non-binary. For others, it may change throughout our lives based on what we know about the world and ourselves. Since there is often little to no education about transgender identities or encouragement to explore gender at a young age, many trans folks (including me) have a winding path to discovering their gender identities.

Folks whose gender identity matches their sex assigned at birth are cisgender ("cis-" being a Latin prefix that means "on the same side as"). Folks whose gender identity does not match their sex assigned at birth are transgender ("trans-" being a Latin prefix that means "on the other side as").

A transgender woman is someone who is born and the doctor says, "It's a boy!" That person grows up and says, "No, I don't feel like a man. I feel like a woman." A transgender man is someone who is born and the doctor typically says, "It's a girl!" That person grows up and says, "No, I don't feel like a woman. I feel like a man."

Let's say you are born, and the doctor decrees, "It's a girl!" You grow up to say, "'Woman' doesn't feel right, but neither does 'man.'" This means you likely fall under the non-binary umbrella. This means something different for different people. For some folks, this means you identify somewhere firmly in the middle of the dial. This is where I locate myself as a non-binary person. For gender-fluid folks, it might mean that your felt sense of gender fluctuates. For agender folks, it might mean the whole concept of gender isn't a defining or salient identity factor, and their ideal way to exist in the world is to be as genderless as possible. Some non-binary folks identify with the term "transgender," and some don't.

BEING TWO-SPIRIT: AN INTERVIEW WITH DR. ROGER KUHN

The Western sex/gender binary is not a universal way to differentiate individuals. Cultures all over the world have traditions of gender that exist outside the binary, such as the hijra of South Asia and the fa'afafine of Samoa. To better understand gender diversity within Indigenous communities in the now United States, I spoke with Dr. Roger Kuhn,* a two-spirit individual and licensed therapist, about connecting to Indigenous wisdom and the long history of gender diversity. In Roger's words:

"I identify as a Poarch Creek two-spirit Indigiqueer gay person. My tribal affiliation is part of the larger Muscogee Nation. Two-spirit is a term that I use to recognize my gender and sexual orientation variants. I've never felt like a boy and I've never felt like a girl, and I didn't have the language as a child to express that. It wasn't until I heard the term 'two-spirit' that I finally found a term I felt represented who I was.

"Two-spirit is an umbrella term that comes from the Northern Algonquin word 'niizh manidoowag,' but there's over 152 terms for gender found in ethnographic literature in Native populations. I might identify as two-spirit and then, within that umbrella, identify as ennvrkvpv, leakey, hayama, batai, or bowtaai. A lot of words were lost because of genocide's disruption of culture and language. Though some Native people use the term 'transgender,' we can't say every Indigenous two-spirit person is transgender.

"Indigenous communities accepted everyone because we knew everyone was needed and had a place. Two-spirit folks were in roles like keeping peace between nations, doing naming and puberty ceremonies, and medicine people. I always say to transgender folks that, in my culture, you're sacred. Your body is sacred."[15]

We've talked about how labels are one of the ways we know ourselves and our place in the world, and I've said before that they are only useful when we apply them to ourselves. With that privilege, it behooves us to be mindful of which labels we claim for ourselves. We get to self-identify our gender while holding a responsibility to not appropriate another culture as our own. For example, Roger is clear that while there is much wisdom we can and should learn from Indigenous traditions, adopting the label "two-spirit" is not okay for non-Native folks.

Transgender/non-binary folks may know they are trans from a very early age, discover more about their gender identity as they get older, or have a gender identity that fluctuates. For example, a binary transgender person might embrace more of their non-binary identity as their life

* You can check out our full conversation on www.gendermagic.com.

experience (and potentially their body) changes. This is a normal part of identity development and exploration.

In my case, I didn't have the language or the capacity to explore my gender identity until I got through several other big identity transitions. I experienced a lot—rejecting fundamentalist Christianity, releasing myself from a marriage, and coming out as queer—before discovering my non-binary identity.

Similarly, I've worked with many clients who could not explore their gender identity at an early age because of things like lack of education and language about transgender identities, lack of visibility of other transgender/non-binary people, fear of violence and harassment and rejection, religious affiliation, or prohibitive life circumstances like a marriage, children, or fear of negative career impacts. Remember: Gender identity doesn't exist in a vacuum.

Everyone's journey is different. Whatever your path and whatever age you discovered your authentic gender identity, you are valid and right on time.

A NOTE ABOUT SEXUAL AND RELATIONAL ORIENTATION

Folks often mash up gender identity and sexual orientation or get extremely confused trying to label the sexual orientation of a couple with one or more partners who are transgender or non-binary. We'll talk about this a bit more in part 2 when we talk about pleasure, but for now, understand that gender identity and sexual orientation are both constellations. Separate but connected stars. The labels we use for our sexual orientation are our own, just like our gender identities. What feels the most salient for describing our sexual orientation is up to us, regardless of who we are in a relationship with currently.

Dial #3: Gender Expression

While your gender identity is internally focused, your gender expression is how you choose to display your gender to the world. Your gender expression may be congruent with your assigned sex at birth and align with societal expectations of your gender identity. Or it may not. This is true for both cisgender and transgender/non-binary folks.

Gender expression includes things like physical appearance, fashion choices, and medical transition but also encompasses norms around "masculinity" or "femininity" such as—but not exclusive to—body language, values, attitudes, energy, ways of speaking, hobbies, career choices, distribution of labor in the home and at work, and even expectations around people-pleasing.

In chapter 5, we will dive deeper into how to find a gender expression (including names and pronouns) that feels like magic, design gender experiments, and make decisions about medical transition. In the meantime, what I want you to know about gender expression is that it is play. Exploring gender expression can be a place of joy and curiosity and settling into yourself in a new way. It's likely what you came to this book to do, and fear not: I'll show you how.

Adjusting the Dials

Looking back at all the dials, the dial of sex assigned at birth is out of our control. You can't choose what the doctor puts on your birth certificate as a baby.

The dial of gender identity also isn't a choice but may change over time as you discover more about yourself. You might choose to experiment with whether "male" or "female" or "non-binary" or another term altogether feels right to you.

How you turn the dial of gender expression, though, is completely up to you, regardless of your gender identity or sex assigned at birth. You can identify as male and wear dresses just like you can identify as female and wear dresses. It's totally up to you.

Whatever your unique constellation of identities is, you are 100 percent normal.

That said, sometimes finding a gender identity and gender expression that feel authentic to us requires adjusting our dials. If and when someone decides to adjust the dial of gender identity, that's called gender transition.

Gender transition is the process of leaving behind the gender associated with your sex assigned at birth and transitioning into a different gender identity, whether this identity is binary or non-binary. It also may or may not involve changing your gender expression and social/medical/legal transition.

The societally expected narrative of gender transition is a very linear journey from a binary sex assigned at birth to another binary gender identity with a defined "point B" that includes social, medical, and legal transition. It also implies that you must always have known you were transgender, hated your body, and experienced intense gender dysphoria.

While that narrative has been useful for building empathy for the transgender community and emphasizing the necessity of legal protections and medically necessary care, it doesn't reflect everyone's experience.

There are many transgender people who do not feel intense gender/body dysphoria, discovered their identity later in life, are non-binary, or do not have access to social/medical/legal transitions. Similarly, there are lots of transgender folks who don't hate their body, and who don't want to undergo social, legal, and/or medical transition.

Right now, suffering and self-hatred are assumed to be part of the experience for all transgender people, so much so that I've had many clients in my office who doubt their transgender identity because they haven't "suffered enough" or simply because the dominant narrative doesn't reflect their lived experience.

If that's you, know this—you are trans enough.

WHAT'S GENDER DYSPHORIA?

As defined by the *DSM-V*,[16] gender dysphoria is psychological distress that results from an incongruence between one's sex assigned at birth and one's gender identity. The *DSM-V* conceptualizes gender dysphoria as "a strong desire to be rid of one's primary and/or secondary sex characteristics because of a marked incongruence with one's experienced/expressed gender," "a strong desire for the primary and/or secondary sex characteristics of the other gender," "a strong desire to be of the other gender," and "a strong conviction that one has the typical feelings and reactions of the other gender."

Like our overall cultural narrative around gender transition, the *DSM-V* definition of gender dysphoria centers on distress and impairment. It is also worth noting that the diagnosis of gender dysphoria comes from a history of pathologization and gatekeeping in the medical field. This creates a reliance on the medical system to "correct" gender dysphoria.

There are three general parts to gender dysphoria: cognitive dysphoria (how we feel and think about ourselves), social dysphoria (how we feel out and about in the world), and body dysphoria (how we feel about our body).[17]

In saying that it is possible to transition your gender with ease, I do not want to ignore the lived reality of many transgender and nonbinary folks who struggle with severe and sometimes debilitating gender dysphoria. This is *not* a personal failing in someone's ability to love themselves.

These three parts and the *DSM-V* definition focus on the individual factors of gender dysphoria. However, much of gender dysphoria comes as a reaction to a binary, policed gender system based on sex assigned at birth and societal transphobia. While we live in a transphobic culture and systems of oppression that negatively impact transgender individuals, I don't believe it is possible to erase gender dysphoria completely.

Setting a Course for Gender Freedom

The point of framing sex and gender as a spectrum or mosaic is not to erase gender. I don't want us to all live in "gender-neutral" burlap bags or to say that all bodies are exactly alike. How boring (and itchy)! Also, have you ever been to a queer party? The looks! The gender fuckery! Swoon. The point of doing away with the sex and gender binaries is to embrace the diversity of bodies and identities we have. It's to have fun.

Gender freedom is not about erasing gender, but allowing it to be a playground, full of richness and individuality and freedom for everyone, cis and trans alike. Activist and bestselling author Jacob Tobia calls this "gender-chill," where everyone can define what their gender identity and expression look like for themselves without gendered expectations.[18] I like to call it gender freedom—imagining all that's possible when we show up for ourselves and the world from our authenticity and deep self-knowledge.

Like transgender/non-binary folks, cisgender individuals have an opportunity to look intentionally at the way the gender binary has both privileged them and hurt them. To understand the ways they express gender automatically that aren't serving them and feel constricting. This creates space to make different choices about gender expression and deepen their understanding of what authenticity means to them.

Gender transition and gender freedom are about self-growth, your unique gender identity, and how you choose to express that gender identity to the world. Transition has less to do with any sort of defined path to social/medical/legal transition and more to do with moving toward the most authentic gender identity and expression for you, as defined by you.

Because transition isn't the point.

Gender transition is simply transitioning to your most authentic, lit-up version of yourself *so that* you can go on and be the best, most bold version of yourself in the world. When folks can show up to life without the dark, brain-consuming cloud of gender dysphoria over their heads, it creates room for them to be more present for the people they care about, causes, arts, and their career.

And most importantly, they can be more present and loving to themselves.

I'm here to help people transition (whatever that means for them) with less suffering and more ease. If gender transition is a process of self-growth, it can also be a process of curiosity, joy, and gender euphoria. And I'm going to show you how, starting with foundational mindsets and coping skills that work.

MAPPING YOUR GENDER GALAXY

Now that you understand the basics of sex/gender, you can begin to explore your own galaxy of gender. Whether you are transgender/non-binary or cisgender, these questions are a starting point for exploring your unique gender constellation. I encourage you to grab a notebook and write down your answers. Don't think too hard; just brain dump onto a page, and don't worry about trying to figure out every detail of your gender identity and expression from this exercise. Be curious and give yourself permission to explore. You might walk away with clarity about a shifting gender identity or expression, more questions than answers, or simply more intention about an existing gender identity. Whatever the outcome, I invite you to take this feeling of curiosity and awe with you through the rest of this book. Whatever comes up for you, let yourself feel awe and wonder in the process. After all, this is about the journey, not the destination.

1. When have you felt awe in your life? What does it feel like in your body? How can you tap into that feeling as you explore gender?
2. How did learning about the diversity of biology in our hormones, chromosomes, brains, and differences in sexual development impact your perspective about the gender binary?
3. How has the gender binary negatively affected your life? (*Think about times you were "punished" for behaving in gender nonconforming ways, limiting beliefs you hold about yourself, gender discrimination, feelings and desires you suppressed, etc.*)
4. How have your intersecting identities influenced your experience of gender identity and expression? (*E.g., race and ethnicity, culture, differences in sexual development, differing abilities, size, class, etc.*)
5. When did you know your sex assigned at birth did or didn't match up with your gender identity? Describe what it was like. This could be a lightbulb moment or a slow realization.
6. Does the term "woman" or "man" feel accurate in describing your gender identity? If so, why? If not, describe what your gender identity feels like. This could be literal (*I feel non-binary and that means X*) or metaphorical (*I feel like my gender is a neon light and that means X*).
7. What assumptions have you held about how you were "supposed" to express your gender to the world? (*Think about how you dress*

and behave, roles, competition and collaboration, relationship to feelings, interests, careers, etc.)

8. What aspects of gender expression are you curious about exploring for yourself? (*Think about how you dress and behave, values, interests, roles, relationship to feelings, etc.)*
9. What makes you feel lit up and authentic in the way you identify and express your gender?
10. What makes you feel off and not like yourself in the way you identify and express your gender?
11. What does gender freedom mean to you? How can you create more of it in your life?

CHAPTER 2

Mindsets for Gender Freedom

If gender exploration and transition feel hard for you, it's not a personal failing, nor is it an accident.

Throughout history, white men (cis, straight, nondisabled white men, to be specific) have clung to their power and status by creating and actively maintaining systems that (surprise!) serve only themselves—systems like laws, healthcare, policing and prison, education, and immigration. Our identities don't exist in a vacuum, and the more nondominant identities we hold, the more these systems negatively impact us.* This is what Kimberlé Crenshaw named "intersectionality," but women of color have been talking about these concepts since the 1800s.[1]

Folks are trying their damnedest to make things happen for themselves. When even just ordering a coffee / going to the grocery store / something else that seems mundane feels like it's too much, it's easy to feel defeated and assume that *you* are the problem. Why bother if these slings and arrows are all that are going to meet your efforts? But let me say it again: You are NOT failing because these stressors and systems make you want to scream-cry into a void. Nope. It's fucking hard and confusing when the systems are literally set up to work against you.† These harmful

---

* Examples include policing gender norms, racism, sexism, a fear of difference, ableism, fat phobia, as well as a system of criminalization and punishment and norms around work and housing policies that disproportionately affect transgender/non-binary people of color.

† As you can imagine, these messages—along with the stressors and microaggressions caused by them—add up over time and manifest in health disparities, poverty, chronic illness, underemployment, struggles with mental health, substance use, and suicidal thoughts. Stressors based on identity can range from everyday "paper cuts," or microaggressions (like getting misgendered by the grocery store clerk), to physical violence.

ideas, biases, and assumptions creep into our collective consciousness as truth and reality. The most insidious thing is that those messages we get about ourselves, reinforced by institutional systems, sink into our bones and influence our beliefs about ourselves.

Reclaiming our power—our agency—is how we move from feeling helpless to taking back control of our lives.

So how do we develop a sense of agency while dealing with systems and stressors that are often out of our control? We shift our mindset.

Don't worry—this is *not* a chapter about how to "love and light" the way through gender exploration and transition. I am not here to say, "Just think positive!" or to tell you that life is perfect and the only problem is your perception, or to say all your problems will be solved if you just get your mind right. We all know that's a bunch of BS.

Instead, this chapter will show you how to move out of your reactive survival brain and into the part of your brain that is proactive, goal oriented, and controls more complex thoughts, behaviors, and decision-making. These three mindsets—self-efficacy, self-love/self-compassion, and self-growth—are the fuel for your journey of gender exploration. If you can embrace these, no matter where life takes you, you'll have the inner resources to navigate systemic barriers and stay in the driver's seat of your life.

The Energy to Survive

Recently a friend of mine cut someone off at a stoplight. It was an accident, but even so, the person in the car behind them got out with a shotgun and started walking toward my friend's car. *Yikes!*

Luckily, he had a turbo button on his dashboard, giving the car a burst of speed and power. My friend raced away from this dangerous situation unharmed. Our brains, being the smart little buggers they are, also have a turbo button. You've probably felt its power before: It's commonly known as the fight-or-flight response, though these days we also add the freeze and fawn.*

* "Fawn," as defined by therapist Pete Walker, indicates a people-pleasing response to physically and emotionally unsafe environments to the detriment of one's own boundaries and needs.

Our fight-or-flight response is the domain of the sympathetic nervous system, which is part of our limbic brain. This part of our brain developed to handle brief and specific threats—to give us that turbo boost out of perilous situations. It makes connections between things quickly, creating shortcuts that alert us to future danger, and reacts without much cognitive thought. These shortcuts are called triggers—and can be a huge help in life-threatening situations. Going back to the example of my friend, the moment his eyes saw the gun, he reacted, hitting that turbo button. His brain knew what to do (flee!) in a split second because a gun is a clear danger trigger.

When our brain enters fight/flight/freeze/fawn, our body reacts physically. For example, we may breathe rapidly. Our heart rate speeds up. We become hypervigilant, feeling on edge and like our body is vibrating with energy. We might even get sweaty (to make yourself more slippery to the threat), and blood flow is redirected to prioritize your muscles, brain, legs, and arms. In the case of freeze, we might feel numb to avoid physical pain as our heart rate slows.

Our brains and bodies have responded this way for millennia, and it's worked, since, you know, humans still exist. It's brilliant. However, the problem with our fight/flight/freeze/fawn response is that:

1. our brains don't know the difference between man-with-shotgun and chronic stressors like transphobia and racism, and
2. our brains aren't meant to stay on turbo.

If you tried to run your car on turbo all the time, you'd run out of gas really quickly, right? Our brains are the same. So if you're struggling with gender transition right now, it's likely because your brain has been stuck on turbo too long and your tank is empty.

When faced with chronic and uncontrollable stressors like transphobia, transmisogyny, microaggressions, and how gender norms are both literally and figuratively policed (on top of stressors like racism, ableism, etc.), we start to run out of gas. So our body often activates its final survival strategy: freeze.

Going into "freeze" is your body's most adaptive response when faced with an uncontrollable stressor. Like the fight and flight responses, the freeze response is active and physically taxing on our body even though it looks a little different. When we freeze in response to a physical threat, we might feel numb to avoid physical pain, our heart rate slows, and we might hold our breath or restrict breathing. However, when we freeze in response to an emotional stressor (and have reactions like procrastinating or feeling depressed), we often get labeled as "bad" or "lazy" by ourselves and others.

The anxiety and stuck feelings that come with our freeze response often manifest in thoughts like these:

I feel hopeless.
I'm so lazy I just want to lie in bed all day.
I'm so overwhelmed and confused.
I feel like a burden.
I'm so scared of judgment/rejection/regret that I can't move forward.
I feel like I don't deserve to transition.
What if I'm not "trans enough" to transition? I feel like a fraud.
I don't feel valid as a [your identity] because _______.
I feel like I don't have control over my own body or this process.
I have doubts and don't know if I can trust myself.

We often believe the things our brains tell us without question, especially when they are negative and loud. But our thoughts aren't always true, and negative, hurtful thoughts like these often come from a place of fear and self-protection: Stuck in freeze, our brains want to stay small and still to survive.

In order to discern which thoughts are true and which aren't, we need to understand that our limbic brain is less like a 911 dispatch and more like an overzealous bodyguard tasked with keeping us safe. Imagine someone who is tall and has big muscles named...Tiny. They are a great person, but Tiny's afraid of the dark and isn't always the most accurate when assessing risk and danger. Similarly, the strategies our brains have used to keep us safe in the past are not always the strategies we need to thrive.

For instance, let's pretend that, instead of a gun, my friend's trigger is getting misgendered by a family member. For the sake of this example, let's say the family member is not a physical threat.

Sometimes, my friend's instinct to "run away"—flight—could work. Leaving an emotionally unsafe situation is valid, though it might be a little strange if they just took off running, leaving the front door banging in the wind. The "fight" instinct might not be great either. Imagine if you punched your grandma every time she got your pronouns wrong. "Play dead" also probably isn't a long-term coping strategy. Going a little numb to get through a hard situation can help, but it does nothing to resolve the situation, and everything feels a little foggy. "Fawn" would have you shove down all your feels in order to make the person who misgendered you happy, but I think we can all see why that would feel shitty.

Even in the case of becoming triggered by a legitimately dangerous object—a gun—it's not helpful to remain on edge and hypervigilant against the threat once we've already survived it or it's no longer a threat in the moment. Yet that is often what happens in a brain that has been traumatized, whether that trauma is a singular experience or a life of living under multiple, intersecting systems of oppression.

When Triggers Become Traumas

Back in the day, researchers studied the impact of mild shocks applied to mice (sad, I know), which they had assigned to one of three boxes. The first group received no shocks. Lucky ducks. The second received shocks but had the ability to escape the shock by moving into a different but connected cage. The third group received shocks but were unable to escape.

The mice in the group of inescapable shocks understandably displayed anxiety and froze. Here's the important part: The freeze response continued even when these mice were placed in the cages where they *could* escape the shock. Despite having a way out in the second experiment, these mice couldn't discover it. In the past, they had no control, so they believed they'd *never* have control. They gave up.

In contrast, the group of mice with escapable shocks in the first experiment didn't have a stress reaction to the shocks after they escaped. Interestingly, these mice also didn't go into a freeze response when they were later placed in an *inescapable* shock environment. Even though they didn't have control in that particular instance, they *expected* to have control, and that expectation alone "immunized" them against a freeze response.[2]

See where I'm going with this? The helpless, frozen feeling becomes our default defense mechanism when we don't see a way out. And it's smart as hell... right up to the moment when we've become so used to believing that we don't have a choice or agency that we forget there might be a way out we simply can't see yet.

COMPLETING THE STRESS CYCLE

Our bodies are designed to handle a stress reaction in a very specific way: Your brain recognizes a specific threat and activates your sympathetic nervous system. You (hopefully!) escape the threat by fighting, fleeing, or freezing, physically discharging all that adrenaline in the process. Big sigh of relief. Knowing you are safe again, you can shake out any remaining energy, connect with your loved ones, and relax, knowing that you're safe and the danger has passed. Cycle complete.

But these days, it's rare that we need to physically run away, fight someone, or literally play possum, so we're often left with that energy vibrating inside us instead of finishing the stress cycle and moving back into a calm and grounded state of mind.[3] In the security line at an airport, a woman behind me (unmasked in the middle of Covid) stood so close to me that I could feel her breathing on my neck. I asked her to back up, which apparently was a wild request. She yelled at me to calm down, got closer, and proceeded to spew transphobic comments. I shot back some choice words with my best don't-fuck-with-me vibe (hey, I'm human too) and spent the rest of my time waiting to board my plane shaking and relishing the idea of dumping a large slushie on her head, wondering if that would land me in Florida jail and how bad could jail be in Key West anyway? The energy was stuck in my body with nowhere to go.

Unless and until we discharge that energy, it vibrates around in our bodies, impacting our ability to access our higher-level thinking and make decisions and just generally making us feel shitty. So, what do you do when you can't *actually* extinguish the threat of things like transphobia, no matter how personally satisfying dumping a slushie on someone's head might be? Emily and Amelia Nagoski talk about this extensively in their book *Burnout*, and they share that the easiest way to complete the stress cycle in our modern world is to do something mildly strenuous with your body—run, bike, dance, etc. Other options to move the energy through your body are to spend time breathing deeply, tense up all your muscles and then relax them, laugh till you pee just a little, make out (yes, I'm telling you to go make out with someone for your mental health—you're welcome) or hug or cuddle someone, make art, or put on Pixar's *Up* and cry it out.[4]

Completing the stress cycle brings us back into our prefrontal cortex, helping us move from surviving to thriving, while still leaving room for our limbic system to react quickly to threats. This part of the brain gives us the ability to think more clearly, make better decisions, and move toward a goal (like feeling affirmed in our gender) rather than just running away from a risk (like being misgendered).

For transgender and non-binary folks, the list of threats is long: disproportionate rates of violence (especially against Black transgender women); employment discrimination; housing discrimination; rejection from family, friends, and communities; financial disparities; medical gatekeeping; frequent microaggressions; and just trying to go to the damn bathroom unbothered.

Here's what I want you to know. While some of these threats truly do require the limbic system, many do not. The work of gender exploration, transition, and living as our most lit-up selves requires that we be able to discern between the two.

And while we can't control all the systems, structures, people, and experiences that cause us trauma, we *can* use our brains to support us in moving through our stress responses with agency and kindness to ourselves. Completing the stress cycle physically (as best we can) is one bridge to a calmer nervous system. Intentionally cultivating more powerful mindsets, and the actions to back them up, is another.

By shining a light on our self-protective negative thoughts and working to shift our mindset, we can impact our emotions and behaviors and help our nervous system chill out.

Self-Efficacy, Self-Love/Self-Compassion, and Self-Growth

The way we think, the stories we tell ourselves, and our belief in our ability to do hard things make an enormous difference in our quality of life and ability to cope, handling and moving through with challenges in a grounded way. Again, we're not going to Pollyanna our way through transition and gender exploration. This is hard and it asks a lot and the barriers you experience are real. That said, there are three mindset shifts that will help the journey feel better every step of the way: self-efficacy, self-love/self-compassion, and self-growth.

These mindset shifts are the cornerstone of exploring and transitioning your gender with more ease, and they are foundational to every other skill and idea in this book. While they are simple concepts, they aren't always easy to live out. Be kind to yourself and remember it's a process.

Mindset Shift #1: Self-Efficacy

When Parker, a biracial transgender woman in her late forties, came to work with me, she was feeling intense anxiety about moving forward in her transition. She had been exploring her gender on her own for a while and wanted to continue but felt overwhelmed at the "bigness" of it.

When we started working together, Parker had only spoken about her gender identity to her wife, who was struggling with the revelation. She worked in a male-dominated industry and worried about what coming out might mean for her job. She was also concerned about how her mother's religious family would react. And she was scared about what it would mean for her safety to be visibly transgender in our world today.

"I just want to sit in bed and not have anyone look at me," she said to me with tears in her eyes. "I wish it was just okay to be me in the world."

For Parker, every step that came with her gender transition—starting hormones, coming out to family, changing her name, coping with a divorce, coming out at work, navigating public spaces—kicked up a new round of anxiety. Each step forward became the "hardest thing" about transition.

But each time we worked through the painful emotions and she came out on the other side, her confidence in herself grew a little bit more. "I've done eight 'hardest things' already this year," Parker said in one of our sessions, laughing. "I guess I can do one more."

Your belief in your competence and capacity to figure things out—which we call "self-efficacy"—influences not only what you think is possible but also how hard you try to reach a goal and how likely you are to succeed, especially when obstacles come up. It's difficult to change negative thoughts about yourself or move forward in the midst of challenging circumstances if you're having trouble believing that you are resilient and have a measure of control in your own life.

While we may still feel big feelings, self-efficacy prevents fight/flight/freeze/fawn reactions from getting the best of us.[5] That fundamental belief that you can do hard things gives you an ability to choose how you want to respond to a situation. It takes your brain off turbo, gives Tiny a break, and grants you access to your prefrontal cortex so you can assess potential danger more effectively and come up with creative solutions to keep yourself safe.

For example, it's easy for me to go into fight/flight/freeze/fawn mode when my parents say or do something homophobic or hurtful. It took a lot of work, but now I'm able to notice when I'm triggered and remember I can choose to respond and take care of myself in ways that are safe and supportive to my mental health instead of spiraling into trauma land. I know I can handle it.

No matter what barriers you're facing, you have more choice than you think. And you can affect your experience more than you think. This doesn't mean the barriers and obstacles you face aren't real. They are. We are going to hold that together, grieve it, and then ask, "How do you want to handle it?"

This question allows us to change the tone of our life story from helpless to empowered.

The benefit of being human is that, regardless of our conditioning, we can tell ourselves a different story. There's a woman named Tammy, described in a study about transgender women of color, that I love.[6] Tammy was formerly incarcerated and had a vision of herself financially independent with a husband and a home. She knew that employment would be a challenge with a history of incarceration and didn't know how to reach her goals, but she started taking steps toward this imagined future anyway.

She noticed a bridal boutique close to her home and was determined to work there. After getting a job at another clothing retailer to gain experience, she took a deep breath and went into the bridal shop to pitch herself even though she was terrified of being rejected. In her cover letter, she shared her dreams for herself, what working at the bridal shop meant to her, and how she wanted to help other women achieve their dream wedding. She got the job! And even though she hadn't reached her goal of being in a partnership or home ownership at the time of the study, she felt confident and excited about the future and her ability to take steps toward her dream.[7]

It's easy to think that self-efficacy is something you either have or you don't, but it's actually a belief you can build and reinforce over time. At the outset, Tammy felt hopeless about her dream of financial independence (and eventually having a spouse of her own). Each step she took proved to herself that she had some control over her life, even with significant barriers in her way. Her future wasn't exclusively defined by her current circumstances. She had more choices than she thought.

In his amazing book *Man's Search for Meaning*, psychiatrist and Auschwitz survivor Viktor Frankl writes,

> Between stimulus and response there is a space.
> In that space is our power to choose our response.
> In our response lies our growth and our freedom.[8]

Remembering that we always have choice helps us find the space Frankl describes and choose a response—even if that response is simply to remember who we are in the face of an uncontrollable obstacle. That space is how we move *out* of feeling frozen and *into* our own power, but it's not always easy to do when we feel overwhelmed, stressed, or confused—so I'm going to help you out.

We've talked about how our struggles are not because of personal failures but rather the result of the oppressive systems we live in and how we've internalized negative messages about ourselves. Fighting those systems feels like an unwinnable game—and often it is. But awareness of that context can move us out of our freeze response (as well as guilt, shame, and internalized transphobia).

Think of it this way: How many TV shows, movies, or books can you name where humans are put into uncontrollable environments that threaten their lives? I mean . . . *Squid Game*, *The Hunger Games*, *The Matrix* . . .

In these stories, characters are asked to do horrible things to each other, to perform, and to comply with the system in order to "win" the game. But what moves the character from helpless to hero is always the same: They recognize it's a game and stop. playing. the. game.

By recognizing the game is rigged,[9] characters in these films realize that playing by the rules only serves their oppressors, and they shift their attention toward a bigger goal: freedom. For our characters, sometimes freedom is an individual escape and sometimes it's liberating the whole damn country (with impeccable fashion).

If the status quo and feeling frozen is the blue pill, then context and agency are the red pill. Once you take the red pill, you're free to make different choices, to chase your own freedom and the freedom of others, and to see more clearly what you want, unclouded by society's "can'ts" and "shouldn'ts."

In order to feel self-efficacy, you have to name what you're moving toward. Many people are afraid to take step one of gender exploration and transition because they can't envision what step ten is. The good news is that you don't have to have it all figured out to feel self-efficacy. You just need to know a general direction. Moving toward a goal, any goal, activates your thinking brain—the prefrontal cortex. Instead of fleeing, fighting, fawning, or freezing (which activates your survival brain), you're directing your brain's attention to what you want. Your brain can't move toward and away from something at the same time.

Remember Parker from earlier in the chapter? When I asked her about her goals for transition, she looked out the window for a moment, considering, before she said, "I want to feel like me in new, more authentic ways. I want to be comfortable with myself." With that goal anchoring her, she worked to notice what felt good in her gender expression and develop a support system around her (including at work) rather than put her focus on the negative reaction of her partner and fear of harassment. Saying clearly that she was moving toward a more authentic, visible gender expression helped her decide to come out to a trusted colleague and some close friends, as well as find gender-affirming clothing stores to explore.

Becoming the best version of ourselves isn't something that happens by accident. In order to grow, you have to prioritize it, surround yourself with people who also want to grow, and take intentional steps toward the person you want to be. Having a goal that lights you up, makes you feel excited when you say it, and centers on how you want to feel in the world can be your anchor on the days that feel hard.

The number one skill for coping with gender exploration and transition is what I call a bias to action. This doesn't mean taking giant leaps that feel panic inducing and potentially unsafe, or doing anything you don't want to do. But it does mean that you're more likely to act than not. It means taking one small step at a time.

Taking the first step toward gender transition can feel like you're in a glass elevator to the top of a skyscraper. Once you get in and push the button, you have no choice but to ride it to the top, highly visible to everyone around you. But gender exploration and transition aren't elevators; they're staircases, and you get to take each step as you're ready. We may not get to choose our gender identity (even though it may shift and change over time for some folks), but we do get to choose how to express that gender identity to the world and at what pace we go.

There is power in a tiny step.

ACTING "AS IF"

Building our self-efficacy is a lifelong process, but when we want to change thoughts or emotions, often the easiest and most accessible place to start is to change our behaviors.

And how do you do that? Well, you fake it. Sort of.

Consider this: If you were a person who believed you had agency, choice, and confidence, who trusted yourself and knew that you could do hard things, how would you behave differently?

What choices would you make?

How would you treat your body?

What resources would you use?

You can use these questions to guide your choices in any situation—from deciding what to wear to get a latte to choosing who gets to be in your life.

"Acting as if" isn't about pretending.

It's about choosing who you want to be in a certain moment and taking action that reflects that, even if you aren't feeling it just yet.

Mindset Shift #2: Self-Love and Self-Compassion

Gender exploration is an act of radical self-love for all of us, cis and trans alike. By intentionally engaging with gender instead of mindlessly accepting the "manual" we were given for our sex/gender assigned at birth, we are declaring we deserve to be our most authentic self in the world.

In *The Body Is Not an Apology*, Sonya Renee Taylor discusses radical self-love as an innate part of us, leading us to our highest selves.[10] I love this frame for self-love because it speaks to a larger truth: Self-love is about expanding into who we already are. The goal isn't to *make* ourselves love ourselves and our bodies by doing a million self-care tasks. It's about choosing to believe that the highest and most authentic version of ourselves is worth the growing pains, and knowing that we deserve to live our one and only life as *ourselves*.

In other words, our most authentic self is not what we *strive* for. It's who we get to *relax into* as we work through the layers of personal and cultural goop that keep us disconnected from ourselves and feeling small.

Self-compassion is how we evidence that love to ourselves. You cannot have one without the other.

Self-love and self-compassion are about

1. how you talk to yourself,
2. how you treat your body, and
3. how you let others treat you.

Let's take them one at a time.

How You Talk to Yourself

We talk to ourselves constantly, telling ourselves stories about our thoughts, feelings, and the circumstances of our lives. As we've already seen, those stories shape the way we move through the world, and if we're not mindful, we can be real jerks to ourselves, letting thoughts like *I'm a lazy, hopeless fraud and ugly to boot* run the show.

Researcher Kristin Neff talks about three elements of self-compassion: self-kindness, common humanity, and mindfulness.[11] Basically, it means not being an asshole to yourself when you aren't perfect, you "fail" at something, or things go wrong.

Instead of beating yourself up because you feel overwhelmed, ashamed, confused, frozen, scared, or doubtful, self-compassion helps us guide our thoughts back to a place of kindness and understanding. It teaches us to look for context: Why might you be thinking or feeling the way you are? How do culture and your life circumstances play a role? In what ways can you show yourself kindness, warmth, and understanding?

For example, if you're feeling shame or frustration about not moving forward with a goal like filling out name-change paperwork, showing yourself self-love and compassion might look like acknowledging your boss has been a nightmare at work or that you've been struggling with a chronic illness flare-up, and the paperwork is confusing as hell. Ain't nobody got spoons for that.*[12] When you see your struggle in context, it makes complete sense that you don't have the time, resources, or motivation you need!

It's also helpful to step back and recognize that many humans have experienced this (whatever "this" is) before. Seek those stories. You are not alone, whatever you are feeling or experiencing.

How You Treat Your Body

When you don't feel at home in your body, it can feel hard to feel love or even compassion for it. This is true for many people, thanks to diet culture, patriarchy, and narrow Western beauty standards, but it's especially true for transgender and non-binary folks who experience gender dysphoria. The good news is that self-love and self-compassion toward your body don't have to be about how your body *looks*. They're about respect for yourself as a physical being in the world.

When I spoke with Dr. Lindo Bacon, a white, non-binary trans person and author of *Health at Every Size*, they told me that

> some people are never going to get to a place of loving their body. That's an unrealistic expectation in the world we live in, and when you lay that expectation on people, it is just another reason for them to feel like there's something wrong with them. It may be way too much to ask of people to love their bodies, when there's so much stigma placed on certain bodies. Body respect feels like a more realistic goal... You don't have to love your body, but you can still treat it kindly.[13]

In other words, the question isn't "How can I love every inch of my body?" The real questions are "How can I accept my body as it is at this moment, while also wanting to change it? How can I show my body care and respect right now?"

---

* "Spoon theory" is a metaphor used to describe energy limitations for those with chronic illness.

Even if you don't always (or ever!) love how your body looks, tapping into the things you can respect about your body besides its appearance can allow you to treat yourself with care and appreciation. After all, our bodies do plenty of amazing things for us—the way they move, how they function to keep us alive, how soft they feel, how they let us speak up about the things we care about, how they rest, how they play, how they can experience pleasure.

Treating our bodies kindly and with respect is essential (and not just a nice thing to do sometimes) because, well, we live there. Until someone invents a way to upload our consciousness to the cloud, we get one body and one life. When we don't treat our bodies with respect and kindness, we often end up hurting ourselves in various ways. For instance, as someone with rheumatoid arthritis, I used to ignore my body's signals that I was pushing myself too hard, leading to days and weeks where I could barely walk (or think). Showing kindness to myself now means paying attention when I need to rest or get off my feet, and my quality of life is much better for it.

If you want to thrive, there is no more important relationship than the one you have with yourself and your body.

How You Let Others Treat You

Self-love and self-compassion directly impact how you let others treat you. When you don't feel love for yourself and your inner critic is the loudest voice in your head, you're more likely to accept bad behavior from others. Asking for what you need and setting boundaries with others is an important outcome of greater self-love.

If you have lots of practice shutting down parts of yourself for the benefit of others, you're not alone. Many people do. That's why focusing on yourself and your own needs when you start the deep work of exploring gender can be so uncomfortable. Setting boundaries and asking for what you need (like being called your correct name and pronouns) can feel like you're being a burden on others. You're not. We can't expect people, especially those unfamiliar with trans folks, to be perfect right away, but we *can* expect them to try and do their own work to continually get better.

Mindset Shift #3: Self-Growth

Adopting a growth mindset means that we teach ourselves to value the process, not the outcome. I have good news and bad news, my loves: You're never going to arrive at your most authentic self. And that's a good thing. Imagine for a minute who your most authentic eight-year-old self was. Would you want to be that person forever? No offense to the little me whose hobby was airbrushing T-shirts and forcing my neighbors to buy them and who thought a mocha caramel-drizzled Frappuccino with extra whipped cream was the crowning glory of life (that caffeine and sugar intake and my third-grade P&Ls explain a lot, now that I think about it...), but probably not! We're always growing and changing into more of who we are.

Stephanie Budge, a researcher at the University of Wisconsin–Madison whose research focuses on improving treatments and access to care for two-spirit, trans, and non-binary people, defines self-growth as "consistently working towards being the best version of yourself."[14] To me, self-growth is intentionally and consistently investing in yourself—your healing, your authenticity, your passions, your relationships, and your skills. As a result, you make space to play, to wonder, and to get to know yourself and explore your gender identity and expression. Leaning into a self-growth mindset allows you to put less pressure on achieving a certain transition goal and more into enjoying the journey of being an ever-evolving human being.

Because if you're going to bet on anything in this life, bet on yourself.

Many folks feel they are "behind" in their goals of transition because they didn't understand their identity at a young age or weren't able to socially transition earlier in their lives. Likewise, lots of transgender folks feel both internal and external pressure to have every piece of their identity figured out and a clear picture of their end goal before they take a single step forward in their transition. An attitude of self-growth turns down the volume on this pressure because the focus is on one tiny step at a time instead of rushing toward a perceived "finish line." There is no "behind" in a self-growth journey. There is no timeline. Wherever you are right now is the perfect place to grow from.

With a self-growth orientation, the "shoulds" of what your gender identity, expression, and/or transition are expected to look like become less important since a journey of self-growth looks different for everyone. A self-growth mindset is simply putting effort into being a student of yourself—learning and growing more into who you are and how you want to show up in the world. Playing with gender exploration naturally springs from getting to know yourself better. From this perspective, "success" isn't based on hitting particular milestones, or on how others perceive you (though having a supportive community *is* a large part of resilience). Rather, success is measured by how you feel about yourself.

Remember: Transition isn't the point.

Here's what I want you to know:

> Your struggles with gender exploration and transition are not a personal failing. You are not broken.
>
> You have not "failed."
>
> Your brain and body have been doing their best to keep you safe, and even if those tactics might no longer be useful, you can treat yourself with love and compassion as you choose to respond in new ways. Ways that give your brain space to think, write, create, make, and innovate. Space to just be.

When you give yourself permission to invest in your own growth with curiosity and joy, you have the capacity to invest in your relationships, experience pleasure that leaves you turned on and fired up, dance, live out your values, and simply exist.

Because when you show up as your most authentic self, free from confusion and self-doubt related to your gender, you light up the room. You have space to breathe.

And that's the world I want to live in.

In the words of Lizzo, "If I'm shinin', everybody gonna shine."

LETTER FROM YOUR FUTURE SELF

This is one of my favorite exercises to do with my clients.[15] It's adapted from designer Debbie Millman, and it is a powerful tool to help you tap into your why for transitioning and increase your feelings of self-efficacy, self-love, and self-growth by creating a hopeful vision for your life—a north star to guide you.

Your objective is to imagine that you are yourself but ten years in the future and write yourself a letter sharing a typical day in your life. This future self is the best and most lit-up version of you that you can possibly imagine. The world is your oyster, and you slurped that baby up. You are happy, content, and feel good in your own skin.

Take your time with this one. You can write the whole letter in one sitting or take some time and create multiple drafts until it feels right. Just kindly tell any analytical and perfectionistic voices in your head that you don't need their help. It's cool. You've got this.

After you've written your letter, read it over slowly and intentionally once a week for six months (bonus points for reading it out loud!).

As you read through it, take time to visualize living the day you've just described. Feel it in your bones, with all of your senses. At the end of those six months, reflect on what has shifted for you.

Oh, and come curious to this exercise. It's kinda magic.

Set the Scene and Gather Your Supplies

Grab a pen and paper. Really! An old-school pen and paper. Writing by hand activates important parts of your brain related to memory and learning.[16] As an alternative, grab your phone and voice record your thoughts and have them transcribed. Likewise, we are less likely to censor ourselves when we record ourselves talking.

Find a space where you can focus and that feels pleasurable to you. This might mean alone in your room or in a coffee shop with a nice, subtle buzz of conversation. This might mean taking a moment to tidy up and declutter.

Wherever you are, fill your senses with pleasurable things. Play some music, light a candle or some incense, make a cheese board or grab a chocolate bar (my favorites), sip on something yummy, put on your favorite clothes.

Take a few deep breaths.

Start Writing

Begin your letter by describing the moment you wake up and finish with the moment you go to sleep. Give all the details from the minute you wake up, brush your teeth, have your coffee or tea, all the way through until the minute you tuck yourself in at night. What is that day like for you? Where do you go? Who do you see? What do you surround yourself with? Give as much sensory detail as you can! I want you to be able to vividly see, hear, taste, smell, and touch your experience of the day.

Your work as you write this letter is to dream big—dream without any fear. Write it all down without judgment. No one is holding you to it, and you don't have to share it with anyone—don't let what feels "possible" constrain you.

As you start, reflect on the life you're trying to create for yourself and what you anticipate will be different about your life when your gender identity doesn't take up as much brain space as it does now. If you're feeling stuck or uncertain about what to include, I recommend you consider some of these questions and use them in your depiction of the day:

The Feels

- How do you experience pleasure in your life? If sex is important to you, what's your sex life like?
- How do you incorporate play into your life? What do you do for fun?
- What excites you about your life currently?
- As your future self, what are you looking forward to in the next six months?
- What emotions or thoughts are most present for you?

The People

- What is your community like? What spaces are you in? How are you helping to uplift and support your community?
- Who are your chosen family? What does intimacy look like with your chosen family?
- Who has your back when things are hard? Who celebrates your wins?
- Do you have a significant other(s)? What are they like? How do they treat you? How do you connect romantically and sexually? How do you play?
- Who do you live with?

- Do you have kids? What are they like? How old are they?
- Do you have pets? If so, talk about them.

The Details

- What's your style? What sort of clothes do you wear?
- What kind of hair do you have?
- Do you have tattoos? Piercings?
- Do you have hobbies or creative pursuits? What are they? What are you creating?
- What are you reading or watching or playing?
- How do you like to move your body? How do you feel in your body?
- What are you eating and drinking?
- Where do you live?
- What is your home like (*e.g., style of the furniture and décor, belongings, etc.*)?
- What is your bed like? What are your sheets like?
- How do you get around? Car? Bike? Yacht?

Gender Things

- What is your name?
- What are your pronouns?
- How do you identify your gender?
- How are you expressing your gender to the world?
- How do you feel in your body?
- How do you experience pleasure in your body specifically?

Your Work

- What's your primary source of income?
- Where do you devote your intellectual and emotional energy?
- What goals do you have for your career?
- What impact do you want to make in the world?
- Do you work for yourself or others?
- How do you want to feel every day at work?
- What do you want to spend your days doing?

CHAPTER 3

Unearth Resilience

Gender transition is a *wicked problem*.*

And no, I don't mean "wicked" like the Wicked Witch of the West. A wicked problem is one that is complex, interdependent, and has a lot of intersectional factors, making it difficult or impossible to resolve completely.[1] The hallmark of these problems is that they don't have tidy solutions. There is no one, single, perfect, universal answer that will cut through the complexity of homelessness, or climate change or, in our case, why gender exploration and transition can feel so difficult, confusing, and full of anxiety. Navigating the transphobic culture we live in is hard as hell.

In the last chapter, we talked about how accepting the reality that oppressive systems exist helps us see them for what they are. Acceptance lets us develop a critical eye and choose how we'd like to contribute to collective liberation from a grounded place while still prioritizing rest, pleasure, and joy.

Most of all, accepting gender transition as a wicked problem frees up our brains to focus on problems we *can* solve about gender exploration and transition from both individual and community-based perspectives. Through those three mindsets of self-efficacy, self-love/self-compassion, and self-growth, we put our brains and nervous systems in a space to

---

* Wicked problems come from social planning and human-centered design—a subset of the larger design world that focuses on applying design thinking to how we create our lives and world. When I came across human-centered design in an interview on *The Tim Ferriss Show* with designer Debbie Millman from the letter exercise in chapter 2, my nerdy soul lit up, and I knew this was a missing piece of the puzzle for my work.

respond rather than react—to name the wicked problem before us, create space to grieve the reality of living in a transphobic world, and start to answer that all-important question: How do we want to handle it?[2]

The way we choose to cope—which is to say, the way we handle hard things—determines the way we move (or don't) through our journey. Viewing gender transition as a wicked problem acknowledges why it's complex to navigate while also offering a hopeful path forward that focuses on creativity and agency. In other words, it puts us in the mindset of the mice (from chapter 2) that *didn't* freeze in response to a shock because they believed they had the ability to escape.

Coping with gender exploration and transition is about finding "good enough" solutions, instead of perfect ones, that work for *you* and center on self-growth. By choosing strategies that center on your agency, you can make space to find and develop the best of you right now.

Coping Skills That Work

We all use coping skills on a daily basis, whether we're conscious of them or not. We have a lot of ways to cope—some are helpful, some are less helpful, and some are helpful in one moment and not helpful the next.

What makes a coping strategy effective is that it keeps us moving forward (remember that bias to action?). Dr. Stephanie Budge, from the previous chapter, calls this facilitative coping.[3] "Facilitative" comes from the Latin word "facilis," meaning "ease," and is proactive, self-growth focused, and goal oriented.[4] Bringing more ease into your gender-exploration journey involves learning new skills, creating new patterns of behavior, building and using resources, and working toward a positive vision of your future.

Finding coping skills that work isn't about giving you boatloads of new tools that will magically make everything better. The secret to transitioning with more ease is believing you already have everything you need. Because you do. Your body and brain are intuitively wise, but a casualty of living within a system that causes trauma is that we often feel disconnected from our bodies, our desires, our inner wisdom, and wisdom from our transgender/non-binary (or Indigenous) ancestors. After many years of logically mulling over top surgery and telling myself all the reasons I shouldn't get it or that it wasn't the right time, my moment of clarity happened when I got still and felt the calm in my belly and excitement in my chest as I thought about life without boobs.

Our innate resilience is still there, ready to be unearthed.

Here's the thing, though: What really helps us in the face of our problems might not be pain-free at first. For her book *Burnout*, I spoke with Emily Nagoski[5] about effective coping. As I described to her, taking care of ourselves is sometimes like taking care of a skinned knee. Most folks know what to do when they fall off a bike: They wash the gravel out with water, spray some antiseptic on it, bandage it, and maybe elevate it with some ice. Even though this is exactly what needs to happen for your knee to heal, getting the gunk out of it stings and the knee still hurts for a while. Effective coping doesn't always take away the pain immediately. But it *is* what you need to heal.

Research tells us the early stages of gender transition are generally the hardest.[6] We also know that transgender/non-binary folks early in transition tend to use avoidant coping strategies—things like substance use, hiding their gender identity or aspects of gender expression, and even suicidal ideation and attempts—to numb out and shove down the difficult emotions that come with gender exploration and transition, or deny a transgender or non-binary identity altogether. Wicked problems quickly feel overwhelming, and often that leaves us wanting to avoid them. And an avoidant response makes total sense! It's natural, strategic, and a sign that your brain/body is trying to keep you safe.

Here's the problem: Shoving down emotions doesn't make them go away. It just builds up pressure until it feels like we're going to explode.

Avoidant coping often comes from a deep fear that we will be rejected and unloved because of who we are. We would rather suppress, ignore, or numb ourselves to a situation than face it just in case our worst fears are confirmed: That we will always feel as lonely as we are right now. That we are too much and not enough at the same time. Sound familiar? If so, you aren't alone.*

Shoving down difficult emotions like fear, sadness, grief, and anger (or gender dysphoria) doesn't help us either. The ideals of toxic positivity state we can solve all of our problems by denying we are experiencing difficult emotions and just focusing on love, light, and #nobadvibes. This is a recipe for disaster.[7]

If you've been pushing your emotions down for a while, it's like a buildup of water pressure behind a dam. The pressure builds up on one side of the dam over time, and eventually, a crack will appear in the wall and the water *will* find a way out. Most likely, it won't just leak out in tiny amounts but use the crack as a way to explode out of the dam, dramatically creating a giant rush of water. It can feel like big feelings will consume you if you let them out a little bit.

This can be scary. And the wild rush of water doesn't last forever. It's a temporary state of release that comes as the result of built-up pressure. As that first gush settles down, the water on both sides of the dam becomes more still. As you learn to sit with and process your emotions, you will experience less of that wild rush—because you have less pressure built up. Eventually, you'll be able to ride your own waves of emotion like a pro surfer does the ocean.

DISTRACTION OR AVOIDANCE?

Sometimes we need to zone out to our favorite show surrounded by treats and pets. In the middle of an intense emotional experience, we need time to rest. To put down the heavy thing, relax, and let our brain have a break.

Distraction and avoidance can look similar since many of the *activities* are the same. The difference is in the intention. In avoidance, the

* Sometimes avoidant coping and a fear of rejection come from real safety concerns about being visible as a transgender person. We will discuss in chapter 4 how strategic gender expression can be a facilitative coping skill.

intention is to shove down emotions and bury your head in the sand. In distraction, the intention is to take a *break* from the emotionally intense experience with a plan to come back to it later when the intensity might be a little lower.

For example, distracting yourself by having a couple of drinks or a joint with a close friend while you listen to great music and laugh about the latest antics of their dog, David Rose, likely feels recharging. But avoiding your feelings by going to a bar, downing four shots to numb out, and stumbling home to drunk text your ex about returning the sex toys you left at their house? That'll just continue to drain you.

It is okay to take breaks from thinking about gender. In fact, I encourage it. These breaks decrease the emotional intensity, helping you recharge and make more grounded decisions. Rest is necessary for moving through gender transition in a way that feels sustainable.[8]

Designing Effective Coping Strategies

A lot of the advice out there for exploring gender centers on thinking and journaling about your past and present experiences of gender. While this reflection time can be useful and bring up important insights, folks often get stuck here endlessly mulling over the same questions and doubts, spending months or years considering why or if they might be trans or trying to figure out solutions to sticky or impossible problems (like how to make sure you won't experience *any* rejection) before taking a single step forward.

That stuckness makes perfect sense: After all, it's hard to imagine a positive future as a transgender person when we haven't seen it reflected in our culture. This is where a bias to action comes in.

We get to try things. Some of those things might work and some won't. That's all part of the process. Creativity, play, and testing out possible solutions for where you feel stuck are *essential* for building an authentic, lit-up life. Every day when you wake up, the choices you make (and don't make) design your life whether you do them intentionally or unintentionally.[9] So let's do design our lives intentionally.

Focus on the Journey, Not the Destination

The two biggest questions I get asked by clients are "What if I'm trans?" and "What if I'm wrong about being trans?" But these are the wrong questions. They're unhelpful to most people because they're so big and often rooted in anxiety.

Figuring out if you're transgender, non-binary, or cisgender is the *answer* to a bigger, more important question: "What makes me feel more open, more myself, more free?"

This kind of question will be your best guide.

As you explore possible solutions to complicated problems that come with gender exploration and transition, it's helpful to stay away from thinking about "the finish line."

Instead, ask yourself questions like "What is the next easiest step I can take?" and "What are all the possible solutions to this problem?" Write down all your wild ideas—don't judge or censor yourself. You might be surprised at what flows out of you.

Do the Thing

It can be scary to think about taking a step forward when you don't know where you're going. However, the beauty of design thinking is in "doing the thing."

Essentially, this means the best information we can get about coping with gender exploration and transition comes from trying things out and seeing how they feel.

I encourage my clients to start with the next easiest, tiniest step. This often means taking baby steps (like asking a close and supportive friend to try out a new name for you in private) until you feel comfortable taking a bigger leap (like changing your name at work).

We are aiming for what education theory calls the "zone of proximal development." Imagine a bullseye. The center is your comfort zone, where you feel safe. It's cozy in our comfort zone, but we often don't take the risks that allow us to move forward if we stay here.

The outer edge of the bullseye is the "flooding" zone. This means the step feels so big that you haven't developed the skills or the resources to handle it in a grounded way. It's likely going to feel like standing naked in front of your entire high school. Flooding might look like coming out on social media spontaneously before you have come out to close and supportive friends and then spending the next few days in a mild panic attack with a sense of dread every time your phone notifications buzz because your cousin told your grandma who called you to ask about "the surgery" and tut-tut about how "you'd be so pretty if you grew your hair out." AHH.

The section of the bullseye between the comfort zone and the flooding zone is the zone of proximal development.[10] This is the zone where we take a step that gives us butterflies in our stomach. It feels both scary and exciting.

The truth is that *being* safe and *feeling* safe aren't always the same thing.

A few years ago, I went on a retreat in the mountains. The facilitators led us to a crumbling dam in the middle of a forest where a river used to run, informing us that we were going to jump off it. Our first challenge was to climb a sixty-foot ladder to reach the top, which only caused my heart to race if I looked down. Once at the top, I carefully clipped a climbing rope to my harness and shuffled along a tiny ledge to get to the center of the dam, where a helper was waiting. Watching a few small rocks go over the edge as I inched along the ledge, five inches between me and the dry riverbed below, I realized I hadn't taken a breath in about thirty seconds. Sixty feet looks very different when you're standing on five inches of crumbling rock looking down. The helper looked at me in the eyes and said, "Repeat after me. Even though I don't feel safe, I am safe."

I could feel my sweaty hands and pounding heart. A voice was yelling in my head, "GET DOWN. DO NOT JUMP." But I dutifully repeated the phrase.

Even though I don't feel safe, I am safe.

As I did, I noticed the thick ropes securely attached to my harness. There was someone below to let me down gently. My heart didn't slow down, and my hands were no less slippery. But I felt the fear shift into something else—excitement.

"Now jump!" And so I did.

Even though I don't feel safe, I am safe.

This is the level of discomfort we are aiming for. In this zone, we can learn and take risks that challenge us, but not to a level that would be emotionally overwhelming or physically unsafe. We have the skills to navigate the risks in a way that may not be comfortable, but we believe we can handle it without falling into a heap of despair on the bed. For me, this meant having a supportive community before I came out to my parents, who I knew would be unsupportive, and I let my people know I might need to call them when the day came. The experience was still difficult, but I wasn't alone, and that made all the difference.

USE YOUR RESOURCES

Using your resources means considering internal resources, like emotional-regulation skills, and external resources, like supportive and knowledgeable people/groups or knowing the legal protections at work.

When your brain is in a helpless, hopeless, and overwhelmed place, it's difficult to accurately assess what resources and supports you may already have or could gain access to. You feel alone and stuck and like you just want to crawl into a hole and live there forever. I've been there.

It's true that many trans folks lack easy access to many resources. I've also seen clients (and friends and myself) discount potential resources, supports, and action steps because they aren't the perfect solution to the problem. The truth is that accessing support, coping skills, and resources is an imperfect process.

And you have more resources than you think, both internally and externally. You've likely been using some instinctive and adaptive coping strategies without even realizing it—like, because of rheumatoid arthritis, I choose to not take the stairs at work because I need to save my energy for rock climbing later in the day.

Bringing attention to these can help you use them more intentionally when things get hard.

In a conversation with Dr. Stephanie Budge, we discussed how impactful accessible resources can be—like taking in positive transgender stories, mindfully enjoying moments of joy and pleasure, and simply being around other transgender people (virtually or in person).[11]

Communicating about a trans identity and getting social support is one of the biggest sources of resilience for transgender/non-binary folks.[12] This support could be an affirming therapist, coach, online forum, support group, friends, or family. Transgender, non-binary, and queer spaces are often life changing for folks who have felt isolated (I discuss how to find places and people like this in chapters 10 and 12).

Remember: You aren't alone.

You Can Do Hard Things

Taking risks is scary. Uncertainty about gender identity, the path forward, as well as a fear of regret and detransition (which we'll talk about in chapter 4) leave many individuals feeling frozen and stuck in their gender journey.

But when you focus on curiosity, reframing negative thoughts, focusing on the journey instead of the destination, using your resources, and doing the thing and *not* on whether you're trans enough (you are), if you're behind (you're not), or if anyone will ever love you if you're trans (they will), you can explore gender and transition with more ease, curiosity, and pleasure. It allows you to acknowledge the wicked problem of gender transition while actively moving forward toward a life that lights you up with more confidence and curiosity. It gives you space to breathe and play.

You are innately resilient, adaptable, wise, and magical. You already have everything inside you that you need. And figuring out how to access that wisdom and resilience isn't something you have to do alone.

Let's do the thing.

HOW DO YOU WANT TO HANDLE IT? SOME REFLECTION QUESTIONS.

If you find yourself feeling stuck, frustrated, or overwhelmed, these questions can provide a catalyst, a portal, for moving into more effective and easeful coping. Most importantly, don't let the answers get stuck in your head. Use these questions as a jumping-off point to intentionally move toward your most authentic, lit-up self with self-compassion.

Come Curious

- What do I know for sure about my gender identity and expression?
- When do I feel the best in my body? What is "best" to me? (*Describe with as much body-based detail as possible—shoulders relaxed, loose, open chest, settled, etc.*)
- How is what I'm feeling connected to broader contexts of systemic oppression / internalized transphobia / family and friend dynamics / work dynamics / a binary gendered society? How can I have more compassion for myself in light of this?
- Are my negative thoughts in line with my values and what I truly believe?
- Which younger version of me is scared? What age are they? What was going on in my life then that made me afraid? How can I show compassion for that part of myself? How is that younger, scared voice in my head no longer helpful to me now?

Reframe

- What are the facts?
- What is the context?
- Is this thought true? Is it possible to know if it's true?
- Is this thought in line with my values?
- Is this thought useful to me?
- Is this thought kind to myself? What is a more compassionate way to say this?
- How can I bring more nuance into my thought?

Focus on the Journey, Not the Destination

- What do I desire?
- What makes me feel more open, more myself, more free?
- What tiny step might help me feel more open, more myself, more free?

Use Your Resources (Internal and External)

- What internal resources do I have? (*Examples: grounding skills, connection to ancestors, the ability to self-soothe, addressing negative and untrue thoughts, self-efficacy, self-growth, and self-love/ self-compassion.*)
- What external and community resources do I have or could fairly easily get? (*Examples: finding a therapist or coach, a local LGBTQ center, LGBTQ and transgender affinity groups in companies, online forums and support groups, supportive friends and family.*)
- Is it possible for me to travel to a trans-affirming conference/city/ event/friend?
- Who affirms me already?
- Are there ways that I'm not accepting the support and resources available because I feel like I'm not "trans enough" or worthy?

Do the Thing

- What is the next easiest, tiniest step I could take to move toward my goal?
- Even though I don't feel safe, am I safe?
- How do I keep myself physically, financially, and emotionally safe if I take this step? (*For example: Do I have a way to leave the situation? Will there be financial impacts that I'm not able to handle right now, like my parents cutting off my tuition payments from university or being fired from a job?*)

CHAPTER 4

The Boogeymen of Gender Transition

If questions like "What if I regret transitioning?" and "How can I be sure I won't want to detransition later?" have made you lose sleep and fall down rabbit holes of Reddit and YouTube, you aren't alone. Fears related to regret, detransition, and rejection are some of the most common anxieties I hear from my clients.

I call these the boogeymen of gender transition not because they aren't real or to minimize the impact of these fears, but because these topics, especially detransition, have reached the status of urban myth. Like the man with a hook on his arm menacing young lovers "parking" in the woods, these stories are used like cautionary tales, meant to ward off such "dangers" as premarital sex or, in this case, gender transition. They take on a life of their own far out of proportion to reality.

What's real is that everyone, regardless of gender identity, experiences uncertainty, regret, and rejection at some point in their life. Since these feelings are going to come up no matter what, our task is to decide how we want to relate to and handle them instead of trying to avoid them altogether.

I've found the best way to vanquish a boogeyman is to shine a light into the dark corners where shadows create monsters. This chapter will do just that, deepening your capacity to do hard things by helping you to reframe and get curious about some of the scariest "monsters" of gender exploration—fear of regret, uncertainty, detransition, and rejection.

Reframing Regret and Detransition

In *How to Train Your Dragon*, the movie's hero, Hiccup, encounters what he thinks is a terrifying monster—yep, you guessed it: It's a dragon. But not just any dragon: This one is the stuff of myths, never seen by any Viking alive in his village, famed for incredible flying speed and the ability to go invisible. But even as he fears death by fiery inferno, Hiccup gets curious about the dragon. He offers him a fish, which he quickly gobbles up, and in time the two become best buds. Where am I going with this? Sometimes the things that scare us are more frightening in theory than they are up close, and if we show them a little curiosity, they can transform from unthinkable monsters that scare the bejesus out of us into something that we can live alongside (and even befriend).

Approaching the topics of regret and detransition with curiosity can take away much of the emotional charge of fear and give us space to explore from a grounded place. Moving *through* these fears requires courage and a willingness to embrace complexity and uncertainty. But remember, you can do hard things.

These topics are multifaceted and politicized. Stories of folks detransitioning or regretting an aspect of their transition are often used as "proof" that a transgender identity isn't valid or as fuel for anti-transgender legislation, often targeting medically necessary care for youth. This doesn't change the need for more medical and mental health providers to work from an informed consent model instead of putting up barriers to accessing medical transition care.

One of the difficulties of discussing regret and detransition is a lack of clarity over what *exactly* we're talking about. Whenever a nuanced topic gets wrapped up with politics and media, it becomes one-dimensional, black-and-white, flattened. It's the uncertainty of not knowing what is lurking in the dark that's the scariest. So, let's get to know our "monsters."

Regret is a feeling of sadness about a decision that you've made and/or a wish that an outcome could have been different and better. Sometimes we regret our choice—like saying something mean during a fight.

Other times, we feel regret because the outcome didn't turn out the way we wanted—like regretting getting married because you're getting a divorce.

Detransition is the process of leaving behind a current gender identity and/or expression and transitioning "back" into a previous gender identity or expression. This may include social/medical/legal transition or it may not. Folks who identify as detransitioners may no longer identify as transgender, or they might still identify as transgender but have chosen to live as their sex assigned at birth.

The missing piece in this conversation is *why* someone might feel regret and then detransition. Because it isn't a simple answer. The dominant narrative about regret and detransition assumes that someone, who now identifies as cisgender, made a "mistake" in once identifying as transgender and now regrets transitioning, with a heavy emphasis on medical regrets, and that individual chooses to walk back one or all those changes. This narrative is true for some individuals, but it leaves out context and nuance and presents a skewed view of the reasons people may choose to "detransition."

Research on the experiences of transgender/non-binary folks isn't well funded, but it is studied. Luckily, we do have enough data from both trans-specific studies and general research on medical regret to start putting together a more nuanced and hopeful picture.

Here is what we know:

We know the rate for detransition and regret for adults ranges from less than 1 percent to roughly 4 percent.[1] In a survey sent out to surgeons providing gender-affirming surgeries, 49 percent of respondents had never encountered a patient who regretted their transition. Surgeons reported that, out of 22,725 patients who received gender-affirming surgeries, only 62 patients, or 0.2 percent, reported regret or expressed a desire to detransition. Out of these patients, only 22, or 0.09 percent of total patients, reported a change in gender identity.[2]

In multiple studies, the authors found that regret and/or the decision to detransition often are *not* about a change in someone's gender identity. Instead, they are more often because of the following:[3]

- living as a transgender or non-binary person and dealing with transphobia became too difficult (this represents the majority of folks who detransition)
- a lack of social and family support
- regret about an outcome of surgery, aesthetically or because their view of themselves wasn't significantly changed post-surgery
- medical complications or pain
- regret over a medical decision made because of the intense pressure to conform to a binary gender identity and "prove" legitimacy
- family/career/financial/health/incarceration issues forcing someone to detransition
- an evolving identity to non-binary transgender identity
- expectations about passing/blending were not met

Do you notice how many of these reasons aren't about the choice to transition itself but a reaction to the transphobic society we live in? Feelings of regret are often connected to a wish for gender freedom to be celebrated and supported, a desire to be seen for who we are, and feelings of loss and sadness about how difficult navigating the world as a transgender/non-binary individual can be.

Ongoing research suggests that not only are the numbers for detransition low, but regret over transitioning is often not about someone's identity as a transgender/non-binary person. This is a less exciting headline for Fox News, but it's great news for us as we ground ourselves in facts, curiosity, and nuance instead of viewing detransition as a spooky monster under the bed.

Regret Isn't as Scary as You Think

Fear of regret is a connected but unique boogeyman that often holds folks back from exploring and transitioning their gender. Regret is a feeling like any other feeling. Yet we put regret on a pedestal as an emotion that must be avoided at all costs instead of treating it like any other unpleasant emotion we experience and move through.

Regret—or at least the possibility of regret—is inevitable. There is potential regret in any large life decision, especially medical decisions. If you never make a decision you might regret, I would argue that you aren't taking any risks. The goal shouldn't be to have no regrets in life. In fact, studies consistently demonstrate that people are more likely to regret actions NOT taken than actions taken.[4]

Regret is often about an unwanted outcome more than the decision itself. When people feel regret, they often assume they made a bad choice, and it brings up self-doubt and shame. However, good decisions can be regretted if the outcome isn't what we hoped for. In reality, most decisions are fairly neutral.

Let's consider, for example, the decision to move to New York City.

You've dreamed of moving to New York your whole life, and you're finally able to do it. You have a job offer there and a little money saved up. The city is everything you dreamed of—there's great food, you love the hustle and bustle, and you find a beautiful community of people. You will look back on your decision to move to New York and say, "Wow! That was a great decision."

Now, let's say you make the same decision to move to New York, but it doesn't turn out quite the same. You still have the job offer and a little money, but the apartment you rent is a studio in a five-story walk-up. Brutal. Everything is expensive, and because you're working long hours, you have trouble making friends and you rarely get to experience anything you'd dreamed about doing. In this case, you are more likely to look back at the decision to move to New York and say, "I made a bad decision and I regret it. And now I feel ashamed that I made a bad decision."

But the decision itself wasn't bad. Either of these outcomes was a possibility, and the choice itself was carefully considered. My point is, you can experience disappointment at an outcome while still trusting you made the best decision possible given the information you had.

Wrapped up in regret is the belief that life would be better if you hadn't made a particular choice, but that's not usually true either. In the aforementioned example, there is a reason you moved to New York. Something about where you lived before wasn't working for you. If you had stayed, there is no guarantee that your life would have been better. In fact, you'd have been just as likely, if not more so, to regret *not* moving to New York than moving to New York.[5]

I also question why, as a culture, we are so focused on transgender folks avoiding experiencing regret about a permanent to semipermanent body change but not cisgender folks. There is not the same policing, fear, demand to prove "legitimacy," and professional conversation about liability and gatekeeping with cisgender individuals who choose to undergo plastic surgery to change their body. Similarly, we do not have the same reaction to someone's choice to change their body with laser hair removal, LASIK eye surgery, hormonal supplements, or other body-altering decisions.

But when the aim of surgery, hormones, or another bodily change is related to gender identity and expression, suddenly the stakes seem higher. Why? You guessed it: transphobia and transmisogyny. And it's often hidden behind sentiments such as, "I just want my child/friend/partner to be safe and happy, and I'm worried about them." Part of the bias and narrative about regret and gender-affirming surgeries is that culturally, we don't actually believe it's a good thing.

The conversation would look very different if

- we truly believed gender freedom is the goal for everyone;
- changing your name, pronouns, body, and/or appearance to feel more authentic was just another part of self-growth celebrated in our culture;
- we applied "my body, my choice" and a belief in bodily autonomy to gender and not just reproductive health. Wait...

QUESTIONS TO REFRAME REGRET

No matter how many times you read these studies, the fear-of-regret boogeyman will likely make an appearance or two in your journey.

When it does, instead of asking yourself, *Will I regret it?* try on one of these questions instead:

Am I making the best decision I can, given the information I have in this moment?
Do I have good reasons for wanting this?
Do I reasonably understand the risks and rewards of this decision?
Is this decision consistent with my values and life plans?[6]

Navigating Worry and Uncertainty

When fear and anxiety are ringing loudly in our ears, it makes sense to want to protect ourselves. We worry in an attempt to feel some control over our anxious feelings, eliminate uncertainty, and come up with answers to the questions we think are the most important. Questions like...

What if gender transition doesn't "work"?
What if I never feel like [gender identity]?
What if I don't look the way I want to look?
What if I never feel legitimate? Am I ever going to be enough?
What if I'm wrong about wanting a particular aspect of social/medical/legal transition?
What if I hate ______?

Our brains think that if we worry long and hard enough and eliminate all uncertainty, we will be able to move forward with confidence.[7]

It's a lie.

When I hear clients bring up this jumble of worries, I hear the fear that all the wrestling with gender and effort to be authentically themselves in the world will be for nothing. That at the "end" of transition, they will still be unhappy and not seen or loved for who they are. I also hear a lack of trust in themselves.

I understand how scary and painful those feelings can be. I know what it's like to be so frozen with the what-ifs and anxiety that your brain reaches the inevitable conclusion that you're destined to die alone in an alley eaten by cats (cue "Circle of Life").

And yet, research shows that transitioning dramatically decreases gender dysphoria and increases mental health.[8]

We also know the overwhelming majority of folks who transition their gender experience positive mental health benefits:

95 percent had better life outcomes as a result of medical transition,[9]
80 percent reported significant reductions in gender dysphoria after hormonal and surgical transition,
78 percent reported significant improvement in psychological symptoms,
80 percent reported significant improvement in quality of life,
72 percent reported significant improvement in sexual function.[10]

A small, qualitative study by Dr. Stephanie Budge found that 100 percent of respondents did not regret their transition and felt that transitioning was the best emotional decision they had made *despite* also reporting emotional hardship and difficulty coping with rejection.[11]

That said, gender transition won't solve *all* your problems. You will likely still experience dysphoria sometimes. Your mental health will not be perfect, because you aren't a robot. People will still misgender you (ask my transmasculine friends with full beards), and you'll still experience microaggressions.

I do know two things:

1. You don't need to change a thing to be loved and seen for who you are. Beyond your own self-love and self-respect, there are people out there who will affirm you *today*. So if "become worthy and lovable" is still floating around on your to-do list somewhere, cross it off now.
2. Giving yourself an opportunity to exist in the world as the most lit-up version of yourself (to the best of your ability, given whatever circumstance you're in) creates space for more affirming and supportive people to show up in your life.

Remember: Transition itself is not the point. *Gender freedom* is the point. And sometimes chasing freedom requires making bold choices when we can't know the outcome, despite our best efforts to understand and control as many risks as possible.

QUESTIONS TO REFRAME WORRIES

If you find yourself stuck in an anxious what-if headspace, try considering the positive what-ifs as well.

What if this went well?
What possibilities have I never or rarely considered?
What would it feel like to not have to shove down parts of myself?
What would it feel like to be affirmed at work / by my partner / by my loved ones?
What could having a strong and supportive community look like?

Do the Thing: Navigating the Boogeymen of Gender Exploration

Now that we've shone a light on the boogeymen of fear of regret and detransition, let's take a look at a few ways to navigate them.

Talk about It

Often, folks think they are alone in their swirling thoughts. This can bring up feelings of shame, which, as Brené Brown says, thrive in the dark.[12]

Just like boogeymen.

Talking about these common fears and questions (which are, by the way, exceptionally unexceptional and normal) with trusted and affirming folks in your life takes away their power and normalizes the experience.

Get Good Information

When you're trying to make a decision, you need enough information to figure out potential risks and benefits. Getting community wisdom from other transgender/non-binary folks is an important, and often necessary, part of transgender culture and solidarity. I've also seen how the search for information, validation, and an answer act like catnip for anxiety, at best leaving you overwhelmed and more confused and, at worst, giving you bad or outdated information.

What I recommend is to gather as much objective and accurate information as possible from credible sources and then check in with the community for more nuanced and personal experiences. For example, if you're concerned about bottom growth related to starting testosterone, instead of scrolling down Reddit forums for hours trying to decrease your anxiety, you can ask your prescribing doctor about the timelines for changes and typical growth patterns they see. Armed with this information, you can ask folks online about their experiences of bottom growth from a more knowledgeable and secure place.

Make Grounded Decisions

Regret won't kill you. I promise. You can do hard things, and I know you can grieve and heal and move on from choices you regret. It can even be a positive thing in the long run, clarifying your values and impacting future decisions.[13] But while I will always remind you that regret isn't something to be feared at the level we do so, and that people are more likely to regret action not taken than action taken,[14] there *are* ways to approach decision-making that can minimize the likelihood of regret.

We call this hot-and-cold decision-making, and it's all about giving ourselves the space, time, and nervous-system regulation we need to make a grounded choice, instead of shooting from the hip.

Carey arrived at their top-surgery consultation in a flurry of activity. Almost late, they sat down in the waiting room, tapping their toes quickly on the floor. They felt a pressure in their chest, and their heart raced as they waited. Once in the doctor's office, they zoned out during the surgeon's detailed explanation of the procedure, daydreaming about how top surgery would take away their gender dysphoria for good. They interrupted the doctor to ask about the earliest available surgery date. They knew it would be difficult to figure out time off work, finances, and how to manage recovery while living alone in that short of a time period but couldn't stand the idea of feeling like this one more day.

Oof, Carey is coming in *hot*! "Hot" decisions can best be described as making decisions from a place of anxiety, scarcity, or urgency. While there is often an intense desire for gender-affirming surgeries and other identity-affirming choices, there is a difference between desire and making decisions from an agitated or heightened emotional space. When people are "hot," they tend to make choices they think will quickly "fix" their feelings. This can lead to folks not understanding the risks of the choice and overestimating its likelihood for success. Definitions of "success" in a hot state often include unrealistic expectations, like never being misgendered again after surgery. So it's unsurprising that people are more likely to experience regret from decisions made in a hot state if the outcome is worse or different than what they imagined.[15]

In contrast, a "cold" decision is a decision made from a more grounded and balanced state of mind. In a cold state, people can turn down the volume on urgency and breathe. They can think and talk through the risks and possible outcomes of the choice, get clear on their expectations and criteria for "success," and make the best decision based on the information they have, in line with their values and desires. This doesn't mean folks have zero anxiety, but they are able to stay present and trust themselves throughout the process.

Carey in a cold state arrived at their top-surgery consultation with time to spare and excitedly made themselves a tea in the waiting room. Noticing the nervousness and pressure in their chest, they took a deep breath, pushing their feet into the floor to ground themselves. Once in the doctor's office, they listened closely as the doctor detailed the procedure, and they pulled out a list of questions gathered from other transgender friends they had spoken to and a few articles they had read about surgery techniques and outcomes. They looked at the doctor's result photos and determined the surgeon's technique was a good fit for what they wanted. Carey could barely contain their excitement and relief as they scheduled the surgery for a couple months out. Even though an earlier date was available, they knew it would be easier to plan for time off and secure financing. They walked out of the office with the information packet about pre- and post-surgery details and started thinking about what support systems they would need for an easy recovery.

If you're currently in a hot state, know that you're completely normal.

No matter how good our coping skills are, we all experience a hot state from time to time. The goal isn't to never experience a hot state but to *notice* when you're feeling hot and make the choice to slow down. It's okay to take the time you need to regulate your body and emotions before making a major decision. Turning down the emotional temperature can look like taking a walk or going on a bike ride, doing a mindfulness exercise, focusing on breathing, journaling, or tapping into your support systems by talking to a supportive friend or other transgender/non-binary folks who have been through a similar experience.

Through the regret section, we understood this "monster" as simply a feeling and brought it back down to a manageable size. But underneath that fear of regret is often a fear of another feeling: rejection.

The Boogeyman of Rejection

When the tiniest hint of a mood shift rolls across someone's face, my brain immediately panics: *What's that? What's wrong? Are you mad at me? Clearly you no longer love me.* Someone close to me gets moody when their feet are warm, and I used to assume every time they would get quiet or snippy that it was my fault. I would ask ten thousand times what was wrong while racking my brain to figure out what I had done to offend them... *when their damn feet were just too hot.*

We are wired for connection. Rejection, perceived or real, hits on primal buttons related to belonging and survival. As babies, rejection by a parent can be fatal. We carry this longing for connection with us into adulthood, and the possibility of rejection often feels intolerable. Unfortunately, experiencing rejection at some point in our lives is an inevitable and profoundly human experience. It's unrealistic to believe that every single person we encounter will see and love us for the totality and complexity of who we are.*

* The experience of not being fully seen for who you are in all your various identities is not specific to transgender/non-binary folks. Cisgender folks also experience this, especially folks who are BIPOC, disabled, or have other intersecting identities.

That feeling is painful. But even though it hurts, when I've experienced rejection, I've survived every time. I bet you have too, since, you know, you're currently reading this book. And on the other side of these painful experiences are better boundaries, more wisdom and self-worth, deeper and better relationships, and less tolerance for people who are not compatible with who you are.

When I hear fears related to regret and detransition, I often hear the underlying fear of rejection, which can be summed up by the question "Will I be loved for who I am?"

Here's the great news: Being seen and loved for who you are and having confidence in yourself are available to you right now without changing a thing about yourself. Validation of your identity is important and powerful, but what your body looks like has nothing to do with whether the people who love you will respect your identity and see you for who you are.

And by the way, "the people who love you" includes yourself. Too often we forget that, ultimately, how you feel about yourself comes from within. Many of us try to avoid experiencing rejection by people-pleasing and being hypervigilant to *any* sign of potential rejection. We make ourselves smaller and more "digestible," often apologizing for simply existing, and put aside our needs and boundaries for others' comfort (remember the fawn response?). Your job is to bring that focus and attention away from an anxious people-pleasing response and put it back on your own mental health and joy.

It takes courage to show up in the world as *you* and risk being rejected. Showing up authentically and in line with your values, with boundaries and self-respect, isn't always popular with others. It rocks the boat. But the boat needs to be rocked.

Rejection can be a gift.

Every rejection makes more space for the people who are your biggest fans, who have your back, and who celebrate who you are. Because they are out there. I promise.

It's also easy to assume that feeling rejected is about your gender identity or expression when, sometimes, what we perceive as rejection is just someone's feet being too hot.

And for the record, you are so lovable.

The Ultimate Boogeymen Defense: Self-Trust

I've worked with transgender and non-binary clients for more than ten years at the time of writing this book. In that time, I've never once had a client who regretted transition or wanted to stop moving forward. Even during some of their hardest times, they expressed that living as their authentic self was a source of strength and joy through those emotional trials.

I'm not saying that no transgender or non-binary person will ever experience regret or decide to detransition (whatever that means to them). But when we are guided by questions like "What feels good to me? When do I feel most lit up? When do I feel the most like myself? When do I experience joy and pleasure?" it's hard to go wrong.

I believe that regret, rejection, and detransition aren't things to be feared. Feeling uncertainty, self-doubt, anxiety, and fear are normal parts of exploring your gender. It doesn't make you less trans, and it doesn't mean a decision is wrong. Moving through these difficult feelings is part of the process.

And remember, transition is *not* an elevator. Yes, some medical changes are permanent, but you always have agency over how you identify your gender and how you choose to express it to the world.

Sometimes the hardest part of gender transition is learning to trust yourself to make good decisions. But if you are making a decision about social/medical/legal transition from a grounded place, have right-size expectations, know the risks and the facts of the change you are making, and are checking in with your gut, you can trust yourself to make the best choice possible.

You can choose to trust that you know what is best for your own life.

Remember the mantra *Even though I don't feel safe, I am safe*. When your heart is beating out of your chest and your hands are sweaty, look around to see if you are, indeed, safe. Even if you're also scared.

Then, if you want to leap, leap. Because wanting it is enough.

WORRY DATE

In order to build trust with ourselves, sometimes we need to get the brain poo out of the way. When we're dealing with intense anxiety and worry, it's easy to want to bury our head in the sand (aka avoidant coping) or endlessly think think think about all the terrible things that could happen. Ironically, getting it all out on paper can help us look at our worries more objectively and trust ourselves enough to say, "Thanks, brain. I hear and appreciate the ways you're trying to keep me safe. I still want to leap—and I trust that we're going to be able to make a good decision together."[16]

So, let's make a date with worry. A worry date is a practice of making intentional space for worry in your life and containing as much worrying as possible to *just* these times.

This exercise can be done on an ongoing basis. But to start, commit to worry time for at least one week. Pick a consistent time and place to do worry time and set a reminder on your phone. (*Pro tip: Don't do worry time in your bed.*) Grab a notebook and a pen and set a timer for fifteen to thirty minutes (no more!).

Then, brain dump on the page. Everything you're worried about and all of those swirling thoughts in your head—get them on paper. Don't worry about making sense or even making full sentences. Give that worry free rein, pour it all out on the page, and try not to stop until the full fifteen to thirty minutes is up, even if you feel you have nothing else to say.

When the timer goes off, put your notebook away and do something that will shift your energy—like taking a walk, petting your pittie, or drinking a cup of tea.

Your brain is predictable when it comes to anxious thoughts. After about a week of doing this, a few things often happen. You might start feeling bored and struggle to fill the time. You might start noticing patterns in your thoughts and realize that the big swirling mess in your head is really three to five core anxious thoughts. You might notice that you have more ability to "postpone" worry until these times. Most importantly, you get some space from and perspective on these thoughts so they don't feel as overwhelming.

Whatever the outcome, worry dates provide a valuable outlet and intentional time to let out and process all those worries that tend to rattle around in your head like a monkey swinging and occasionally flinging poo.

May we all have less brain poo.

CHAPTER 5

Find Your Magic

As a teenager, I only wore black band shirts, Goodwill finds, a studded belt, and Chucks. I collected buttons and dyed my hair purple. I wasn't out as queer or non-binary, even to myself, but I knew I felt out of place.

Growing up in a one-stoplight Louisiana town where the only time church was canceled was to celebrate our hometown hero, country star Tim McGraw, I used my clothing as a signal of solidarity to anyone else who felt different, the misfits. Trying to fit into the status quo would have either killed me or bored me to death. Either way, it wasn't an option. My vibe is a little different today, but I can see the roots of my penchant for black clothes and leather and my love of dancing around in a crowd of sweaty queers in those early days of adolescence.

We expect teenagers to explore different identities and ways of expressing themselves as they get to know who they are. Growing up, I never felt pressure to Decide with a capital *D* who I was and how I wanted to express myself forever. Yet, there is often pressure for anyone exploring their gender identity (at any age) to Decide who they are and how they want to express themselves as soon as possible and for that Decision to never change.

But identity doesn't develop like that, and the pressure to "pick" takes us out of the natural flow of exploration and self-discovery. While gender identity isn't a choice, how we label, understand, and express our gender is often fluid and changes as we get more comfortable with ourselves over time. I was non-binary in my twenties and I'm non-binary in my thirties, but what that means to me and how I express my gender has shifted. And that's a good thing! It's a sign that I'm growing.

Our heteropatriarchal culture has made any exploration of gender and how we want to express it into a very *serious* thing. But what if it wasn't?

Gender exploration can and should be fun. If you've ever styled a gender-bending look that made you go, "Dammmnnn," or tried embodying energy that is against the "rules" for your assigned gender and felt on top of the world, you know what I mean!

In this chapter, we'll explore what makes you feel like magic when you show up in the world and how to take the pressure off gender exploration as a Very Serious Thing™ while bringing in more play. This chapter—and the whole book, really—is not going to offer every piece of information you need to capital *D* Decide on a gender identity and expression that feels good to you. Instead, we're going to focus on developing ways of thinking to support you as you experiment, explore, and make decisions about gender identity and expression—including names, pronouns, and gender-affirming medical care—with more ease and less anxiety.

I Think You're Magic

I started signing off most correspondence with "PS: I think you're magic" several years ago. It's my way of telling people I think they're special, mesmerizing, interesting, powerful, and different from the ordinary. I'm delighted by them. As the *Cambridge Dictionary* says simply, magic is "when you think something is very good and you like it a lot."[1]

In this case, reader, it's you. I like you a lot. It takes strength and openness to be here reading this book, exploring gender, and letting yourself grow into the incredible human I already trust you are.

Our work in this chapter is to figure out what makes you feel this about *yourself*.

Now, no one can feel like magic 100 percent of the time. But the more we notice when how we feel, how we act, what we believe, and who we are at our best are in alignment, the more guideposts we have to make decisions and focus our attention on what matters.

The way we find our magic is to play—trying things on and trying things out, organically building on each moment of "Yes!" and seeing what sticks.

Spaghetti-Wall Mode

Ask most transgender/non-binary folks (me included) if their journey was straightforward and clear, and they'll laugh in your face. Recent research has challenged the widely held assumption that you define your gender identity and *then* figure out how to express it in a neat and tidy way.[2] Rather, discovering your gender identity and actively exploring how you want to express your gender are linked. You learn who you are by taking action to explore who you are and then simply paying attention to what feels good.

In other words, there's room to play.

Rather than a one-and-done Decision, gender exploration is a series of tiny steps and experiments that lead you closer to your authentic self and the magic that makes you who you are. To come up with our own steps and experiments, we can use what I call "spaghetti-wall mode."

When you cook spaghetti, one proverbial way to check if it's done is to throw a few of the noodles at the wall. If they stick, they're done. If they don't stick, no big deal—just keep cooking them until they do. The brilliance of this approach is that there's no failure. You just keep throwing spaghetti at the wall until you've got what you need.

Testing out different ways of expressing your gender identity doesn't mean we are going to get it 100 percent right the first time or that it will never change. But there's no harm done in the trying: If the proverbial spaghetti doesn't stick, we simply keep cooking.

We've talked before about the importance of shifting our focus away from the end result of gender exploration or transition and instead focusing on the next tiniest, easiest step. As my friend and colleague Dr. Lucie Fielding puts it, is this a "feels good, yes!" step or a "feels bad, no!" step?[3] If it feels good, take another tiny step. If it feels bad, or is too intense for you, slow down. Take a step back or try a half step instead.

If you're not sure what the next step looks like, a grounded starting point is to ask yourself what you already know for sure about your magic.

For example, you may not know exactly what pronouns feel right to you, but knowing you don't like "she" or "he" is a great place to start. Likewise, you might not feel like you have your gender expression on lock, but you do know that you love wearing flowy outfits. How can you build on the things you know for sure about yourself?

MAGIC UNDERWEAR AND TEAMMATES

While we often think of gender exploration as something deeply internal and solitary, exploring or transitioning with more ease is not just an individual process.

After my divorce, I did what most people do: I threw myself onstage in front of strangers with nothing to say and started taking my clothes off.

In other words, I joined an improv burlesque team.

I learned that improv is really just sneaky life skills. We learned to take risks and jump onstage, before we knew what we would say or do, and trust ourselves and our teammates to support us if we got stuck.

As part of our show, we played a game where three of us got inside a giant pair of underwear as a three-headed expert. The audience would ask us a question and we'd offer them life advice, one word at a time from each of the three heads. The answers were as absurd as you can imagine, but we pulled it together to form actual sentences. We trusted each other to listen and have one another's back, and we were always trying to support each other like three people in one pair of underwear should.

When applied to gender exploration, trusting your teammates is knowing who has your back and involving others in your "spaghetti wall" experiments. To get through the hard stuff—and revel in the fun stuff—we need each other. This is especially true when faced with the reality that "finding your magic" isn't always celebrated in our world. Having a soft place to land in your support system where you can be reminded that you're magic makes the greatest difference I've seen between surviving and thriving.

What Is "Success"?

Emphasizing process (and play!) instead of the outcome is very different from how we typically think of "success" in gender transition. When I ask my clients what successful transition would look like to them, many are laser focused on passing or, a preferred term, blending. I like this term because it reflects what I find my clients want the most: to exist without their transgender identity defining them. They want to stand at a bus stop and not be stared at. Or walk down the street and not be afraid of violence.

Sometimes there are real safety concerns related to one's desire to blend, and that's valid. Likewise, microaggressions like being misgendered, stared at, or not called by your correct name hurt. It can feel like death by a thousand cuts, and I'm not here to minimize how painful it can be.

And yet.

Gender exploration and transition are about *you*. Strangers on the street or the grocery store clerk should not get to define your self-worth or your gender's validity. And if your main criteria for "successful" gender transition is blending 100 percent of the time, you're giving away your power to people you can't control. This is where we get to change our definition of success.

Successful gender exploration is *active* gender exploration—consistent, intentional action to find the magic of having your actions, your beliefs, and how you show up in the world match up. Joyfully. It's the journey, not the outcome.

When our measure of success becomes our own internal happiness and a continued effort to grow and change into more of who we are over our lifetime, the pressure's off. There is no handbook, no rules to follow, so it's impossible to do gender exploration "wrong." As long as you're doing it, you're doing it right.

Managing Internal Discomfort

Growth is uncomfortable. And sometimes finding your magic means being uncomfortable in the present, knowing you are investing in long-term satisfaction over short-term comfort. Growing sometimes involves grief and the ambiguous loss of those who aren't celebrating us along the way. But every step that moves us toward the most authentic version of ourselves also brings pleasure and joy. We can hold both.

When you're feeling uneasy, anxious, uncomfortable, nervous, or unsettled mentally or physically, this discomfort is often a clue that something needs to change. For example, if my shoe is uncomfortable, I likely need a different size.

Discomfort is also the feeling you get when you're pushing yourself enough to grow but not so much that it's overwhelming.[4] If I'm learning to throw a pot on a potter's wheel, I might feel frustrated as I squash my tenth misshapen pot in a row. That discomfort is okay because I can't learn how to do something new without being bad at it first. The same goes for exploring gender and managing the emotions that come along with it: You're learning something new about yourself, you're experimenting and playing, and it's not going to be or feel perfect the first time.

I know I've done my job right when, at the end of a session, a client laughingly says, "Fuck you. Thank you." It's their way of saying, "You're asking me to do something hard and uncomfortable, but I know it's a good thing, so thank you for the push."

Hard is not always bad. Discomfort inside can feel really challenging and even scary, but it's not harming you. I'm here to tell you it's normal and expected when you are changing your life and doing something new like exploring your gender.

Learning to differentiate if discomfort signals growth or the need to change something takes practice. It's helpful to slow down, ground yourself, and ask your discomfort what it wants to tell you.

EVERYONE HAS BAD DAYS

We all have days where things feel like too much. Sometimes you're growing, sometimes things suck, and sometimes it's just a bad day. In the movie *Captain Marvel*, there is a moment when all seems lost. Captain Marvel is on the ground and losing the fight. As she struggles to get up, a montage plays, showing her as a little girl falling down multiple times. We see her get back up, each time brushing off the dirt and scrapes, and look resolutely into the camera. You see, Captain Marvel's true strength didn't come from her superhuman abilities. It came from her ability to get up after a fall. Success doesn't mean never falling or having difficult moments. It's how you choose to pick yourself back up that counts.

Taking Tiny Steps

While it's true there are many barriers to transgender and non-binary folks thriving in the world, I've also seen how people's own limiting beliefs and fears can hold them back. Accurately assessing safety is a necessary skill, but our assumptions about what is or isn't possible aren't always true. Without new information, our brains will continue to assume these negative, limiting thoughts are true, so the way we start to change them is—you guessed it—by taking tiny steps. Let's look at an example.

Ella, a Black transgender woman, came to me because she wanted to work on presenting her gender authentically at work. Specifically, she wanted to wear a rich, red lipstick (aptly called "Brave"). She knew the lipstick made her feel like a million bucks from wearing it at home, but the thought of wearing it outside of her house left her frozen in fear of how others might react. The story she was telling herself was that she would be ridiculed and physically hurt for wearing a bright lipstick.

First, we assessed for safety. Ella's fear of physical harm when presenting as more traditionally feminine stemmed from alarming statistics on violence against Black transgender women. However, Ella worked in a suburb of a large city, at a popular shopping center. The parking lot was well lit, with a constant flow of people. Her workplace was progressive and had policies protecting LGBTQ+ staff from discrimination. So, while her fears were not unfounded, we could assume from her context that wearing lipstick to work was a low safety risk.

I also discovered that Ella was spending a significant amount of time online reading stories about transgender violence. I challenged Ella to limit the amount of time she spent looking at these stories and to spend the same amount of time weekly reading stories of transgender people thriving.

Knowing that it was likely safe for her to do so, as her therapist, I wanted to challenge Ella to do things that scared her a bit, but not too much. Remember that zone of proximal development we learned about in chapter 3? My goal was to find a way for Ella to wear the lipstick where she would be stretched but not overwhelmed, and together, we got creative about how she could do this without it causing significant anxiety.

Our first step was for Ella to put on lipstick at home and bring makeup wipes to take it off in the parking lot at work. Next, she wore lipstick in the car, wiped it off before walking through the parking lot, and reapplied it in the work break room to wear for the day. She was surprised that no customers said anything negative to her. One even complimented her lip color.

Once she built confidence that she could keep herself safe and handle the anxious thoughts that wearing lipstick in public brought up, she started wearing the lipstick walking from her car to work. The first day, she was nervous, so her homework assignment was to get herself a special treat after work for doing a hard thing. She also texted her friend before leaving the car and after getting to work as a safety precaution and for some encouragement.

For our final phase, she wore the lipstick to a Starbucks in the shopping center. This was a big deal because Ella assumed that wearing lipstick in public, away from the relative safety of work, would be too anxiety provoking. She wasn't sure if she could handle potentially being stared at, and she feared strangers saying transphobic things. While we discussed that these outcomes were possible, we also reviewed all the ways she had built up her capacity to manage her anxiety and the support systems she had (including her manager at work), as well as how she wanted to handle it if someone said something transphobic. By taking these graduated steps, we were reality testing for safety and building her capacity to handle the anxiety that came up slowly. No step felt overwhelming.

I remember when she came into my office, glowing, to say that she had worn the lipstick to Starbucks. She was treated respectfully by the employees, and no one said anything to her. She described noticing one person staring at her but proudly talked about how she didn't get stuck in her head about it.

Every tiny step she took built her confidence and challenged her to reimagine what was possible, letting how she felt with each tiny step (in the car, at work, in the parking lot) take her further than she'd originally envisioned: all the way to the victory of a gloriously lipstick-stained Starbucks cup.

Designing a tiny-step experiment is how we learn what "feels good, yes!" or "feels bad, no!"[5] These experiments are how we get the information we need to find and own our magic.

DESIGN YOUR OWN TINY-STEP EXPERIMENT

This exercise is intended to help you design your very own tiny-step experiment. A word to the wise before we dive in: When you're thinking through tiny steps, remember that I really do mean *tiny*. We are talking about minuscule, itty-bitty steps toward bigger goals.

While it's useful to bring in a therapist or friend to help you implement your experiment and confront what you've been avoiding, you can also do it on your own. The following questions are prompts to help you get curious about your fears related to gender exploration and get to the root of them (while also assessing for safety). The most important thing to keep in mind as you go through these questions is the last piece: Take a tiny step. Assess how it feels. Repeat.

What Would You Do if You Weren't Afraid?

This question is your best clue to discovering your magic. Be bold and honest in answering it. If you start to feel a tingle, a feeling of openness in your body, or notice you're holding your breath, you might be on to something. Explore it.

What's Your Biggest Fear about That Action?

What evidence do you have that your fear is likely to happen, either from your own life or outside sources? Is there a range of possible intensities for how your fear might happen? For example, there is a big difference between getting screamed at by a stranger on a sidewalk and hearing them mutter something under their breath. Are there controllable factors that would make your fear more or less likely to happen?

If What You Fear Happened, What Would Be the Result?
Some things are legitimately unsafe. Others we make assumptions about and limit ourselves unnecessarily. Often, we are afraid to take the risk because we are afraid of "failing" at it, we don't feel _______ enough, or the imagined consequences are so dire. Take a moment and ask yourself questions like these:

Would your physical or financial safety be at risk?
How can you keep yourself safe?
What do you imagine you'd feel like?
Is there a range in how bad it might feel?
If you fear experiencing shame or embarrassment, how long do you imagine you'd feel these things intensely?
Have you felt these things before and survived?
What skills did you use to move through these feelings?
How would you talk to yourself if your fear came true, even partly?
How would you handle it?

What Positive Consequences Might Happen if You Do This Thing?
We've spent some time thinking about the negative consequences and imagining them in great detail. Now I want you to spend the same amount of time considering what positive effects this action might have for you. What if everything turned out beautifully? What if this was the best decision you ever made?

Why Do You Want to Do the Thing That Scares You?
When an action feels hard or scary, it can be helpful to recenter ourselves on why it's important to us. How do you feel not being able to take this action? What is the cost to you?

What Are Some Simple and Small Ways You Could Experiment with This Action?
How can you test out your assumptions as safely as possible? What is the safest place to try it out? Who can you enlist to help you as an accountability buddy, safety check, and cheerleader?

Break it down into smaller steps than you think you need to and be creative. You might feel silly taking such tiny steps, but that's part of building your confidence. But remember, the point of this exercise is to significantly decrease your anxiety in doing a scary thing. Feeling bored because you're going "too slow" is great news! Trust the process.

Take one tiny step. Repeat.

Sometimes experiments are an immediate "YES!" like an affirming haircut. When this happens, it feels like magic right away. The trick is to notice when you feel this way and intentionally incorporate more of what caused you to feel like magic into your life. Keeping a note with these moments can be a powerful way to create a menu of gender-affirming actions you can take.

Finding Your Unique Magic

Now that we've talked about the importance of mindset and taking tiny steps in finding your magic, it's time to get specific about what this means for labels, names, pronouns, gender expression, hormone replacement therapy, and surgeries. As you go through these next few sections, keep in mind the spaghetti-wall metaphor and keep throwing those noodles! Give yourself space to play.

Finding Gender Identity Labels That Feel Like Magic

A lot of folks get hung up on gender identity labels. They feel heavy and like a Decision they'll be stuck with forever. But labels and the things that define us often change. I like to ask folks, "What identities do you hold that are important to you?" I love this question because it tells you a lot about what parts of themselves people value. Some people only list labels related to identities that are unchangeable, like race. But most others also list labels related to things that currently define them, some of which will likely change over time, like religion, gender, sexual orientation, work, sports, culture, fashion, hobbies, artistic pursuits, and our intimate relationships.

I always want to be digging more into the question of "Who am I?"

over my lifetime, and I *hope* the answer changes as I grow. Imagine if you were stuck with the labels and self-identity you had ten years ago. Our relationship to things that define us and the labels we use to describe ourselves are dynamic. Over my lifetime, I've called myself straight, cisgender, Christian, monogamous, bisexual, queer, pagan, polyamorous, non-binary, and transgender, to name a few. I've changed in big ways throughout my life, and as I change, my labels change with me. It doesn't mean I was wrong about my previous labels at the time. I just grew out of them as I discovered more about myself.

If you view gender identity labels as just another experiment rather than a static Decision, or an immutable fact of your identity, you get to see what feels right for you. Folks often find out more of who they are by "trying on" a label, even just to themselves. Noticing how your body reacts (light, heavy, butterflies, warm, tense, etc.) and how you feel (euphoric, sad, curious, avoidant, happy, etc.) when you say the label are good clues. And best of all, it's impossible to be wrong. We can hold it loosely.

The thing about labels is they are only useful when you apply them to yourself. They can be powerful, affirming, and connect you to communities of people who identify their gender similarly, and that can be a beautiful experience. But no one else gets to decide them for you, now or in the future.

How to Find a Name That Feels Like Magic

My name has been legally changed twice and unofficially changed once. I was named by a social worker in the hospital (no last name, Beyoncé style), had my name changed by my adoptive parents, changed it again when I got married, and kept my new last name after my divorce. And started going by Rae a few years ago.

I've had friends, cisgender and transgender alike, who have changed their name once or even twice in the time we've known each other (this was surprisingly helpful in the case of a couple of exes who used to have the same name). Every time a friend has changed their name, legally or otherwise, there has been a short period of adjustment, and then, most of the time, I have a hard time recalling their old name.

I've also been a performer in burlesque where everyone has two names: their stage name and their "muggle" name. I have no clue what many of the other performers' legal names are. And now I have friends casually named Crocodile and Queerella. I know multiple grandmothers who go by a name different from their legal name and will give you a death stare if you dare utter anything else.

If you choose to change your name legally, it's a fairly obnoxious process to go through to get all your documents moved over, and it can invite some extra cost, confusion, and a lot more paperwork into your life. But thousands of people change their name each year for a myriad of reasons, including cisgender folks who change their name *simply because they want to*, like my friend who changed her given name in high school because she preferred Bailey.

While intimidating, changing your name or going by a name different from your legal one is not that big of a deal.

Still, folks who want to change their name struggle to choose one that is *just* right. They get stuck in their heads trying to find a perfect name. However, a new name is unlikely to feel perfect immediately. My name, Rae McDaniel, feels like magic to me. But it didn't always.

I spent many months curiously rolling "Rae" around in my mouth, squinting at myself in the mirror and saying my name out loud to get a gut feeling for it. I started small, asking my partner at the time to try out my name. I noticed the shivers that went down my spine when she whispered it in my ear right before kissing my neck. I gave it as my name at Starbucks and for take-out orders. I started asking close friends to try it out when we were together. For a while, their voices awkwardly went up an octave every time they said it. But after a few months, it just felt like . . . me.

Finding names to try on can come from a variety of sources, both meaningful and random. Choosing a family name or involving a parent or partner feels important for some folks. Others find their name through a baby name book, a favorite character, or simply a word they like. For me, I chose a name that was a shortened version of the name my social worker gave me in the hospital, the first act of love I received, and was close to my legal name. Only later did I discover that Ray McDaniel was my biological grandfather's name, a little piece of unexpected magic.*

Your name might change multiple times over your life as well. Who knows? And more importantly, who cares? It's *your* name.

How to Find Pronouns That Feel Like Magic

Similar to names, many folks get stuck trying to decide what pronouns they'd like to use. The thing I want you to know about pronouns is you don't have to choose one and stick with it forever. You can also use multiple pronouns, like they/she, if a rotation feels the most aligned for you. Experimenting with different pronouns and potentially changing them over time is a normal part of self-growth and development. As with names, asking people close to you to help you test out new pronouns can be a helpful and low-risk way to see how you feel about the pronouns.

YOU ARE NOT ASKING TOO MUCH

Asking others to respect your name, pronouns, and identity is not asking too much. It's not even asking a lot. It's basic human decency to call someone by their name and respect their identity. It's not too hard to learn a new name or new pronouns if even a little effort is applied, as evidenced by the lack of fuss toward anyone who has ever gone by a new nickname or changed their name when they got married. Also, humans can learn new words and how to use words in a new way fairly easily, like the singular "they," and integrate them into vocabulary. It's not "too hard." Ask anyone who has ever uttered the word "TikTok."

Finding a Gender Expression That Feels Like Magic

Gender expression, our third dial in our spaceship to the galaxy of gender freedom from chapter 1, includes your physical appearance, as well

* Yes, that means my ex-husband's last name is the same as my biological grandfather's. There's no relation—believe me, I checked!

as your values, your interests, and how you move through the world. Basically, anything that feels connected *to you* expressing your gender is gender expression.

Finding an authentic gender expression involves critically questioning gender norms. Masculinity, femininity, and androgyny are constructs that change over time and culture. For example, did you know that heels were created for Persian men to keep their feet in stirrups and not as the pinnacle of femininity they are today?[6] Or that actress Katharine Hepburn was so insistent on wearing "masculine" pants in the 1930s (when it was expected for women to dress exclusively in skirts and dresses) that there was a paragraph dedicated to it in her 2003 obituary?

There is not one right way to embody these ideas, because that's all they are—ideas. Whatever forms of expression you experiment with don't have to be on the traditional end of a masculine/feminine spectrum or even match up to how others define these ideas at all. You don't have to be masculine to be a man, feminine to be a woman, or express androgyny in a certain way to be non-binary.

Will, a white, non-binary person, told me they feel the most connected to powerful energy they define as masculine when they wear a dress and makeup. They also expressed how the freedom to fluidly express themselves as more traditionally masculine or feminine on any given day felt like the most accurate reflection of who they are.

It is not necessary to "prove" anything about your identity by stuffing yourself back into a box that feels constricting to you. The important thing is how you *feel* while experimenting with expression.

Some aspects of physical appearance to consider playing with are style choices, hair and body hair, nails, binding, and tucking.

There is still magic in "failure," though I don't believe in "failing" at anything related to gender expression. Experiments might feel frustrating if you can't get to that internal "Yes!" right away and you have to keep cooking the spaghetti. I had a months-long existential hair crisis during quarantine. My hair had been in a swept-back, high-fade style for years, and I decided to experiment with trying to grow my hair out. I *hated* it. It took going to a new barber for some fresh eyes to figure out a different short style that felt like me, but now I have valuable information about what I don't like. It wasn't a failed experiment because I didn't like the first outcome.

It's easy to take an experiment not feeling like magic right away, make it mean you "failed," and feel hopeless or frozen because of it. In chapter 2, we talked about how our freeze response prevents us from fully accessing our prefrontal cortex, the "thinking brain." Recognizing the context and reframing a "failed" experiment as simply information can move us back into a mindset of self-efficacy. You may also notice you have a belief like "I can't wear this because...," which is a sneaky way self-imposed limits show up. Actively reframing these limiting beliefs can help you move from feeling stuck to gender expression feeling authentic and like play.

For example, many transgender women feel pressure to dress hyper-feminine every time they leave the house. But if we get to the root of the assumption and reframe their thoughts, we can move toward what feels more free and powerful. Like this:

Negative thought: *If I don't dress traditionally feminine and wear makeup when I go to Target, I'll never get gendered correctly, because I'm not "woman enough."*

Reframed thought: *Lots of women wear sweatpants and no makeup to Target. And what I wear and if I wear makeup doesn't change who I am. Being misgendered is about the other person, not me. And damn if these sweatpants aren't the most comfortable thing on the planet.*

Feeling silly or frustrated because an item of clothing doesn't fit your body properly might mean it's not right for you. *Or* it could mean society has put unrealistic and highly gendered expectations on us about what we are "supposed" to look like. The fashion world isn't exactly known for its great work creating clothing that fits a variety of bodies.

So, we get to get creative: Is it possible to find more inclusive brands or get items tailored? For example, I have the narrowest shoulders on planet earth. It's almost impossible to find off-the-rack shirts that fit me properly. So, I find shirts (often thrifted) that don't have shoulder seams, get shirts tailored, or just accept the way it looks on my body.

Playing with gender expression also involves testing out things besides physical appearance that feel gender euphoric to you. This might be a particular style of dancing or moving your body, taking time to explore hobbies and interests, ways of having sex or the roles you take in the bedroom, your mannerisms, and how you want to express your values. After all, who you are is way more than how you look. Transgender and non-binary folks often shut down parts of themselves at a young age because they got messages that their behavior was too masculine or feminine for their assigned gender. It can feel healing to rediscover and reclaim childhood interests—like camping or ballet or playing with Legos or blowing bubbles in the park—you never had "permission" to explore.

How to Make Decisions about Hormone Therapy That Feel Like Magic

Starting hormone therapy (HT) tends to be a turning point in the gender transition journey, and shifting body chemistry to be in more alignment with your gender identity is one of the most affirming things many transgender/non-binary people experience. While starting hormone therapy won't solve all your mental health problems or erase gender dysphoria, many folks do see immediate positive mental health benefits.

Deciding to go on hormone therapy *is* a big decision, but not as big as you think. The most common fears that keep people frozen in indecision are fear of feeling out of control as their body changes and an assumption that starting HT is a lifelong commitment. At the core of both these fears is an inability to sit with uncertainty and assumptions that can be easily reframed.

Instead of getting stuck in your head, actively exploring or starting hormone therapy is often the best way to figure out if it's right for you. Taking a tiny-step approach to HT allows you to explore this aspect of gender expression at a pace that feels less anxiety provoking and more easeful.

My client Alice is a great example of how to walk through the tiny-step process for yourself. When they first visited my office, Alice was agonizing over whether they wanted to start hormone therapy. They were stuck in their head about potential unwanted body changes and uncertainty about whether hormone therapy was right for them.

So, we designed a tiny-step experiment.

First, we explored the fear of unwanted body changes. I asked Alice to reflect on their gut feelings and emotions to gather more data. At the same time, we also gathered accurate information about common timelines for body changes and side effects, using that to develop a list of remaining questions. Then, Alice made an appointment with a doctor so they could ask their questions, do blood work, and get a prescription.

Once Alice filled the prescription, the next tiny step was simply to put it on their dresser for a while with the expectation that they never had to take a dose if they didn't want to. As they stared at the medication every day for a few weeks and assessed how they felt about it, Alice was able to get clarity that they *did* want to try hormone therapy. They called a friend to come over to offer support while they took their first dose. With every dose, Alice and I reaffirmed that the changes were feeling good and they wanted to continue.

Going through this process, Alice felt more confident in their ability to make other decisions related to their gender identity, like top surgery. The next tiny step for them was researching surgeons in the area, looking at reviews, and asking to see their result pictures.

If you are thinking about hormone therapy, you can do exactly what Alice did. Or some of it. Or none of it. Let me reiterate: You have not started hormone therapy until you . . . start hormone therapy. It's true that all bodies respond differently to hormone therapy, and some changes are permanent (the most frequent concerns I hear are about genital growth or change in sexual function, which we'll talk about more in part 2). However, there are general timelines for body changes, and bodies do not drastically change overnight. There are many steps between setting up a doctor's appointment and taking your first dose. And even after your first dose, there's more space than you think to consider if the changes you're seeing are in alignment with your gender identity and to change your dosage or stop hormone therapy altogether. Just like gender transition, hormone therapy is not an elevator. You can stop, restart, or change the dosage at any point in your journey. As a non-binary person on testosterone, I fully expect that I will go on and off hormone therapy throughout my life.

YOU ARE TRANS ENOUGH

You don't have to have gender dysphoria about your body to be transgender or non-binary. I spoke with queer and trans researcher Lou Lindley about the needed shift away from understanding gender dysphoria as only body-based distress.[7] Social dysphoria, or distress over not having your gender seen and respected by others, is an equally important factor regardless of whether or not you want to change your body.

You also don't have to *hate* your body to want to change aspects of it. We tend to think of dysphoria as an extreme emotion. But like we've talked about, sometimes social and body dysphoria can feel more like the rub of a too-small shoe that turns into a blister over time. Experiencing dysphoria happens when an aspect of how you are being perceived or how you are showing up in the world is out of alignment with who you know yourself to be. It's valuable data for your gender experiments.

What makes you "trans enough" to consider gender transition, whatever that means to you, is simple: The answer to, "Do you want to transition? is "yes."

How to Make Decisions about Surgeries That Feel Like Magic

The number one question I get about gender-affirming surgeries is "How do I know if _____ is right for me?" For better or worse, the only one who can answer that question is you. Making a permanent decision about your body is an exercise in self-trust and cannot be rushed. We talked about hot and cold decisions in chapter 4. Deciding whether to have a surgery with ease means taking the time to make sure you are making a grounded (cold) decision.

Often, folks get stuck in the loop of trying to figure out if they want a surgery before taking *any* steps forward. As with other aspects of gender expression, much of our important information comes from actively engaging with the process. One tiny step at a time. You are not having surgery until you are in a preoperative room with an IV in your arm making you sleepy. Every step before that is an active choice, and you can change your mind at any time.

I've had many clients who wrestled with a surgery decision for months or even years before making a doctor's appointment. Sometimes, the act of making an appointment (and often the wait before the consultation) brings the clarity someone needs. Taking the steps to gather accurate medical information by asking a doctor your questions, seeing photos of the doctor's previous surgeries, and discussing implications of the surgery specific to your body will help you decide from an informed and grounded place. This process, as well as talking to other transgender/nonbinary folks who have gone through the same surgery, can also help you gain clarity on both expected and unexpected positive and negative outcomes for surgery and make the best decision for you.

Like we discussed in chapter 4, most decisions are fairly neutral, but we tend to make meaning out of them based on the outcome. When we make a decision from a grounded place after gathering as much information as we can, we are making the best decision possible and are less likely to experience regret regardless of the outcome.

Making the decision to have a gender-affirming surgery *is* a big deal in the sense that you are making a permanent decision about your body. However, the anxiety and panic from both ourselves and others over gender-affirming surgeries is largely based in transphobia. Cisgender folks have body modification surgeries all the time without feeling the same level of intense pressure to make the "right" decision.

SEXUAL PLEASURE AND GENDER-AFFIRMING SURGERIES

One primary concern in top (chest) and bottom (genital) surgeries is a loss of sexual functioning or sensation. This is a real concern, and many doctors still view sexual pleasure and functioning as a secondary goal to aesthetics. When gathering information and choosing the right doctor for you, it's helpful to talk explicitly about your priorities with regard to sexual sensation and functioning. A good doctor will be able to address your concerns and come up with solutions that feel good to you. For example, nipple sensation is a major source of sexual pleasure for some, and there are surgery techniques that leave critical nerves attached. However, when I got top surgery, I decided to go with tattooed nipples instead because this sensation wasn't important to me. This not only met my goals for top surgery but also gave me a memorable answer to introductory questions like "Please tell us an interesting fact about yourself."

Finding your magic is about committing to discovery, committing to a self-growth mindset, and committing to keep throwing spaghetti at the wall and experimenting and noticing what lights you up—then shamelessly chasing that. It's confidently naming your desires and believing you are powerful and worthy enough to move toward them. Just like looking up at the Milky Way on my grandfather's ranch, I want you to feel awe at all the exciting things you *get to* discover about yourself.

Magic isn't about struggle and hustle and white-knuckling it through life to make something happen. Owning your magic is acting as if what you once thought was impossible is inevitable.

Because after all, why would you fight so hard to get out of a box just to put yourself back into one?

PS: I think you're magic.

THE FIVE WHYS

This exercise is simple but powerful and can help you understand why you are stuck or feeling anxious about making a decision. The five whys are exactly what they sound like.

You are going to ask yourself why five times.

As simple as it gets, right?

Here's where the power comes in.

Each time you ask why, take it one level deeper. This helps you quickly get to the root of the issue, ask the right questions, and get to solutions faster.

For example:

1. Why am I feeling anxious and stuck deciding if I want a surgery?

   I'm worried it's not right for me.

2. Why am I worried it's not right for me?

   I'm not 100 percent certain of the outcome, so I'm worried I'll regret changing my body permanently.

3. Why am I worried about regretting changing my body permanently?

   I feel uncomfortable with any amount of uncertainty and don't trust myself to make good decisions about my body.

4. Why do I need to be 100 percent certain of the outcome to move forward with confidence?

   I believe if I don't have absolute certainty, things will turn out badly and I'll regret my decision. I believe if I am 100 percent certain of the outcome, I can protect myself from all potential discomfort.

5. Why don't I trust myself to make good decisions about my body if I can't know the outcome of my decision with absolute certainty?

   Because I've had to shut down my intuition for so long to be able to survive in a transphobic world that it's hard to know what I really want. I've been nervous to take a step forward to get the information I need to make an informed decision because it feels scary.

   Because there's a part of me that still doesn't feel like I'm "trans enough" to change my body. I'm afraid others will think I'm a fraud and judge me.

All right! That's great information. Now we know what we need to work on to move through the stuck feeling. In this example, our first step is acknowledging moving forward toward surgery is scary instead of shoving down the feelings. Once we can name it, it becomes less powerful. Then we can work on building self-trust and self-efficacy, reframing being trans enough (you are!), and finding affirming support while working through the fear of judgment. You don't have to feel zero fear or imposter syndrome to move forward, but starting the process of naming and working on the deeper core beliefs keeping you stuck creates space to take more tiny steps.

Next steps could include setting up an appointment with a doctor to get your questions answered, reframing uncertainty and regret, and addressing the internalized belief that you aren't trans enough to have a surgery (again for the folks in the back: You are!).[8]

CHAPTER 6

Coming into Your Magic

In the last chapter, we talked about finding your magic by doing tiny experiments. Finding your magic for yourself is essential and exciting, and part of the joy of doing that work is the desire to share it. When you feel authentic and share who you are with the world, you attract people who love exactly who you are instead of a smaller, more digestible version of you.

This chapter will focus on sharing your gender identity and expression with others, even if you don't have all the answers yet. Two of the biggest anxieties I hear from clients are how to come out in various aspects of their lives and how to navigate family, work, and other relationships once they do. This chapter is all about how to do just that.

Reframing Authenticity

Before we talk more about strategies to come out to friends, family, colleagues, and other loved ones, I want to offer a friendly reminder: No part of transition is an elevator. Even if you know that they/them pronouns make you feel like magic, that doesn't obligate you to change your Facebook name and pronouns, call your grandma, and come out to your partner all on the same day. You can choose *how much* and *to whom*.

We often think of authenticity as being your full self, loud and proud, everywhere we choose to go. But I believe the idea of authenticity has more nuance. For example, sometimes the most authentic thing to do is to keep yourself safe, and that might mean not being out in every context of your life. When I say "safe," I don't mean that it will always be comfortable—we all know by now that gender exploration and transition require leaning into the unfamiliar and taking some risks. But your physical, financial, and emotional safety are important and have to be prioritized.

It's important to start with the fact that living with authenticity can include what Lou Lindley calls "strategic gender expression."[1]

Strategic gender expression means picking and choosing where you decide to show up as your full self. That might look like being out with your partner but not at work, or wearing gender-affirming clothing most of the time but wearing something more neutral when you visit your conservative grandparents. Sometimes coming out in all areas of your life is physically unsafe or likely to create financial instability (for example, you might lose a job or have college funds taken away), or you can reasonably assume that you will experience emotional abuse that you can't escape.

Sometimes the cost of asserting your identity isn't worth the effort, is dangerous, or doesn't help you meet your goals in the moment. There are many reasons one might choose to not assert their identity and instead prioritize safety, or simply not deal with trying to educate someone else.

As a non-binary person myself, this is a choice I make frequently. I do not "blend" as a cisgender man (and don't want to) and get consistently gendered as female. For example, I recently had dinner with a group of friends at a restaurant. Three of us are non-binary, using they/them pronouns, and the rest are cisgender. After getting called "ladies" at every turn, my cisgender friends asked us the best way to be an ally in that moment and if they should correct the server.

While everyone's answer is different, and I would gladly stand up for a transgender friend if it felt supportive, all of us at the table expressed that it generally didn't feel worth the effort to try to explain they/them pronouns to a server when our goal was to enjoy the meal. In our experience, asserting our identity led to microaggressions and emotional labor to educate others. I just wanted to enjoy my mac and cheese. (We did, however, request to be called kings instead of ladies, which seemed like a nice compromise.)

It wouldn't have been worth my time to try to nicely educate this guy. I don't always want to be nice and appeasing and the perfect educator when microaggressions, or just plain aggression, are directed my way. Sometimes, I just want to be happy and move on with my day.

Should transgender/non-binary folks have to make these trade-offs simply to exist (and eat mac and cheese) in peace? No. But, to borrow a phrase from disability justice, sometimes you just don't have the "spoons" for it, and self-care looks like prioritizing your own comfort.[2]

We also have many parts of us that we value and are authentic, and because of the world we live in, sometimes these values are in conflict—like valuing close family relationships and not hiding our transgender identity. There are no perfect choices, only the best choice you can make in a given moment based on your priorities.

I also want to say for the record that "coming out" is an unfair expectation on transgender/non-binary (and queer) folks. There's only a closet to come out of because the closet was necessary to avoid discrimination and violence. That said, we still live in a world where folks' gender identity and pronouns are often wrongly assumed, and coming out is a way to be seen in a world that insists on compulsively gendering . . . pretty much everything.

When you do need or want to assert your gender identity, the most important question to ask yourself is, "How do I design this experience to keep me safe, stay in my thinking brain, communicate my identity and boundaries well, and meet my goals for this interaction?"

Hannah is a fifty-five-year-old Latinx transgender woman who worked with me to explore her newfound identity. She was employed as her church's administrator for the last fifteen years, and a great deal of her community came from the relationships she cultivated there. She knew the church would not be accepting of her transgender identity and that it would be difficult to get another job at her age and experience level. She was also limited in her gender expression by the fact that she lived in the same conservative area, so it could potentially be physically unsafe to wear something like a dress.

She wanted to prioritize staying in her church community and connected to her neighborhood, so we worked to figure out how she could express her gender freely and safely and get support within this context. Hannah found a transgender meetup group in her town, far enough away from her neighborhood to feel safe. She had a couple of close, supportive, out-of-town friends that she could visit and with whom she could wear whatever she liked. Hannah was also able to come out to her neighbor, and they would have dinner together frequently in her home.

At work, Hannah played with ways to express her gender without putting her financial safety at risk. She experimented with wearing women's underwear under her traditionally male clothing and getting a manicure. She started a low dose of hormone therapy, and when her breasts started to develop, we explored ways to flatten them at work, like wearing a compression shirt or a binder and looser tops.

She also played with ways to express her vision of femininity through her actions. Things like baking and bringing treats to work, listening well and supporting others, and prioritizing being kind. At the end of the day, she created a routine of changing clothes and putting on makeup as soon as she got home from work to bookend her time spent not being able to express her full self.

When I asked Hannah how it felt to make these choices, she said, "It's not perfect. But it's enough and I'm happy."

STRATEGIC GENDER EXPRESSION GUIDING QUESTIONS

Making decisions about what you want to share about yourself in a particular moment can feel stressful. Here are some questions to help guide you in quickly assessing a situation and showing up in the most authentic way—in line with your needs and goals. Remember, you can always change your mind and choose something different next time.

Is it physically, emotionally, and financially safe (enough) for me to share more about myself? *(Your physical safety should always be prioritized. If it's not emotionally or financially safe, you might want to still share more about your identity later, but you need to take extra steps to keep yourself physically safe first.)*

What do I need to prioritize? *(Do you want to prioritize sharing more about your gender identity, or are there other priorities, like* *connection to family or enjoying time with your friends, that feel more important right now?)*

Is the person I plan to share with likely to be willing and able to affirm my transgender/non-binary identity? *(Be honest. If they aren't willing or able, your goal might need to shift, since it's not helpful to go for an unattainable goal.)*

If the answer is no, is it worth my energy and the consequences of coming out at this moment, knowing it likely won't change their behavior? *(It's okay if the answer is yes, but consciously choose it.)*

What is my goal in this situation? *(What outcome are you hoping for?)*

Which problems do I want to choose at this moment? *(There are rarely perfect or easy choices, so which problems feel the most manageable right now—expressing your gender identity more fully or coping with not expressing your gender identity the way you'd ideally like to?)*

A Simple Framework for Coming Out

Coming out can feel BIG. Becoming more open about your identity can signal a major turning point in your life, and being vulnerable about an important part of who you are can feel that much more stressful when you aren't 100 percent sure how people will respond. To make it manageable, I use a very simple framework borrowed from the journalism world: You're going to ask yourself who, what, when, where, and how. We will dig into specific strategies for coming out to different groups like employers, partners, and families of origin starting on page 103, but these five questions can guide you toward an authentic, safe coming-out experience in any circumstance.

Who?

Starting with "who" instead of "what" is essential because it guides the rest of the questions. For example, coming out to your boss will require a different approach and vibe than coming out to your mom.

I encourage you to start small and with people you can reasonably assume will be supportive. If you have the right supports in place, coming out in a big way (like a letter to your family or on social media) could be the next step that feels right to you; however, if the idea of coming out still feels so scary that it pushes you into fight/flight/freeze/fawn, notice that and take smaller steps.

At this stage, identifying the resources and support systems you already have or could easily get access to will make the greatest difference in your experience.

WHAT TO DO IF SUPPORT FEELS SCARCE

Knowing who has your back helps you feel supported and grounded when faced with coming out to folks who aren't supportive or validating. If you don't have those people in your life (yet), there are many online groups with other transgender/non-binary folks who can offer encouragement and support. In our era of Zoom, there is also greater access to therapy, coaching, and support groups online.

If none of those supports are available to you for whatever reason, try focusing on giving yourself what you need—for example, wrapping up in a weighted blanket, visualizing a future self and how they would give you care in this moment, or using a tool from somatic therapies, like self-holding (putting pressure on specific body parts that help calm your nervous system).[3] Most importantly, be kind to yourself. This shit can be hard, and it's okay if you need to fall apart sometimes. You're not a robot.

What?

When thinking about coming out, the transgender and non-binary folks I work with often feel like they need to defend their identity, pulling evidence from childhood and expressing how difficult it has been to live being seen as cisgender, in order to convince loved ones that their identity is valid.

You don't.

Coming out doesn't mean that you need to prove anything about your identity. It's simply letting people know who you are and how you want to be treated and addressed. You aren't required to have everything figured out. You don't have to know or share about your plans for hormone therapy or surgeries. You don't have to give your life story.

You are, of course, welcome to share any and all of those things with folks if that feels good, but your emotional safety and boundaries take precedence over someone else's comfort, confusion, or curiosity. You get to decide what and how much you'd like to share. Saying something like, "I appreciate the question, but that's something I'd like to keep private for now," can be a helpful redirection.

DECIDING WHAT TO SAY

Deciding what you want to say about your gender identity can feel overwhelming since so much about gender identity and expression is nuanced and personal. These questions will help you think through what you feel comfortable sharing. I encourage you to write these things down and take them with you. You may not use them, but it's comforting to know you have a list of your key points if you get tongue-tied.

What points do you want to make? *(Is it just your identity, name, and pronouns, or do you want to share more about your journey? If so, which parts?)*

What do you want to keep to yourself? *(Example: plans for medical transition, childhood experiences of gender, trauma, mental health struggles, fertility plans, your sex life, etc.)*

What are your concrete asks? *(Example: using new name and pronouns, getting a new email address and name tag at work, being referred to as a son/daughter/child, verbal affirmation and celebration of your identity, etc.)*

What are your boundaries, and how do you want to handle it if someone pushes them? *(What types of responses will cause you to leave the situation or take a break? What do you want to say if someone asks you questions you don't want to answer?)*

When?

It can be easy to think there will be a perfect time to come out to someone. A moment when astrology is in your favor, everyone is stress-free and in a great mood, and you are invulnerable to any negative reactions. But there's never a perfect time—only a good-enough time.

Remember in chapter 2 when we talked about having a bias to action? That gut feeling to take a tiny step will take you far in deciding your *when*. If coming out to a particular person feels like too much, a tiny step might be engaging them in a conversation about trans identities in a more neutral way, like listening to a podcast together and discussing it or watching a show like *Pose*. This can also be a way to assess their openness to the conversation as you think about strategic gender expression and safety.

You'll also want to be mindful of when someone is likely to be receptive to hearing about changes in your identity. I want to be clear: You cannot read anyone's mind, and you are *not* responsible for anyone's reaction. But coming out to a spouse in the hour they have between work and taking the kids to the park instead of on a walk together on a weekend can make a big difference in how they process the information. Do your best to choose a time when you know they will be more calm, grounded, and present.

Where?

Finding a time where you have the most control over your environment helps establish safety. As Q said to James Bond, "Always have an escape plan."[4] In the context of coming out, this means that it's wise to know your options to get out of a physical space before initiating a conversation. Even if someone is affirming, the experience usually feels vulnerable, and taking some time for yourself afterward to let your body calm down can feel grounding.

When I visit my parents, I always have a rental car available. Knowing that I have the ability to leave makes me feel safer in that environment. Other resources for an escape plan are having a friend who can pick you up or let you stay with them, using a rideshare app to take you somewhere safer, going on a long walk, or asking friends to provide some mutual aid to get you a plane ticket or a hotel.

How?

There are many different mediums you can use to come out, like letters, emails, a phone call, text, social media, and in person. None is better than the other. Your safety, both physical and emotional, is the most important factor in how you choose to come out. Your decision will likely include thinking about how the other person might receive it best, but your preferences matter. If you communicate best in writing, it's okay to choose an email, even if the other person would likely prefer an in-person conversation. I've also had clients who wrote a letter that they read in person. One effective strategy I use to complement any of these approaches is an FAQ letter, which you'll learn how to create in the exercise at the end of the chapter.

DISCOMFORT IS NOT HARM

All growth requires some amount of discomfort on both a personal and a systemic/cultural level. When we are trying to be the best, most authentic version of ourselves, it's absolutely okay to ask that of other people as well...and the best version of someone is never full of hate.

I can't guarantee you that everyone will respond the way you hope when you come out, but that reaction does not mean that you're harming them. It is not harm to ask people to call you by a new name and pronouns, to set boundaries around respecting your gender identity, to use a bathroom that aligns with your gender, or to stand up for your basic human rights.

Harm is feeling like you have to shove down or hide a fundamental piece of your identity for your own safety or the comfort of others.

Let me say it again: Discomfort is not harm.

Putting It All Together

Rob is a twenty-three-year-old multiracial transgender man and a client whom I walked through the process of coming out to his family. His parents were conservative, but not overly so, and Rob could reasonably assume he wouldn't experience verbal abuse, even though they would likely say hurtful things and ask inappropriate questions.

Since he had graduated from college the previous year and had a full-time job, Rob was no longer reliant on his parents for money. He also had a few supportive and close friends he could lean on. We talked about the points he wanted to make—telling them he was transgender, sharing a little about his gender journey, letting them know to expect physical changes, and focusing on the positive effects of gender transition.

Rob decided he didn't want to answer any questions about possible surgeries, didn't want to defend his identity by answering questions like "Why are you trans?" and that he would leave the situation if he no longer felt emotionally safe. His asks were simple: call him Rob, use he/him pronouns, and do not refer to him as a woman.

Rob decided on writing an email to his parents, partly because he communicated in writing well and partly because he didn't want to see his parents' initial reaction. In the email, he shared his boundaries and asked if all of them could sit down the following week and talk in person. This gave the parents a chance to process the news, hopefully do a little googling, and come to the conversation after the initial dust had settled. He let them know that he didn't want to talk about this again until then.

TOOL: BOOKENDING

Bookending is a practice you can use to regulate your nervous system in any situation you anticipate will be emotionally difficult. In practice, it means designing a grounding and validating experience before and after a challenging one—hence, the term "bookending."

What constitutes a grounding, validating situation will mean something different to every person. Some people will find being surrounded by friends most affirming, whereas others need to have a therapy session and a spa day planned. The key things to focus on are being in affirming spaces, connecting with your support people, and treating yourself compassionately and well.

In other words, treat yourself to something that brings you pleasure, and make sure your cup is filled. Feeling as good as possible before going into a potentially stressful situation will help you feel more in control, and knowing you have a friend date at your favorite restaurant soon after gives you something grounding to look forward to.

Applying the Coming-Out Framework

Beyond the general framework of who/what/when/where/how, there are some additional things to consider when coming out to strangers, work, partners, kids, and family. These are the main groups of people you'll come out to and that typically cause the most anxiety, so I want to give you a little extra support.

Coming Out to Strangers

The most common experience of coming out to strangers is as a correction if you get misgendered. The important questions to ask about coming out to strangers, like a server or a grocery store clerk, beyond the general considerations discussed earlier, are "Do you have the capacity?" and "Does it meet your goals at this moment?" Sometimes it might feel the most authentic to correct them, and other times you just want to buy your Amy's frozen burrito in peace and move on with your day. There is no right answer here, just a choice you make in the moment based on your needs.

These interactions with strangers are not a reflection on you, your identity, or your appearance. Misgendering someone says more about them than it does about you.

Coming Out at Work

Many companies have made great strides toward transgender/non-binary diversity and inclusion, creating explicit non-discrimination policies that support their employees. Even in conservative areas, there are generally pockets of businesses and larger companies that are LGBTQ+ affirming and that have national policies around LGBTQ+ anti-discrimination and support. That's not to say that coming out in some workplaces won't hold risk, especially with regard to financial and job instability, and it's no secret that transgender and non-binary folks can be actively discriminated against when seeking employment, regardless of policy or legality.

Coming out at work or while seeking a job requires being strategic and thoughtfully considering what is going to meet your goals and needs the best.

I recommend you start with a trusted and supportive colleague. It can feel less overwhelming as a first step, and knowing that someone has your back at work often lets folks breathe a little easier.

Finding your resources is also especially important. Before coming out at work in a broader way, I always recommend you start by researching your company's non-discrimination and LGBTQ+ inclusion policies. Staff handbooks and a quick google will often give you at least a sense of where the company stands.

In the worst case, you now know that your employer is not transgender/non-binary affirming, and you can make more informed decisions from there. In the best case, human resources can significantly reduce your personal burden and handle annoying logistical things like changing your email to your new name. Some workplaces, particularly at larger companies, have experience with transgender/non-binary employees and might already have an employee-transition plan in place. HR can also answer questions related to the company's bathroom policy, but please also check your state and city guidelines for any legal protections or discriminatory laws related to going to a bathroom that fits your gender best. After you've gotten the lay of the land, the order of events is usually to come out to your boss and collaborate with them on how to tell the rest of your team or direct coworkers.

Depending on the size of the company, coming out with a bang to the whole company as trans or non-binary might be overkill. Some folks may choose to simply change their name in the company directory and on Zoom and add their pronouns to their email signature.

The important thing to remember is that it's the company and your boss's job to help you, and it's okay to ask them to do things that will make the coming-out experience easier on you. For example, you might want to collaborate on drafting an email to the team that comes from your boss's email to announce identity, name, and pronoun shifts instead of sending an email yourself (and potentially opening the floodgates for reactions and questions you don't want to manage). One powerful tool for getting ahead of questions and setting firm boundaries is to create an FAQ letter that is distributed to the team or company. I've included some guidance to help you create this at the end of the chapter.

JOB SEARCHING WHILE TRANS

If and when you come out while job searching depends on your goals.

If your goal is to find a workplace that is transgender/non-binary affirming, looking at company policies before an interview and asking about LGBTQ+ inclusion during an interview can help you decide if this is a company that will be supportive of your identity. I've also had clients integrate this research and their identity into a cover letter with a lot of success. For example, "As a transgender woman, I was impressed by your commitment to LGBTQ+ diversity and inclusion and feel I can do my best work where my identity is seen and supported." Remember that an interview is a two-way conversation to see if you and the company are a good fit for each other.

If your goal is to find (or keep) a job as quickly as possible and you're unable to find an LGBTQ+ affirmative workplace, using strategic gender expression can help you continue to feel like you have agency while still meeting your need for financial stability. By reframing your choice to not be out or to "tone down" your gender expression during an interview as an act of self-care to keep you financially safe, you are free to seek validation elsewhere in your life. Besides, it can be a fun reveal when, on day one of your job, you show up with a prominent undercut. Take that, patriarchy! That said, this isn't a perfect solution, and there are no easy choices here. As always, prioritize your safety, your needs, and take a run through the who/what/when/where/how framework if you're feeling uncertain how to proceed.

Coming Out to Partners

Coming out to a partner can feel overwhelming, especially if you've been together a long time and built a life together, but it can also be an exciting way to take your relationship to the next level. The simple truth is that some relationships stay together after a partner comes out as transgender or non-binary, and others don't. Healthy partnerships are built on the desire to see the other person thrive, and in any relationship, partners may grow in ways that create distance or no longer align with each other's needs.

The biggest difference I've seen between the partnerships that stay together and those that don't is an attitude of openness, curiosity, and play from both parties. For partners, this means letting go of preconceived notions of gender roles, engaging with your transgender/non-binary partner with curiosity instead of assuming that a shifting gender identity is a threat to your relationship, and recognizing that sexual orientation is a label you apply to yourself regardless of your partner's gender.

For your part, it means inviting your partner to participate in your tiny experiments as you play with gender (like having a coffee with you where you dress how you like), being curious about any reactions they have (as long as it's emotionally safe to do so), and maintaining an attitude that you're a team.

It's common for someone to experience fear of the unknown and a feeling of loss or grief when their partner comes out. This is a normal part of any big change—and even positive changes, like a wedding or an exciting new job, can cause stress and big emotions to come up. Parents cry as their children go off to college and at their weddings because in any change is also loss; however, we don't assume that the sad feelings mixed with pride and excitement mean that the child's next steps are negative—we can hold both. I invite you to stay open and remember that your partner's initial feelings may not be a sign your relationship is doomed.

That said, while you want to be there for your partner, you are not responsible for their feelings, nor are you obligated to be the primary person who helps them process their initial reaction and potential feelings of loss or sadness. It's helpful for partners to have a transgender-affirming therapist to navigate through difficult emotions and fears related to a partner's gender transition. As you're preparing to come out to a partner, consider what level of emotional support you have the capacity to offer. Coming out to partners also includes discussion of a new sexual landscape, and we'll talk more about navigating sex as a transgender/non-binary person in part 2.

Coming Out to Kids

In my experience working with clients who have come out to children, younger children and teens typically adjust quickly to a parent or grandparent coming out as transgender/non-binary. As education and the cultural acceptance of transgender individuals continues to grow, many children are already exposed to basic education about transgender identities and have much less rigid views of gender.

Providing reassurance that nothing has changed about your relationship and answering basic questions about your identity help ease a fear of uncertainty and provide an important sense of stability for children. Collaborating to find a family term that feels good to both of you is often a part of this process. Some clients I've worked with have made an exception to gendered terms like "mom" or "dad" for their children, while others prefer to find another name.

Coming Out to Family

Every time I hear a story of a parent or other family member embracing their transgender/non-binary child for who they are, it fills my heart with joy. Over the years, I've seen this happen more often as gender-diverse folks get increased media coverage and the cultural conversation expands. Family support makes a significant difference in transgender/non-binary folks' life satisfaction and, in many cases, might quite literally be life or death.[5] When parents are able to engage with their transgender/non-binary children with acceptance, curiosity, and openness, a child becoming more of who they are is an invitation to get to know them on a deeper level.

Sometimes parents experience a feeling of loss or grief as their child changes appearance, names, pronouns, and identity. It's important to remember that, while parents can sometimes consider changing a given name or pronoun a personal affront, it's not about them. Changing a name is about moving toward an identity that feels the best to you, not a fundamental rejection of their care in choosing a name. While their feelings are normal, it is *not* your responsibility to fix them or to take them on as your own. You get to decide both your willingness and emotional capacity to support your parents through any difficult emotions that arise.

Celebrating gender exploration and transition allows us to reframe this feeling of loss as similar to any other developmental milestone. Like a parent who cries as their child goes off to kindergarten, change often mixes loss with pride and possibility.

Even supportive family members will likely screw up from time to time and misgender you or call you the wrong name. Collaborating on how you'll let them know they made a mistake, what they'll do to correct it, and what you need for repair can turn the intensity down on this experience and allow you both to move through it with a stronger relationship than before.

What I want you to know about coming out is this: You don't have to shrink because someone's world is too small for you.

Coming out is not a selfish or burdensome thing to do. It's the most basic of human interactions. Letting someone know who you are is the beginning, and not the end, of a conversation or relationship.

So, what would you *want* if you weren't afraid? What would you *do*?

Because there is no greater feeling than seeing ourselves, than playing, than finding and owning our magic in the vast, awesome galaxy of gender.

FAQ LETTER

The FAQ letter is a tool I cannot take credit for. The idea came from a client many years ago and I was so impressed by the outcome that, with their permission, I started recommending it to my other clients. It is true magic, and the tool has helped many of my clients feel more of a sense of ease while coming out like none other. Now I hope it can help you.

The purpose of the FAQ is to clearly communicate your identity and your asks, answer common questions, and set clear boundaries. I've seen it used successfully for both work and family, since the tone is casual, assumes the recipients will support you, and frames gender transition as a positive change in your life to celebrate.

In other words, this isn't a letter to apologize for putting people out (you aren't!) or prove your identity. It's just a fact sheet. It's usually one to two pages and doesn't go deep into your gender journey narrative. The key components to think through when designing your FAQ sheet are the following:

What do you want to communicate about your identity, and how would you like to be referred to?

- names, pronouns, gendered language
- a few sentences about your story and what has changed for you
- what might shift with a changing gender expression
- how exciting of a time this is for you
- if there will be any changes in client-facing work related to your gender transition

What are common questions that Google can answer just as well as you? Start with the assumption that people will be supportive. Some examples include the following:

- What does it mean to be a transgender or non-binary person?
- What are they/them pronouns, and how do I use them? (*E.g., "They said the TPS reports are ready."*)
- How should I treat you? (*The same! Just with different words.*)
- What can I do to support you?

What are your boundaries around...

- questions related to your body (*e.g., "If we didn't talk about my body before, we shouldn't be talking about it now."*)
- being misgendered and how you'll correct folks if you are misgendered
- people who do not support transgender/non-binary individuals (*e.g., "It's okay if you don't understand or agree with my decisions. I simply ask for mutual respect and for folks to use my name and pronouns correctly."*)
- answering further questions

What further resources do you want to provide for people to do their own learning?

PART II

PLEASURE

CHAPTER 7

Pleasure Yourself

A dinosaur was having an orgasm in front of me. To be specific, my friend, dressed up in a blow-up T. rex costume, was riding a saddle-like sex toy contraption with a vibrating and rotating dildo while enthusiastically orgasming.

I was at a play party at a local dungeon, and I could think of nothing more erotic in that moment than a dinosaur pleasuring themselves while I watched with joy, doubled over in laughter.

When you throw out all the preconceived notions of what you "should" find erotic and what "sexy" is and let yourself play, sometimes what you find pleasurable might surprise you.

So, let's talk about what pleasure is.

Pleasure isn't productive, but it is generative. Pleasure is an invitation to create, and in that way, it's in direct defiance to messages that say our worth is dependent on our productivity.

Eroticism is indulging in pleasure, letting it sink into your bones and fill your chest with the feeling of being turned on and alive. Esther Perel defines eroticism as "pleasure for its own sake" and the "qualities of vitality, curiosity, and spontaneity that make us feel alive."[1] Eroticism includes sexuality, yes, but it's also so much bigger than that. It's about a turned-on life. Saving some of the most delicious feelings for just sex? How boring. Imagine that energy existing in more of your everyday life, guiding choices and inviting you to slow down and remember to enjoy being alive.

Eroticism and pleasure bring connection and intimacy within ourselves, and particularly within our bodies. When you're exploring gender, finding ways to feel pleasure in your body helps quiet dysphoria and self-critical thoughts. Or, at the very least, it helps you realize you can hold both pleasant and difficult feelings and move between them. Pleasure and eroticism help you recharge. They remind you of why you're exploring or transitioning your gender in the first place—to feel good in your skin.

Pleasure and eroticism also connect us to others, whether that is through shared sexuality or shared platonic experiences. Some of the most intimate and pleasurable moments I've had with others have been watching a beautiful performance-art piece or staying up too late laughing and talking about ideas that make our hearts sing.

Pursuing pleasure is a statement about your self-worth, saying you deserve to feel alive—to create, receive, explore, delight, connect—and to experience pleasure for its own sake.

That's what this chapter is about.

You don't have to have it all figured out to start experimenting with pleasure, nor do there have to be dinosaurs and dungeons involved. Finding what brings you pleasure is both an experiment and a form of play. You can't fail at this, because the measure of success isn't about an outcome. It's about the act of being playful. As Emily Nagoski puts it, "Pleasure is the measure."[2]

When I say, "Pleasure yourself," your imagination might go to many different places. The first place is likely to be solo sex, or masturbation, since that's the context we often use this term in. And yes, I will talk about pleasuring yourself sexually. But I'm also talking about pleasure in a more global sense—as a feeling of satisfaction, delight, joy, and indulging in things that make our senses light up.

Maybe your imagination goes to ropes and whips, or perhaps long baths with candles and coconut oil, dancing alone in your room to your favorite song, staring at the ocean, watching an inspiring performance, feeling the wind on your face while riding your bike around town. What brings each of us pleasure is as unique as we are.

Or maybe you can't think of anything. That's okay too. I've been there.

Historically, I've felt disconnected from pleasure and eroticism, especially in my body. Unnamed gender dysphoria played a role, but it's not the whole story. My family and culture were big factors in keeping me disconnected from noticing or pursuing pleasure in my body. In addition to oppressive norms around sexuality (or lack thereof), my family would have agreed with the preacher in *Footloose* about dancing. Growing up, I wasn't allowed to wear a two-piece bathing suit, spaghetti straps, or shorts that didn't graze my knees. Engaging with anything erotic or pleasurable related to the body was actively discouraged.

I also lived in a body with chronic pain and untreated anxiety. My body has been a source of hurt and distress throughout my life. Dissociating from it and dreaming of the day my brain could be transferred to a new, AI-powered body during the robot revolution was a coping skill I learned early. All of these intersections in my life made it difficult for me to discover what it meant to be connected to my body and to experience pleasure in it. Since then, I've done a lot of work (and still do) to connect to my body with more self-compassion and notice what brings me pleasure.

The turning point for me was simple: I decided it was worth fighting for a life where I get to be myself, to feel joy and pleasure, and to be connected to people who love me. I deserve that. And so do you.

Building Your Pleasure Practice

We often think of pleasure and eroticism as something that happens to us—something latent inside us that reveals itself with time. But I find it more helpful to think of eroticism and pleasure as a practice. The key to building your pleasure practice is to slow down and take time to notice and pursue things that bring you pleasure. Our brains pay attention to what we ask them to focus on, which means we can quite literally train our brains to notice pleasure. It's like looking for red cars on a road trip—as soon as you start looking for them, you notice them everywhere.

Getting in touch with our senses and imagination is one of the easiest ways to connect to pleasure in our bodies. There is a reason we call it "sensuality." When we fill our senses with things that are pleasurable to us (good music, a vivid sunset, a hot bath, a cup of tea, a clean house that smells like lemons) and understand what pleasure feels like in our body, we remind our brain to slow down and notice other pleasurable sensations.

For transgender and non-binary folks, there can sometimes be conflicting feelings about experiencing pleasure in bodies that don't feel like they fully reflect who we are. I've had clients express resistance to or guilt about feeling pleasure with certain body parts, sexual activities, or roles because it brings up feelings of being not "trans enough" if those things are outside of the gendered box they are now "supposed" to fit into.

It can be difficult to let ourselves enjoy the body we're in and feel pleasure while simultaneously knowing we may change that body in the future. Complicating this even more are feelings of discomfort at the parts of our physical selves that we can't change.

Remember how we talked about body positivity versus body respect all the way back in chapter 2? Given the world we live in, it's unrealistic to expect that you, as a transgender/non-binary person, are going to feel love for your body all day, every day. However, there is always an opportunity to show kindness to our bodies. And one of the greatest ways to show kindness to ourselves is to pursue pleasure.

Pursuing pleasure is about reminding yourself you want to feel good in your own skin, even on the days when you don't. We can hold it all. You're magic like that.

We've discussed how the way you think impacts gender exploration and the ability to transition with more ease. Likewise, there are important mindset shifts that will help you tap into pleasure while taking the pressure off of any particular "goal" besides "pleasure for its own sake."

Mindset Shifts for Exploring Pleasure

If you're having trouble tapping into pleasure or eroticism, it's not because your vibes aren't high enough or some other silly claim about connecting to your "divine vortex of epic sex." We've talked a lot about how context, histories, and systems have shaped us and created more barriers for folks with multiple, intersecting identities, especially when we're trying to connect to our own and other people's bodies.

Pleasure, eroticism, and sexuality can feel scary. Each requires vulnerability and getting to know sensations that might feel unfamiliar. When we've experienced lots of things that have hurt us, our brain can interpret new sensations as "AHH! SCARY!" instead of the more curious "Oh, what's that?"[3] That's normal.

I say this not to sound depressing but to ground you in self-compassion for wherever you are in your pleasure journey. Let's not judge it. Let's just start there. As we go through the next few chapters and you begin to explore what brings you pleasure, remember your brain can help. The way you're thinking and talking to yourself makes a big difference in the pursuit of pleasure, and by grounding yourself in curiosity and a willingness to take risks, you can turn down the volume on your brain trash.

As always, the most important thing is that you feel emotionally and physically safe. But assuming those two things are present, these two mindset shifts have helped my clients and me explore pleasure and eroticism.

Mindset Shift #1: Curiosity

One of the best guiding principles to get out of your head in the exploration of pleasure is to follow your curiosity. If you've ever gotten stuck in the joy of an internet wormhole and gone running to your partner to randomly exclaim, "Did you know that sperm whales can vibrate you to death with their sounds?" then you know what I mean.

(Only me? Okay.)

Once you notice one thing that piques your curiosity, you can expand on it, just like my journey into the vocalizations of sperm whales had me googling "biggest squids ever seen" late into the night.

Shifting into a curious mindset is especially helpful when we find ourselves judging. A lot of folks get hung up on judgment at some point when exploring pleasure and eroticism—judgment of ourselves, our bodies, our "performance," and of sensations and experiences. Curiosity is an "I wonder..." energy. It's playful, generative, and assumes the best intent of both ourselves and others.

In the show *Ted Lasso*, there's a great scene where Ted has to hit a perfect bullseye to win the round of darts that will determine the lineup of the last two games of the football season (or soccer, to us Americans) that he coaches. His opponent chuckles, smugly assuming that Ted is going to lose. It is, after all, a tough shot. As he goes to throw the dart, Ted talks about how people have always underestimated him, going on to say that had his opponent asked him a couple of questions before he made the bet—instead of judging him right away—he would have found out that Ted had played darts every Sunday for six years with his father.

Then Ted throws the bullseye.

Moving from judgment to curiosity within ourselves is a simple concept but takes practice to apply. Just like noticing how pleasure feels in our bodies, noticing what judgment feels like in our bodies and what our internal dialogue sounds like when we're being judgmental is the first step to changing it. Even if you don't feel curious yet, you can practice acting "as if" until it feels more natural.

In the context of a sexual experience with someone else, this might look like moving from "I'm a failure because I got anxious during sex" to "What happened here? What context and skills do I need to feel more pleasure next time? What do I need from my partner?" Even if you are acting "as if" you're curious before you *feel* curious, practicing this cognitive shift will help retrain your brain to not go to judgment automatically and allow you to pull yourself out of it quicker.

For one client I worked with, those questions helped him decide not to take off his binder during sex because sex felt more affirming that way. Don't overlook the tiny changes that might make a huge difference.

Whether you *feel* curious or not, keep going! Keep exploring. Keep learning. Keep following your budding curiosity and what brings you pleasure. You might be surprised where it leads. There will be days that will feel joyous and euphoric, and there will be days where things will feel harder and frustrating. Just keep swimming.

Both curiosity and pleasure are like snowballs rolling down a hill—as you put focus and intention on them, your pleasure snowball (I know it's cheesy; let me have it) keeps expanding and picking up the pace.

Mindset Shift #2: Flexibility and Willingness to Take Risks

What each of us finds erotic is unique. We each have our own desire templates that are shaped by our identities, our experiences, our values, and our socialization. It's common and completely normal for those desires and interests to shift and change over time as we grow and change ourselves, including during gender exploration and transition.

Discovering what you find erotic, what feels good in your body, and what feels good to consensually do to others' bodies requires flexibility and openness to change. Some of these new discoveries might require you to confront biases and be a little uncomfortable as you unlearn old messages and ways of being.

Exploring pleasure and eroticism often requires a change of scenery and context. Embracing fluidity and growth means being open to new experiences, spaces, and people and getting out of your comfort zone and embracing the awkward. (Your first dungeon party? Awkward. Your first time slowly eating a strawberry in the exercise you're about to do on page 120? Awkward.) But as always, we want to take risks that are challenging but not so challenging that they feel overwhelming.

The mindsets of curiosity, flexibility, and a willingness to take risks are the foundation for exploring the principles of pleasure. Once we get our mind right, everything else becomes easier.

Principles of Pleasure

In her book *Trans Sex*, Dr. Lucie Fielding asks one of my all-time favorite questions: "What would it be to imagine sexuality as a terrain of play and wonder rather than a dysphoria-packed minefield?"[4]

My answer—as you might expect by this point—is that it would feel like exactly that: full of play and wonder. But how do we know where to start exploring? How can we start to identify these feelings? There are four principles that can act as the cardinal directions on our pleasure compass and help us navigate the new terrain.

Principle #1—Pleasure Lives in the Body

We've talked about the challenges of getting stuck in your head in previous chapters, and . . . here it is again. The simple, but not always easy, remedy is to focus on your five senses. Your brain is going to do its own monkey-mind thing and might be all over the place. That's normal. Any time you notice your brain chatter taking you out of the moment, compassionately bring the focus back to what is pleasurable using your senses.

That sounds simple, but if you've felt disconnected from your body for a long time (like I was), your first tiny step is to learn how to reengage those senses and experience what pleasure feels like in your body. The following exercise will help you do just that.

SEXY STRAWBERRY

For this exercise, I want you to find a strawberry (or chocolate or another food item you find delicious) and sit down somewhere comfortable. Your goal is to stay aware of how your body feels when you engage each of your senses. Don't try to force feeling pleasure; stay curious, and pay attention to what sensations come up for you and where you feel them in your body.

Sight: Look at the strawberry closely. Notice the colors and gradients of color. Notice the shape and any irregularities. Notice the different textures of the fruit and the leaves.

Sound: If you rustle the leaves close to your ear or rub your finger across them does your strawberry make any sounds?

Smell: What does your strawberry smell like? Can you identify any fragrance notes like with a fine wine? Do the leaves smell different than the fruit?

Touch: Run your fingers over the strawberry. Notice the different textures. Is it cool or warm? Does the temperature change in your hand? What does it feel like to use a light versus a firmer touch?

Taste: Finally, put the strawberry in your mouth and bite slowly. Notice the juice running over your tongue and the first moment of tasting it. What does it taste like—sweet, bitter, acidic, rich? Finish eating it slowly and notice if there are different flavor profiles as you go.

Once you finish enjoying the strawberry, ask yourself the following:

What did it feel like to be really present and to go slow while eating?
What feelings, body sensations, and thoughts came up?
Did this experience feel like a "Yes!"? What parts?
Did any parts of this experience feel like a "No!"?

Whether or not you identified certain sensations as pleasure, going slow and using *all* your senses help build your capacity for using these skills in more areas of your life. When you do this and your brain and body go, "Yes!" you know you've hit the mark.

Principle #2—Decenter Genitals and Orgasm

Our biggest sex organ isn't our genitals. Or our brain. It's our skin, full of nerve endings all over our body ready to receive pleasure. By decentering genitals, you're opening up a world of possibilities for pleasure instead of having it concentrated in one spot.

It's common to think of orgasm as the point and pinnacle of sex. It isn't. The point of sex is multifaceted, and we all bring different needs at different times, but at the core is an experience that is connective (including to yourself) and erotic. When you center on pleasure and eroticism instead of running toward the goal of orgasm, you're able to slow down and experience more full-body pleasure. You're less likely to get stuck in your head because there's no goal except pleasure. And you take the pressure off any sexual concerns or issues: There's always something else pleasurable to do if your body can't or doesn't want to "perform" like society says it should.

There are many traditions of sexual and erotic teachings like tantra, BDSM, and kink that decenter the genitals and orgasm and can give you ideas for things to explore. And—shocker—the simple way to decenter these things is to focus on pleasure (or painful pleasure) in your five senses.

Slow it down and luxuriate in it. Or speed it up and get a rush. There's no right or wrong way as long as it works for you.

Principle #3—Give Yourself Permission

Skin isn't gendered. It's simply sensation. You don't need to experience pleasure or have sex in any particular way to "prove" your gender to anyone—even yourself. You're already valid. Let yourself enjoy the pleasurable sensations without judgment about what it means.

To be clear, you don't need my permission. (You can give that to yourself!) But in case it helps to hear someone else say it, you have my official permission to enjoy what you enjoy and to explore what you want to explore. You're trans enough, and nothing you do that brings you pleasure or feels erotic invalidates that. Period.

Principle #4—Accept Your Body As Is

When I say accept your body, what I mean is acknowledge the reality of what your body is like right now and show it kindness. I don't mean ignore gender dysphoria, limitations, or other concerns. Those feelings are real, they impact you, and ignoring difficult feelings is rarely helpful. Still. The body you have is the one you've got in this particular moment, even if you change something about it in the future. You don't have to hate your body or be unkind to it to want to change it.

SOME TRUTHS ABOUT BODIES

- All bodies are good bodies.
- Your body doesn't invalidate your gender identity regardless of what medical interventions you may or may not have.
- People will respect your gender identity if you tell them about it regardless of what your body looks like. Not all people. But the ones that aren't assholes, who are also the only ones we want to be hanging around anyway.
- All bodies can experience pleasure and eroticism.
- All bodies deserve pleasure and eroticism.

Accepting your body as is (for now) and working on believing these truths can help you turn down the volume on self-judgment and allow you to pursue pleasure more freely. Again, this is not about ignoring your feelings but about giving yourself a little bit of space to relate to yourself with more kindness. Practicing self-love, self-compassion, and self-efficacy (as described in chapter 2) can help ease feelings of judgment, anxiety, and fear as you work toward accepting your body. We experience the world and pleasure through our bodies, and we deserve to enjoy ourselves along the way.

PLEASURE BATH

One of my favorite homework assignments for clients and a personal practice of mine is a pleasure bath. I love baths (or showers) as a context for exploring pleasure because they take away one of the barriers that folks can get stuck on: being naked. Getting naked in your bedroom can pose a barrier if you aren't feeling comfortable in your body, if you have a partner or kids or roommates who might interrupt you, or if you're simply cold. The wet world is a natural place to explore pleasure since you're already naked and used to touching your body as you bathe.

In a pleasure bath, the goal isn't arousal or orgasm or any particular activity; it's just curiosity. Of course, if you want to get down and dirty with yourself in the bath, go for it! But that's not the point. This is an opportunity to practice curiosity and lean on the pillars of getting out of your head, as well as decentering orgasm and genitals, while exploring pleasure.

To create a pleasure bath ritual, block out at least forty-five minutes and lock the bathroom door. (You hear me out there, parents? Lock. Your. Door.)

Create a pleasurable context. Pick up any clutter. Light some candles or put on music if that's your thing. Or grab a joint and relax. Think about engaging as many of your senses as possible.

Then begin to touch your body with curiosity. Run your hands over your skin. Notice if some parts feel warmer or cooler, rougher or smoother, softer or harder. Experiment with a light touch and a deeper massage. Really look at your body and notice the little details you tend to overlook—curves, the texture, the way the light catches on your skin.

Take your time bathing your body. Massage your head and face. Soap up slowly, touching every inch of yourself.

What sensations feel pleasurable to you?

What feelings or thoughts come up as you explore?

A pro tip: I love using coconut oil in a pleasure bath because many people have it in their kitchen and it's a body-safe oil for our sensitive bits. Throwing a little in your bath or warming it up in your hand during a shower and rubbing it on your skin creates a different (and very pleasant, in my opinion) sensation to explore. Just don't slip and fall!

Hormone Therapy and Pleasure

A common fear I hear from folks who are medically transitioning is that hormone therapy (or surgeries) will change their sexual experience in a negative way.

Here's the truth: It's erotic to be authentic. And folks with all different kinds of bodies, abilities, and hormones are out there having hot and connecting sexual and erotic experiences, both solo and partnered. Changes in desire and exploring new ways to experience pleasure in your body can be an exciting time of growth.

Medical intervention does often change how your body functions and impacts your desire, but the science as well as my own experience as a therapist suggest that this is an overwhelmingly positive change for folks.[5]

Hormone therapy puts your body and mind in an environment where they can thrive.* Even before noticeable external changes start appearing, most of my clients have expressed that simply having different hormones in their bodies dramatically improved their gender dysphoria and helped them feel more comfortable and confident in their gender identity and expression. And confidence is sexy as hell.

Folks often get stuck in their heads about pleasure and hormone therapy, and there are a few misconceptions and anxieties I hear constantly. Much like with our boogeymen from chapter 4, shining a light on these anxieties makes them a lot less scary, so let's take them head-on.

---

* For people who feel like hormone therapy is a "Yes!"

A QUICK NOTE ON TERMINOLOGY

For clarity, I will often use traditional medical terms for anatomy in this section, but please replace any terms that don't feel affirming to you with whatever terms you like best. You can literally cross them out of the book and write your own. Using names for genitals that feel good to you, either all the time or during sex with a partner, can help you drop into your body more fully and create even more pleasure.

Transgender Women / People Taking Estrogen

Many transgender women / people taking estrogen I've worked with feel ambivalent at first about the changes in sexual functioning and desire from hormone therapy. While having more estrogen coursing through their body is deeply affirming, there is a fear they will experience less sexual and erotic satisfaction if it's more difficult to orgasm, there are changes in genital functioning, or their libido, or desire for sex, is lowered.

There are a few fallacies here to address.

First, hormone therapy with estrogen does not kill your libido. It simply changes it. Spontaneous desire is what we usually think of when we think about libido. Think of the feeling of horniness or getting hard or wet with few to no external triggers. This "lightning bolt to the genitals"[6] is what we see pictured in most media when we see desire portrayed.

However, there is another type of desire we don't talk about as much and that is often more common: responsive desire. When we are in a context that is safe and sexy and we give our bodies time to catch up, our bodies will often respond to that context. It's more intentional and just as sexy.

For example, it might mean taking a bath to relax and putting on some audio erotica before engaging in solo sex and giving your body thirty to forty-five minutes of time to feel pleasure instead of jumping on the bed right after work and expecting to have an orgasm within five minutes of furious rubbing.

Slowing down and being intentional about building your pleasure and eroticism practice can open up doors to new and greater pleasure, whether you're taking hormones or not. The transfemme folks on estrogen I've worked with have often described more full-body orgasms and pleasure as well as more awareness and pleasurable sensations in body parts besides the genitals, and they've experienced wonder at how fulfilling their solo and partnered sex lives are. A change in your desire template from more spontaneous to more responsive does not have to be a loss; it can be an expansion.

Second, a soft penis is still able to orgasm and experience pleasure. We are all socialized to believe that the only good penis is a hard penis, but this isn't true. A soft penis has the same number of nerve endings as an erect one and can experience just as much pleasure. Our culture teaches us how to interact with a hard penis (albeit in a very heteronormative way) but not a soft one.[7] Having how your body functions change means it's time to explore new ways of touching and using your body that are affirming for you.

Lastly, if a transfemme person wants to be a penetrating partner but is struggling to maintain an erection, there are lots of options for penetration beyond genitals. Fingers or fists are popular ones. There are also dildos in every shape, color, and size, and strap-ons that have room for larger genitalia.

Transgender Men / People Taking Testosterone

For transgender men / people taking testosterone, there can be uncertainty about "bottom growth," or clitoral growth, and concerns about what an increase in spontaneous desire will mean. Many folks on testosterone experience an increase in the feeling of horniness as a result of the hormones and, just as importantly, new behaviors and increased feelings of authenticity and confidence. As we discussed in chapter 1, testosterone levels are impacted by behavior and socialization more than previously thought, and it's amazing how sexy feeling yourself is. But as folks start to experience greater interest in sex than they might have had before, there can be a fear of becoming a sex-fueled monster.

The answer to the fear of becoming the equivalent of an obnoxious, horny teenage boy is simple. Don't be a misogynistic prick, and you'll be fine. There are lots of people in the world with a lot of testosterone in their body who like sex and are mindful, respectful, and loving, whether with a long-term partner or during a one-night stand. Be that person. Also, for what it's worth, if you're concerned about becoming a sex-fueled monster, chances are you won't become one, because you're already mindful of it (also, that's not how testosterone works).

Increased desire can and should be fun! You're the same person who holds the same values you did before starting testosterone. Remember that eroticism is about more than sex. It's about energy, and energy can be used in many different ways in and out of the bedroom and in solo and partnered play.

Bottom growth is a beautiful thing if it aligns with your gender identity. It can be scary because it's new and unfamiliar and permanent and usually one of the first physical changes that folks notice. And there is space between starting hormone therapy and irreversible bottom growth. If you are uncertain whether you will like it, you have an opportunity to stop or decrease the dosage of hormones at any time if the growth becomes dysphoric for you. In my experience, bottom growth and increased genital sensitivity have been some of the most fun and affirming aspects of more testosterone both in my body and as a partner.

TESTOSTERONE SIDE EFFECTS: DRYNESS AND ATROPHY

A couple of common side effects of testosterone hormone therapy are vaginal dryness and atrophy. Clitoral pain with growth can also be a concern. Often, this is discomfort due to skin growth and will go away with time. If it continues or is especially bothersome, bring in a professional. If you're experiencing any of these concerns, there are a few things you can do.[8]

- Get good-quality lube (check out a local or online feminist sex toy store) and use it consistently for both solo and partnered play.
- Give your body more time to respond to your safe and sexy context.
- Seek out a pelvic-floor physical therapist who can help identify

what muscles might be tight and work with you to gently loosen them up. Pelvic-floor muscles can often be released through internal or external pressure or through things like deep breathing.

- Take deep, slow breaths that expand your belly. You can practice this by sitting or lying comfortably and placing one hand on your belly. Breathe in slowly through your nose while allowing your stomach to rise. As you exhale gently through your nose or mouth, notice how your belly contracts toward your spine.
- If the dryness and irritation is causing your pelvic floor muscles to tense, you can stretch out the pelvic floor muscles with your fingers. Imagine your vulva is a clock. Taking one or two fingers (use lube), inserting them to the first or second knuckle and pressing firmly (but not so much that it's painful) on the "hours" between three and nine is particularly helpful in releasing tense pelvic muscles.
- Talk to your pelvic floor physical therapist and prescribing doctor (or your primary care doctor) about topical estrogen cream to rejuvenate the dryness. Topical creams only impact the area where they are directly applied.

Ideas for Erotic Exploration

All of the mindsets and principles of pleasure we've explored in this chapter lead to something deep and meaningful—hope. Hope isn't about wearing rose-colored glasses or constantly having a smile on your face. Hope is created by having goals (like bringing more pleasure and eroticism into your life), seeing a path to get there, and taking tiny steps toward your goal.[9]

Think of the following ideas as alternately a tasting menu and the proverbial spaghetti to throw at the wall. Some are explicitly erotic (or can be) and some simply focus on pleasure through your senses, play, and inspiration. Everyone's desire template is different, so use these suggestions as a jumping-off point—or ignore them completely and come up with your own ideas. The important thing is that you come curious and let your imagination lead you. Learning that you don't like something can be as powerful as knowing that you do. It's all just information.

Embodied Practices

Moving your body in ways that feel pleasurable or satisfying gives you a feeling of agency over your life and can be a powerfully erotic practice. Dance is a particular embodied practice that has meant a lot to me over the past ten years. Because of my upbringing, I don't think I truly danced until I moved to Chicago (Baptists don't like dancing). Learning to let go of being so controlled in my body and moving it (flailing it?) with the music's rhythm, preferably in a crowd of sweaty queers, is the freest I've ever felt.

As an overambitious Capricorn, I decided to conquer my body issues and continue exploring pleasure by taking my clothes off onstage for strangers while dancing. Graduating from my improv burlesque days, I joined a burlesque class with a performance track and worked my two left feet to the bone learning the moves. "Eyes up!" our teacher would yell roughly a thousand times a class, reminding us to stop staring at our feet and watch ourselves in the mirror. Confidence was the message of the class. Whatever your body looked like, no matter how many dance steps you forgot, no matter what happened onstage with your costume, you had to own it. Because at the end of the day, the audience wanted to see you having fun onstage. Everything else was details.

I've heard clients describe the pleasure and freedom they feel while riding their bike through the city as an erotic experience. Fitness and feeling strong and flexible is a source of pleasure and agency for many, like my friends who run Han Training, a queer, trans BIPOC-led gym in Chicago.

And while it might not sound super sexy, even body-based therapies like somatic experiencing, eye movement desensitization reprocessing (EMDR), and sensorimotor psychotherapy are powerful tools to help folks feel more connected to their bodies when their bodies haven't always felt safe to them.

Solo Sex

Mindful solo sex, or masturbation, is one of the best ways to connect with our bodies. We often think of solo sex as secondary to partnered sex or as a quick release when we don't have a better option. Let me paint a new picture for you.

It's much more helpful to think of solo sex and partnered sex as completely different erotic constructs.[10] Solo sex isn't a consolation prize if we can't or don't want to have partnered sex. It's a different type of sexual experience that is valuable in and of itself. Mindfully engaging in solo sex means taking your time, paying attention to context, and taking the focus off of orgasm and putting it back on sensual pleasure. Solo sex gives you the opportunity to get into a "Oh, what's that?" headspace[11] and explore your body without worrying about paying attention to a partner.

Sexy Snapshots

A sexy snapshot is the result of mining for sexy and safe contexts in an experience or fantasy that was particularly pleasurable and erotic for you. Something that really got your motor running. It can involve sex or being naked, but it doesn't have to. Late author and sex educator Jack Morin calls these "peak erotic experiences."[12]

Getting curious about the factors that contributed to the sexy snapshot can give you important clues as to what feels pleasurable to you. Once you've identified some of the factors, the question becomes "How can I include more of X in my day-to-day life?"

For example, I used to read like a maniac.

Then I went to graduate school, and after all those papers and textbooks, it was hard to get back into reading consistently for fun. As I explored what feels pleasurable and erotic in my life, I experimented with reading novels again for fun, some of them erotic by content but many of them erotic because of the beauty of the words. I lit some candles, poured myself a glass of whiskey, and curled up on the couch with a book and a playlist called "Fuck Me, Daddy."

Thinking of this sexy snapshot reminded me of things I knew I loved on some level but wasn't in the habit of putting together—words, great music, a vibe. I now incorporate more of those things into my week.

Speaking of erotic words...

Erotica and Porn

Finding erotica or porn that resonates with you is a fun and effective way to broaden your erotic imagination. Sometimes finding the right author, performer, or producer can be a challenge, but in the age of the internet, there is something out there for everyone with a little digging.

One of my favorite porn projects is Goodyn Green's Shutter series. Some folks are more visual or auditory, so experimenting with what type of written or video content speaks to you is part of the process. There are also many fantastic and affirming sex how-to books out there that can give you ideas and some great tips. Seeing ourselves reflected in erotic material is powerful and affirming in a world that often seeks to tokenize or desexualize marginalized identities.

However, finding pleasure in words or film is not just about explicitly sexual material. Some of the most erotic words I've heard come from a finely crafted description of the mycelium networks under the earth and Jeanette Winterson's unique ability to blend fantasy with realism or the way Lidia Yuknavitch's words seem to explode from her body and settle into yours.

Finding film and words that bring you pleasure is about chasing curiosity, being open to change, and broadening your erotic template naturally and with ease.

Fill Your Feed

Social media has a profound impact on us in both good and bad ways. Filling your feed with people who reflect your values, promote body respect and pleasure for all bodies, and are explicitly erotic or sexual in nature makes scrolling through Instagram a delight. It can take a little bit of work to find these folks, but I promise they are out there. Once you find a few of them, it becomes a snowball of inclusive pleasure as you start following similar pages and the algorithm catches on.

Erotic Spaces and Art

Shaking up your routines and intentionally putting yourself in spaces focused on eroticism can jump-start your erotic imagination. This might look like explicitly sexual spaces such as classes at your local feminist sex toy store, sensual movement classes, kink conferences and events, play parties, or online groups and discussion forums. It might also include choosing to take in erotic performances like burlesque, circus, or pole dancing or engaging with erotic art. It can also look like going to spaces that bring you pleasure but aren't explicitly erotic, like the ballet, opera, an art gallery, or taking a pottery class (*Ghost*, anyone?) or learning to work with leather.

Brains, Craft, and Talent

Some of the most erotic experiences I've had have not been explicitly connected to anything sexual. I get a lot of pleasure from watching, listening to, and having conversations with people that I find smart, skilled, and talented. I love and am consistently inspired by people sharing their gifts, art, and ideas. I could happily listen to a master maker explain in detail about their craft for hours. Watching talented performers of all types lights me up inside. People's brains and their passions leave me in awe.

The Natural World

Connecting with nature is a source of eroticism and pleasure for many. There's an entire movement called ecosexuality, melding eroticism with environmental activism.[13] The natural world has an endless supply of awe and pleasure to share, whether you literally want to have sex with a tree or simply feel pleasure when you see a beautiful sunset or a mountain peak held by clouds or when you stand in the outer space that is an ocean.

Cheese

There's a reason my only skill in the kitchen is making a cheese board fit for Dionysus. It's a delight for the senses.

Play "This or That"

Imagining new ways of interacting with your body beyond what society tells us we "should" do can be a lot of fun. It's also fun to experiment with new kinds of sensations—like hot and cold, pokey and soft, firm and light. And often, we're surprised by what we enjoy.

The "this or that" game is a great way to explore new experiences. You can play with a partner or on your own. Try two different sensations and ask yourself, "Did I like this or that better?" Repeat.

Reimagining and relearning how to touch yourself or asking a partner to touch you in new ways can feel incredibly affirming. In exploring new terrains in your body, you might ask a partner to try different ways of touching, licking, and sucking that might feel good. You can also experiment with things like ice cubes, body-safe candle wax, something fuzzy, or a Wartenberg wheel (a small wheel of spikes you can roll across your skin).

This game can also be useful for reimagining what you want your bits to be called and finding affirming language for your body. Pro tip: Have a partner whisper them in your ear.

Here's what I want you to know: You deserve pleasure equity. Your body might not feel 100 percent affirming to you, but it's yours and it deserves kindness. Pleasure is accessible no matter what your limitations are, and it's a muscle that you have to intentionally build.

I WANT / I WONDER DANCE PARTY

Saying our desires out loud is powerful. As you discover more about what brings you pleasure, this brainstorming exercise can help get your curiosity and play juices flowing.

For this exercise, find a time when you have some privacy, take a few deep breaths, and turn on your favorite music to dance to. Get warmed up by moving your body to the music for at least one song. As you continue dancing, start brainstorming out loud about things you want and things you wonder about. Don't censor yourself. Don't think too hard. Don't be afraid to be silly. Just let your stream of consciousness flow.

That's it. You don't have to do anything with the answers if you don't want to. But my guess is that you will.

Examples:

I want...

to be desired for who I am

to experience being a top/bottom/dom/sub

to have my partner dress up in a gorilla costume and fuck me with a strap-on

I wonder...

what it would be like to wear a strap-on and have my partner give me a blow job while I watch in the mirror

what words would feel the most affirming when talking about my body parts

what it would be like to feel confident in my sexuality; how would I behave differently?

Pro tip: Try recording yourself saying these things on your phone and have it transcribed (or transcribe it yourself).

We can think faster than we can write, so it's often easier and more authentic to talk it out, and seeing your stream of consciousness in writing can help you see patterns and keep a record of the things you want and are curious about.

CHAPTER 8

Unlock Your Erotic Mind

I once visited a deliciously sexy cave in Portugal.

Touring the Quinta da Regaleira estate is like touring a kinky garden designed by Indiana Jones, with secret passageways and copious grottos for getting into whatever your heart desires. At one point, I found myself alone in a cave with an opening to an underwater pond. It was barely lit, quiet, and darkly beautiful. If the cave could talk, it would have put on smooth jazz and handed me a glass of port. It was hot. And I was into it.

That experience was quite a contrast from my twenties, when you could frequently find me curled up in a ball, sobbing in pain in the bathtub late at night after attempting to have sex with my then husband. When I finally sought medical help and explained to my doctor how excruciatingly painful penetrative sex was, the doctor told me, "Just relax."

Helpful.

I cried to my best friend over snow cones in the East Texas heat about how I wasn't sure I wanted to be married anymore. I sobbed alone as I journaled about how broken and lonely and trapped I felt, not so much by my husband as by the oppressive Evangelical Christian environment we were in that left me feeling like I had very few choices to remedy my situation.

What was wrong with me that I didn't want to have sex with my husband?

What was wrong with my body that sex hurt so much?

Why didn't I feel the pleasure that seemed to come to everyone else so easily?

I felt utterly hopeless. I'll bet some of you feel like that right now. When exploring gender, pleasure—especially sexual pleasure—is often seen as the last frontier. You *might* get to feel good in your body once you figure everything out, once you "fix" yourself, once your body looks a certain way, once you are gendered correctly by strangers 100 percent of the time, and once you're lucky enough to find someone who wants to sleep with you.

That's hogwash.

Wherever you are starting out in your pleasure journey, you too can have embodied experiences of pleasure. When I was in the weeds of sexual pain, disconnection from my body, sexual shame, and exploring my identity for the first time, I never could've imagined being so connected with my body that a cave made me hot and bothered. Or the myriad of other pleasures I've experienced since that painful time in my life.

Like we talked about in the last chapter, tapping into pleasure and the erotic in our lives is not self-indulgent and it's not just about sex. As adrienne maree brown explains, "Pleasure activism is the work we do to reclaim our whole, happy, and satisfiable selves from the impacts, delusions, and limitations of oppression and/or supremacy."[1] Pursuing pleasure is a path toward reclaiming what the systemic oppression in our culture has tried to take away from you: your freedom, your self-worth, your joy, and your imagination.

I'll talk about common barriers to accessing pleasure and eroticism—and remind you that you are 100 percent normal—in this chapter.

Often, folks talk about sex and eroticism for transgender and non-binary folks from the perspective of risk or a deficit. The research talks about STI prevalence, safety, and experiences of gender dysphoria. These are important things to know. But what about all the glorious fun transgender/non-binary people have in exploring pleasure, eroticism, and sexuality?

And trust me—we have fun.

No matter where you are in your process, what barriers you face, your partnership status, or whether or not sex is important to you, you deserve to feel pleasure and eroticism. And the great news is everyone has access to it. I wrote in the introduction about this book being a travel guide instead of a map, and I encourage you to think of your body the same way. You get to explore new terrains and even create entirely new pleasurable, erotic, and sexual experiences with yourself and your partner(s).

As for me, I was eventually diagnosed with a pelvic pain disorder, had surgery, got some help from the miracle workers that are pelvic-floor physical therapists, and started seeing a sex therapist to figure out this whole pleasure thing.

I started looking at how my chronic illness, upbringing, past experiences, and mental health affected my ability to be present and experience pleasure in my body.

Over several years, I also got a divorce, came out as queer and nonbinary, and discovered more about my "Yes!" as I explored sexuality, polyamory, kink, gender, and my body, and simply noticed when something felt pleasurable.

BUT I'M ASEXUAL AND AROMANTIC...

For my asexual and/or aromantic readers: Apply this chapter (as well as chapter 9, where we'll talk about partnered sex) in whatever way feels best for you. You don't have to have the same erotic template as someone who loves sex or romance in order to experience pleasure and eroticism. The principles are all the same, even if the details might look slightly different. Pleasure in your body doesn't need to involve anyone else, sex at all, romance, or certain sexual acts. It's just about feeling good and lit up in your own skin and designing relationships that feel good, whatever that means for you.

Tapping into Your Yes

When we are able to show up in the world as lit-up, turned-on humans who are connected on a deep level to our erotic mind—to our feelings, needs, creativity, and desires—magic happens. I learned a lot of this by reading an essay: "Uses of the Erotic: The Erotic as Power" by Audre Lorde.

In this essay, Lorde—a queer Black woman scholar—says, "We have been raised to fear the yes within ourselves, our deepest cravings."[2] I found this to be true on my journey, and you may feel that way too. I had to unlearn all the ways I had been taught to deny, suppress, and fear my deepest longings.[3] What I want most for you is for you to not be afraid of your yes but to own it, feel its power, and let it guide you.

I learned to allow my "Yes!" moments to inform my path. The process was messy and involved a few panic attacks and plenty of experimentation. But I did find my way to pleasure both in my sexuality and, more broadly, in my body and life, which feels free, expansive, and playful. And, apparently, involves caves.

Intentionally integrating pleasure and eroticism into gender exploration helps you tap into your own "Yes!" and what you are moving toward, rather than what you are moving away from.

After years of shoving down or denying parts of yourself, it can be healing to seek out sensations, experiences, and connections that give you energy and feel good. Tapping into your own "Yes!" as you explore gender puts you in a mindset of creativity, openness, and curiosity instead of fear. Once you've felt the energy of a full-body "Yes!" you sure as hell aren't going to accept a life without more of it.

It's also not just about you. Pleasure and eroticism compel us to action in order to create a world of infinite possibilities we have only caught glimpses of. It's activism, resistance, and defiance—defiance against having others control our bodies, dictate our desires, silence our passion, and tell us that we deserve any less than feeling fully alive.

Audre Lorde says,

> As we begin to recognize our deepest feelings, we begin to give up, of necessity, being satisfied with suffering and self-negation, and with the numbness which so often seems like their only alternative in our society. Our acts against oppression become integral with self, motivated and empowered from within.

In other words, pleasure and eroticism are not the side quest; they're the main campaign.

TRAUMA, THE BODY, AND YOUR "YES!"

This is not a book about trauma, but it is trauma informed. There are many people who have experienced trauma, both individually and culturally, who do not feel safe in their bodies. This is a completely normal response to trauma. As we discussed in chapter 2, your brain is marvelous and protects you from physical and emotional harm by sending your nervous system into fight/flight/freeze/fawn when it senses danger. And when your brain perceives a threat, the last thing on your mind is pleasure.

For those who have traumatic pasts, feeling connected to your body, let alone experiencing pleasure, can feel dangerous even when you want these things and are in a safe situation.

Whatever you have capacity for is okay. If engaging in pleasure and eroticism in a sexual way feels like too much right now, or you're not interested in it, that's okay. *Wherever* you are is okay. Working through trauma is an opportunity for self-compassion, deeply understanding our own boundaries, and building trust and safety within ourselves by exploring at a pace that is slightly challenging but not too much.

Your "Yes!" might be saying no to a sexual experience that you don't want and feeling the pleasure that comes from healthy boundaries. Taking tiny steps toward pleasure and eroticism might look like starting with activities that involve senses other than touch, like lighting your favorite incense, watching or listening to an artist you love, or the pleasure you get from riding your bike or doing gentle stretches in bed. Start where you are.

Working through trauma and its impact on our body is often a lifelong journey, best taken with professionals and in community. If you're interested in more resources specifically about trauma, check out the resources at www.gendermagic.com.

If you're feeling discouraged in your quest for more pleasure and eroticism, I want to reassure you that being transgender/non-binary is not the final nail in the coffin of your erotic life. Many transgender and non-binary folks don't experience body or social gender dysphoria that interferes with their ability to have fulfilling sexual relationships and pleasurable experiences.

On the contrary, many of my clients report having the best sex of their lives and how juicy pleasure feels to them now after they've stopped shoving down huge parts of themselves. Leaning into understanding and expressing your gender authentically often *enhances* your ability to be present in erotic or sexual situations and connect more deeply to yourself and others. I've seen, and know firsthand, how new sexual and erotic experiences during gender exploration can be deeply affirming and a playground to explore identity and expression.[4]

It's also true that pleasure is not equitable.

Pleasure Equity

Cisgender and transgender folks alike, and especially those with multiple marginalized identities, often experience barriers to personal and shared eroticism, pleasure, and sexuality. A glass of wine and a new piece of underwear aren't going to cut it when you're contending with trauma, racism, poverty, violence, anxiety, depression, physical limitations, lack of sex education, fear of rejection, living in a largely sex-negative culture, and the tiny boxes of gender and sexual roles we are told we "should" fulfill.

Many transgender and non-binary folks struggle with gender dysphoria, sexual shame, bodies that don't always reflect who they are, and sex education that only talks about cisgender bodies. For some people, tuning into pleasure and eroticism when your brain is consumed by gender can be difficult. You might be stuck in your head about what your partner(s) thinks of you and your body, and whether they see you for who you are. Safety concerns are also a reality of navigating sexuality as a transgender person, especially for transgender women of color. We will talk more about assessing safety and navigating partnered sex in chapter 9.

If you're dealing with any of these things, know that you're 100 percent normal. There's nothing wrong with you. You're not broken. And a full life of pleasure, eroticism, and fulfilling sexual and romantic relationships is possible for you. I promise. And more pleasure is available to you when you lean into the fact that you deserve a fulfilling erotic and sexual life. The theory on intimate justice explains why believing we deserve these things can be challenging for marginalized identities, including trans folks.

You Deserve Pleasure

"Intimate justice" is a term coined by researcher Sara McClelland. Her research shows that folks from marginalized identities tend to imagine less relational and sexual satisfaction is possible for themselves as a result of systemic oppression, and these same folks tend to think they *deserve* less satisfaction.

When applied to transgender and non-binary folks, this means that many people don't believe they deserve the pleasure, eroticism, or satisfaction in romantic and sexual relationships that they want. Some can't even picture what that would feel like and assume it isn't possible. Erotic imagination is shut down and, with it, the possibility for pleasure.

Many transgender clients I've worked with struggle to feel desirable, as well as "desire-able," a term my friend and colleague Lucie Fielding pulls from disability justice.[5] To feel desire-able means you have the capacity and feel worthy of desiring another, being desired, and having erotic wants and needs (and asking to have them met!).

Historically (and sometimes even today), transgender folks were denied gender-affirming procedures and medication if they expressed anything other than hatred for their bodies or a desire for sexual relationships that were heteronormative. Transgender women are often fetishized and sexualized as a novelty for cisgender men, while also stripped of any personhood or erotic agency. Transgender men are similarly portrayed in media as feeling shame about their bodies and a need to hide themselves from lovers or perform caricatures of toxic masculinity instead of the joyful and affirming sex so many transmasculine individuals are having. Non-binary folks, like me, often get shoved into one box or the other, ironically expected to "prove" our non-binaryness by conforming to some preconceived notion of what our identities mean for how we want to have sex and experience pleasure.

It's time for pleasure equity.

But first, a little science.

Brakes and Accelerators

I first learned about the "brakes" and "accelerators" of sexual desire and arousal from Emily Nagoski's book, *Come as You Are*.[6]

Put simply, whether or not your body is aroused and your brain thinks sex sounds like a great way to pass the time depends on context. Your brakes are the things that turn you off. This includes important things like safety concerns and external contexts like smelly laundry, chronic pain or illness, work stress, and feeling not affirmed in your gender by your partner. Your brakes can also include internal contexts like how you feel about your body, anxiety, worries about performance, shame, and internalized gendered ideas.

Here is the important thing to remember: Brakes aren't inherently bad. They're a critical part of the system that keeps you safe. But when our brakes are calibrated by an oppressive culture, they can sometimes be overzealous in an attempt to keep us safe. Getting curious about what hits our brakes and why can create space to listen to what wisdom they have to offer and engage with the overprotective parts with more compassion.

Your accelerators on the other hand, include all the pleasurable contexts your brain decides are "sexually relevant."[7] This is unique to each person but includes everything in your senses and imagination that your brain says, "Yes!" to. Your accelerators also include having a reasonably secure attachment with sexual partners. You don't have to get married and have babies, you don't even have to know their name, but being able to accurately assess that you can trust them and they have your back, even if for only a brief time, is a pretty big turn-on. In other words, when your context feels safe and sexy, your body and brain are primed for pleasure.

Outside of explicitly sexual contexts, we can also apply the brakes-and-accelerators model to pleasure and eroticism more broadly. Your brakes, in this context, are anything that takes you out of the moment, gets you in your head, and makes your brain scream, "Not safe! Abort mission!" In contrast, your accelerators are anything that helps you be present and in your body and that makes your brain light up and say, "Mmmm... Yes! That!" The feeling I most associate with knowing my accelerator has been pushed is delight. Whenever I feel delight, it's my cue to slow down and savor it.

DISCOVERING YOUR BRAKES AND ACCELERATORS

Some questions to help you discover more about your brakes and accelerators in all contexts are the following:

Do I feel physically and emotionally safe?

What's contributing to my feeling of safety or unsafety? *(E.g., physical environment, relationship dynamics, words of encouragement, a closed and locked door, being affirmed in my gender, etc.)*

What are things that delight me? *(E.g., a hand running down my spine, the sensation of X, novelty, drinking coffee on my porch in the sun, deep conversation with a loved one, a piece of performance art, etc.)*

What helps me be present and tune in to my five senses? *(E.g., a certain smell, taking time to transition out of work mode, knowing the dishes are washed, being outside, focusing on breathing, touching a fuzzy pillow, etc.)*

What's preventing me from being present and tuned in to my five senses? *(E.g., a dirty room, a dog in the bedroom, unclear sexual expectations, work stress, anxiety, body image, gender dysphoria, etc.)*

What turns me on? And by "turns me on," I mean gives me a full-body buzzy, warm feeling of desire. *(E.g., hearing my lover say X; watching my loved one excel; a certain type of touch; dancing to sexy music alone; a long, hot bath, etc.)*

Sex and the Art of Motorcycle Maintenance

I recently learned to drive a motorcycle (sorry, Mom). There are lots of great life lessons to be learned from motorcycle riding, but one of the most important is a great metaphor for working with your brakes and accelerators. Our instructor quickly taught me that hitting the brakes while going around a curve is a no-no. Curves are dangerous, and if you go into one too fast and hit the brakes, you're likely to skid and possibly crash your bike. On the other hand, if you go into the curve too fast and *don't* hit the brakes, you're likely to go screaming over a cliff. Neither of these are good options.

The answer? Take the curves slow.

The way to take a curve safely is to look ahead and assess the risk, hit the brakes *before* you get to the curve to make sure you're going a safe speed, look ahead to where you want to go, then accelerate slightly to maintain the bike's momentum.

See where I'm going with this?

Your brakes aren't meant to help you avoid risk. They're meant to help you navigate that risk safely so you can experience the joy that is going vroom-vroom.

When applied to pleasure, eroticism, and sex, a curve is any context where your brakes will likely come into play. For example, if your house is a mess, your chronic illness is affecting you, or you know that you have a busy week at work coming up, that could be a barrier, a "curve," in your journey to pleasure and eroticism.

There are two things you can do to work with your brakes. The first and most important is simply to notice what your brakes are without judgment. This gives you an opportunity to show compassion to yourself rather than frustration and to ask yourself what you need.

Second, use your brakes to move through curves at a safe pace. In chapter 3, we talked about doing things that are challenging to us but not so challenging that we get into our fight/flight/freeze/fawn response. That's where we want to be when working with our brakes. It can be helpful to slow down when we notice we are about to hit a "curve" and ask ourselves what pace we need to go at for safety and ease while not going so slow that we don't make it around the bend.

Using your brakes as information and a tool for moving through curves safely might look like doing practical things, such as tidying your house, taking a hot bath to help your pain, or talking about what stressful thing is happening at work with your sweetie while on a walk. It can also look like deeper and more long-term work related to knowing your trauma triggers, building emotional-regulation skills, working to unlearn negative messages about your body, and moving through shame. Taking the space to slow down gives you more freedom to hit your accelerator.

When you're riding a motorcycle, where you put your focus is where the bike naturally wants to go. We learned this in class by the instructor pointing to the motorcycle-size dents in the fence and asking, "Where do you think those people were looking?"

When it comes to pleasure, we can ask ourselves the same question: Where do you ultimately want to go?

We talked in chapter 2 about your "why" for transitioning. Hold on to that why (and your why for tapping into pleasure) and keep your eyes on it as you navigate the curves that life brings.

One last note on navigating curves and brakes: I was scared shitless to take my first tight turn on a motorcycle. You have to lean really far over and turn the handlebars in such a way that I was positive I was going to do a slow-motion tip-over as soon as I tried. What helped was listening to my teachers on how to handle new and scary curves that came up and watching my peers take the sharp turns.

Notice I didn't say take the sharp turns and not fall. I watched at least one of my classmates tip over in exactly the place I was scared of. However, I also watched them get up, cringe-laugh, and get back on their bike and take the turn again. They didn't die. No one in the class made them feel bad. We just helped them get back up and try again.

The lesson here is twofold: You don't have to do this alone. And falling down is part of the process and expected as you learn. Just focus on getting back up.

Asking professionals (like therapists), teachers of all kinds, a friend, or a partner to help is a part of resilience. In a sexual situation, you can ask a trusted partner to help if you know there might be some curves coming up. You can let them know if you might need to slow down, how to reconnect with you, and if you might need to change the focus or activity for a bit. You can also enlist their help in taking tiny steps toward things that scare you.

Many of our curves are personal and will require some trial and error to navigate. But there are also two near-universal barriers that I see hit people's brakes: shame and getting stuck in your head.

The Twisty Curves

Going back to our motorcycle metaphor, we can think of shame and getting stuck in your head as twisty curves. They are as challenging as navigating a winding road full of sharp turns down a mountain. Just when you think you've gotten around one curve, another is right around the corner. If you aren't prepared for the quick back-to-back turns, you run the risk of crashing your motorcycle epically. This section will help you anticipate and prepare for those moments when these "twisty roads" are inevitably in our path.

A NOTE ABOUT STRESS

It's outside the scope of this book to talk about all the ways stress impacts our bodies and what to do about it. But it's important! Stress is a pleasure killer. And it's pretty unavoidable in today's world. I'm not gonna lie to you—it can be hard out there. But there can be access to pleasure even in the middle of stressful times if we slow down enough to notice and prioritize pleasure and the erotic.

Short answer? Get rid of as much stress as you can, complete the stress cycle by moving your body, and focus mindfully on the present moment. Make space for rest, laughter, community, and pleasure, even in small ways.[8] You may not be able to eliminate all your stress, but any decrease is better than none. If you're curious and want to know more, I recommend checking out the list of books in the resources section on www.gendermagic.com.

Shame

There's nothing quite like shame to make you hit your brakes.

We've all felt it at one moment or another: the pit in our stomachs, thoughts pinging around in our heads like pinballs—chaotic and directionless—about how we're a good-for-nothing fuckup, rotten to our core, and ugly to boot. Shame whispers, *How could anyone love you? Want you? Think you / your art / your work are worthy or good?*

Brené Brown defines "shame" as "the intensely painful feeling of believing that we are flawed and therefore unworthy of love and belonging."[9] Almost every client that steps through my door talks to me about sexual shame. No matter what the origin of a sexual concern, shame has a way of creeping in, even for folks who value sex and body positivity. To be fair, it's not our fault. Our culture serves us sexual and body shame with the force of a grandma "asking" you if you want a second serving of pie—impossible to ignore and harder to refuse.

Most folks, regardless of identity, have been explicitly or implicitly shamed for something related to sex or their body by family members, peers, religious leaders, teachers, sexual partners, and media. Beyond gender, shame can attach itself to all sorts of things including body size, skin color, ability, STI status, what bodies "should" look like, interest or disinterest in sex, kinks, and wanting relationships that don't fit squarely into a monogamous or heteronormative box. The intersections of identities like gender, race, ethnicity, and disability are on full display as folks with one or more marginalized identities are often stereotyped as overly sexual or "exotic," or desexualized completely.

The best way to begin healing and resolving shame is to understand where it comes from. Among my transgender/non-binary clients, there are four major sources of shame that directly affect their ability to experience pleasure and eroticism.

Leftover Religious Shame

I am well acquainted with sexual shame à la religion. In my family, any *hint* of sexuality was considered dangerous and bad. My dad once confessed the sin of seeing a naked woman...tattoo. Even sex inside of marriage was whispered about as largely something the women put up with but never enjoyed. It started with being shamed for exploring my body as a child, and any PDA or romantic interest in anyone was policed heavily (and sometimes aggressively). I wasn't surprised the first response of most family members to my coming out was (1) worry for my eternal soul and (2) AIDS. While being HIV positive is nothing to be ashamed of, the fear was based on an inaccurate risk assessment and homophobic stigma of queer identities. My grandmother didn't appreciate me explaining, statistically, that her retirement community was more at risk for STIs than I was living my "lifestyle."

In my life today, I don't feel any sexual shame related to my religious upbringing, but those beliefs run deep, and it took many years of therapy and personal exploration to move through and out of them. So, if you're still feeling the repercussions of sex-negative and transphobic religious upbringing, I get it. It's especially frustrating when shame is present even though you don't actually believe those things anymore. It's a process.

If religious shame is part of your brakes, simply being able to name it creates space for it to heal. For me, working with a therapist was key for noticing when old beliefs might be impacting me. I also brought in play and humor as a way to take the power away from the shame. After being told that I'm a child of Satan many times in various ways, I finally decided that if I couldn't beat 'em by convincing the religious naysayers I wasn't a sinner for existing, I would join 'em and embrace my status as one of the fallen. Satan is a queer icon anyway.

Body Shame and Dysphoria

Body size, ability, that weird freckle on your left butt cheek that looks like Texas—shame doesn't discriminate between big and small "reasons" that we should feel bad about ourselves and our bodies.

When we talk about dysphoria, we need to realize that there are two kinds: body dysphoria, where a person's feelings of unease and discomfort originate with feeling a mismatch in their gender identity and their body, and social dysphoria, where the dysphoria is linked to how others perceive and treat someone in the world.

Distinguishing between body and social dysphoria, or at least acknowledging the impact of social dysphoria on body dysphoria, can help turn down the volume on body shame in sexual situations. Kate, a white transgender woman and longtime client, explained how she was avoiding dating and sex because she felt shame about how her genitals looked and functioned. As we unpacked this, we discovered that, while body dysphoria was present, the distress she felt was primarily about an assumption that her body *should* look a certain way to be seen and respected as a woman. In other words, it was society's assumptions about what certain body parts mean about gender identity that was the main issue, not her body itself.

Prioritizing finding a partner who saw Kate for who she was and treated her body the way she wanted it to be treated turned down the volume on dysphoria and allowed her to experience more pleasure and presence during sex. It also allowed her to make the decision to have bottom surgery from a grounded place that was about her comfort and not a feeling of inadequacy or wrongness.

On the other side of the coin, many folks experience shame because they *want* things like erections or penetrative sex and enjoy them. This is an unfortunate outcome of the narrative of gender transition that places suffering and body hate at the center of the story. I've walked many clients through not feeling "trans enough" because they experienced pleasure in their body as is.

Whatever you're feeling, the moral of the story is this: You deserve to enjoy your body. You deserve to enjoy it as it is now, as well as during and after medically necessary care to change it if that's something you want. We can show kindness and love to all versions of ourselves.

There are lots of great resources and voices on the broader topic of body shame that wouldn't fully fit into this book, so I invite you to check out the resources section at www.gendermagic.com.

SHAME OF THINKING YOU'RE HOT

Having erotic fantasies related to gender expression and being turned on by your own body or by clothing you find sexy is not a disorder. Autogynephilia, or the idea (mostly aimed at transgender women) that being transgender is really just a fetish for a certain kind of body, is extremely harmful and pathologizing. It's also bullshit. Whether you are transgender or simply find a different gender expression erotic, it's not a problem. Transgender writer and activist Julia Serano conceptualizes fantasies and erotic desires related to our own bodies simply as embodiment fantasies, or fantasies related to how we experience our own body during sex.[10]

Additionally, because of a lack of representation in mainstream media, many transgender individuals were first exposed to other transgender folks through porn. This is also not an issue.* It's common to be drawn to, curious about, and aroused by bodies and erotic material that resonate with us.

Maybe just accept that you're hot and move on with your day.

Shame about Sexual Roles

How you want to have sex and how you show up energetically isn't gendered. People of all genders can enjoy any role or sexual activity that turns them on.

Even within the queer community, gendered roles during sex run deep. Brett, a white non-binary person in their late twenties, felt like they escaped the assigned box of "female" just to be put right back into another one when it came to their sexuality. As someone whose gender expression leaned on the masculine side, their sexual partners often assumed them to be a top when, in reality, they preferred to bottom. They felt shame about their desires and feared disappointing their partners.

* While it's also true that typical representations of transgender women in porn are highly fetishized and not an accurate representation of how to have great sex, the fact of first being exposed to transgender identities through porn does not mean your transgender identity is a fetish. It simply means there is not enough transgender representation in mainstream media.

Similarly, I've had many transfemme clients who felt shame over enjoying being a penetrative partner and felt like this was a less feminine role. I like to remind folks that femininity can be soft and receptive *and* it can be fierce and dominant. Ask any dominatrix.

Shame of Kink, Non-monogamy, and Other Desires

Similar to the shame of sexual roles and activities, many folks experience shame related to their wants, needs, and desires. This is especially true if those wants, needs, and desires don't conform to strict gender norms or are somehow out of the box of cisnormative and heteronormative sex and eroticism.

Here's the thing: If you don't believe you deserve sexual satisfaction or that more satisfaction is possible for you, how likely are you to advocate for what feels pleasurable and erotic to you? Not very. You're more likely to "take what you can get," apologize a lot, and feel pressure to conform to unimaginative stereotypes of what eroticism, sex, and relationships "should" look and feel like. You're less likely to explore things that might feel great to you—like polyamory or kink or simply a desire to have sex in a different way.

What happens when you believe you deserve sexual and relational satisfaction? You're less willing to accept sexual experiences and partners that hit your brakes instead of your accelerator. You tell people what you want, what you need to feel safe and sexy, and believe your desires are valid and worth pursuing. If you have a partner that doesn't jibe with those wants, needs, and desires, you might get curious about whether they are a good fit for you, or put effort into finding other ways to expand your erotic, relational, and sexual life to get those wants and needs met.

I once had a transmasculine client who had intense shame about a certain kink. Let's say, for the purposes of illustration, that it was being attracted to Tony the Tiger from the Frosted Flakes cereal box. This client was terrified of others finding out about his kink, fearful that partners would reject him and think he was weird and gross. After one experience in the past where he shared his desires with a partner who didn't react well, he shoved down this desire and hid it from all his future partners.

But it was still there, and as we worked together to release shame in other areas of his life related to his gender, the desire to fulfill fantasies related to his love of Tony got stronger. He started getting on dating apps that were kink friendly and talking about his kink to potential new partners. And what happened? Let's say it involved growls and pounces and tails and soft, fluffy things and a whole lot of pleasure.

I can't guarantee that speaking your desires out loud is going to get all of those needs met. But I do know this: Never speaking them out loud is a surefire way to never experience the joy and pleasure that come from getting something you desire. I also know that the world is big and the internet makes it smaller. Somewhere out there is someone who either has the same kink/want/need/desire or would be gleefully down to help you explore yours.

What to Do When You Feel Shame

Luckily for us, there's an effective and easy-to-remember framework about how to navigate shame so it doesn't leave us frozen, brought to us by Brené Brown.[11]

Notice. What does shame feel like in your body? How do you recognize that feeling? Understanding what it feels like to be in a shame spiral creates space to get curious about why shame is coming up and choose how you want to respond to it. It moves the internal conversation from "AHH, I'm a terrible, worthless person" to "I'm feeling shame and it really hurts."

Reframe. Once you recognize you're experiencing shame and have some ideas about where it might be coming from, ask yourself if what is causing the shame aligns with your beliefs and values. Often, it's coming from cultural messages we don't actually believe, like transphobia, misogyny, fat phobia, ableism, racism, etc. Knowing this can turn down the volume or even completely move you out of a shame spiral.

If the feeling of shame *is* in line with your values (like missing the mark on being a good friend, for example), understanding where the shame is coming from creates space for self-compassion and care. Making a mistake doesn't make you unworthy of connection or love.

Connect. Shame loves to live in the dark. If shame moves us away from our own bodies and each other's bodies, healing means moving toward those things. Simply bringing shame into the light by reaching out to trusted others for empathy and care diffuses shame by doing the very thing it wants to keep us from—connecting with other people instead of hiding in our shame cave.

GETTING OUT OF YOUR SHAME CAVE WITH A REFRAME

Reframing is one of those skills that, once you master it, is one of the most helpful life skills to have. If reframing is new to you, it might feel like I'm telling you to answer any negative thought about yourself with "I'm the most awesome human to ever walk the earth," but however true that may be, that's not what reframing is. All we're going to do is say what's true from a more loving, compassionate, and hopeful perspective. For example, let's imagine you said to yourself, "I'm feeling shame because, as a transmasculine person, I'd like to be penetrated by my partner and I'm afraid she won't view me as a man anymore if she does."

You might work through your shame by asking yourself the following questions:

What's beneath this thought?

Maybe you feel inadequate, fear being rejected, or fear not having your identity respected and seen by your partner if you are the "bottom."

What context is important here?

Think about this on an individual and systemic level. Important context in this case would be living in a transphobic culture, living in a culture where being penetrated is seen as a largely feminine role, and the fact that you trust your partner deeply.

How likely is it that the thing I fear is going to happen? What's the evidence?

Your partner is queer, loves you, is trustworthy, and has been supportive of your transition so far. While you don't know for sure if your desires for penetration will change her perspective on you, it's unlikely.

Is this thought in line with my values?

No, it's not. You don't believe anyone is less of a man because they enjoy penetration in any way.

Is this thought helpful to me? What's the cost?

No, it's not helpful. It's disconnecting you from your desires and your partner, and shame feels shitty.

Reframe: "I'm owning that I want to be penetrated by my partner. This is in line with my values and what I desire and has no bearing on my gender identity. It's unlikely my partner will view me as less of a man based on our history and because we are both interested in challenging and working through oppressive and limiting societal expectations on what sex looks like. But even if she does view me differently, I know who I am and give myself permission to feel pleasure any way I like."

Getting Stuck in Your Head

The thoughts that go along with shame, and other difficult feelings, often cause folks to get stuck in their head. When difficult feelings start swirling around, your brain tries to make sense of them by telling you a story.

Sometimes those stories are true and accurate and important to listen to—like if you feel physically unsafe in a situation, need to set a boundary, or ask for something you need. Other times, those stories are just that—stories!—and don't reflect the reality of a situation or our values.

When we get stuck in our heads, it takes us out of the moment and makes it harder to focus on what *is* feeling good. We lose the ability to be embodied and experience a moment because we are too busy thinking about it.

Some folks get stuck in their head by focusing too much on what positive things they "should" be feeling or experiencing. Imagine you're eating a strawberry ice-cream cone. You're enjoying the sunny day and your ice-cream cone and the light breeze, when suddenly . . . you start thinking.

You wonder if you'd like vanilla or chocolate or rocky road better. You start second-guessing if you're getting enough pleasure out of the ice-cream cone. Maybe you made a mistake and should have gotten another flavor. You judge your choice and compare yourself to all the other people around you happily eating their ice cream. Before you realize it, your cone is a drippy mess and you barely even tasted it.

Pleasure and eroticism require presence. You gotta be there, in your body, to experience them. Even if your imagination is leading the way, staying present with your thoughts (and any bodily sensations coming up) instead of letting your mind wander is what creates a moment of pleasure.

Many folks get stuck in their head about gender-related things when it comes to engaging in pleasure and sexuality. When that happens, it's usually because of two things: newness and realness.

Newness

For transgender/non-binary folks who are early in their journey, have started hormone therapy, hit a big milestone for themselves, or have just completed a surgery, there's a lot about their bodies and how their bodies interact with others that feels new. Because it is! When you've had years, decades perhaps, of sexual experiences in a body or identity that doesn't feel authentic to you, it's a whole new world when you're engaging as a more authentic version of yourself.

This can feel overwhelming and jarring as you consider all you don't know. You might feel like you "aren't enough" or just generally feel like you don't know what to do with your hands. You might be nervous or unsure. That's a normal feeling.

But that's also the exciting part.

Clients often share their fears related to engaging in sex again, and we don't sweep those under the rug. We discuss and move through them. And the pure look of wonder or shy laughing as they tell me about this new thing they discovered their body could do or liked to do is priceless.

The full-body orgasms they experienced.

The euphoria that came from asking for what they wanted, needed, or desired and having an affirming partner meet them there.

The freedom they felt.

It's not all rainbows and kittens, and gender dysphoria moments might come up alongside the euphoric moments at times, but the point is that they get to experience the full spectrum of human emotion that comes up around pleasure, eroticism, and sex, including, and especially, the good parts.

When faced with something that feels new and uncertain, the most important skills you need as a lover are not Advanced Sex Skills 301. You can move through this fear by staying present as much as possible, creating a safe and sexy context for everyone involved, paying attention to your own experience of pleasure, and paying attention to your partner's (or partners') experience of pleasure. Everything else is details.

Realness

Some of the biggest feelings to navigate in eroticism and sex for transgender/non-binary folks are not feeling like a "real" woman or man and not being "non-binary enough." These feelings tend to stem from the perception that a body part isn't "right" or a gendered expectation isn't being met, and as a result, partners won't see them for who they are. Within this, I often hear an unspoken belief: "My partner is putting up with so much to be with me; I can't possibly ask for more" or "This is the best I deserve / can get."

So first, let me take a moment to remind you that your identity isn't a burden.

You are simply existing.

The world is the one making your identity a problem, not you. And you do not need to make yourself smaller because the world makes your life harder than the lives of cisgender people.

But when this fear comes up, you have two options: You can take it as the gospel truth and keep shutting down your pleasure, or you can get curious. Is it true that your partner doesn't respect your trans identity, or is it just fear talking?

If it's true that your partner doesn't see you for who you are right now, it sounds like your partner's problem to me. If a partner makes you feel like your gender identity isn't valid, fetishizes you, or doesn't treat your body the way you want it to be treated, they aren't the best you can get. I promise. Similarly, a true partnership means they do their best to meet your wants, needs, and desires, or work with you to figure out a compromise when your wants, needs, and desires don't match up with theirs.

You deserve to partner with people who see you for you who are. And you can be seen and respected for who you are right now, whether or not you have or want to change anything about your body or appearance. And those partners exist, both in new partners and in spouses you've been with for twenty years.

If it's fear talking, and not a partner who is making you feel inadequate, the answer is to do some experimenting. This might look like designing a tiny experiment (remember those from part 1?) to ask for what you want, need, and desire from your partner. It might look like playing with different roles, activities, toys, or names for body parts that feel good to you.

You might be saying, "But, Rae, even if my partner is the most affirming person on the planet, I'll only *feel* 'real' when I have X or look like X."

And that might be true for you. However, as we've talked about in previous chapters, if our measure for success is based on how other people perceive us, we are setting ourselves up for failure because we can't control that.

There is a lot of evidence that gender-affirming surgeries do help self-image and produce a feeling of comfort in your body, and I fully support folks getting them. Yet, without going deep into gender theory (you can review chapter 1 for a little more depth here), being a woman or a man or non-binary has nothing to do with what body parts you have or how you want to use those body parts to have erotic or sexual experiences. It's just simply who you are. You have nothing to prove, love.

And. At the end of the day, the only person who can decide that you are "real" is you. And you are. Real, I mean.

What to Do When You Get Stuck in Your Head

There are many ways to address and move through moments when our mind starts spinning stories and negative thoughts. Here are a few of my favorites:

Mindfully tap into your sensuality. The simplest (but not easy) solution is to refocus on sensuality. Remember that sexy-strawberry exercise? Lean into your five senses and ground yourself in sensation. Don't despair if the brain chatter doesn't stop immediately as you try out this skill. While the concept is simple, like meditation, it's a practice and takes time and repetition to build up your muscles in this area. When you notice your brain getting loud again, the goal is to compassionately guide it back to your senses.

Focus more on yourself. During partnered sex, most people make the mistake of overfocusing on their partner's pleasure at the expense of their own. This does the exact opposite of what we want—to have pleasurable and affirming sex that feels good for both you and your partner. What makes a great lover isn't knowing all the moves or tricks to make your partner orgasm a thousand times. It's being present, paying attention to both you and your partner's experience, and responding to each other's little groans, your bodies pushing into each other, and the feeling of their skin on yours.

Identify the true problem and reframe. We've practiced throughout this book noticing the context and cultural messages that are behind so many difficult feelings and experiences of being transgender/non-binary in the world. Being able to name that your thoughts are coming from a cultural message you don't believe creates space to respond to them differently and takes away a lot of their power.

Communicate clearly about your wants/needs/desires. This is key for moving through and working with your brakes. To use Sonya Renee Taylor's famous phrase, your body is not an apology.[12] Your body is not a consolation prize, nor is it something you have to make up for by saying, "I'm sorry for being trans. Thank you for being with me." You get to have needs and an erotic imagination that's all your own, and you deserve to be able to express that.

Trust your value even when you don't feel it. Sometimes we have days when we just aren't feeling it, and managing shame and negative thoughts feels exceptionally hard. On those days, focus on your behavior. How can you act as if you are worthy of a great pleasure-filled life even if you don't 100 percent believe it at that moment?

Acceptance. Your body is what it is right now. You may not like that answer. And your body may change in the future—and that's great! But right now, as you're reading this book, the body you have is the one you've got. If we can lean into it, acceptance allows us to put attention on the things we can impact instead of focusing on what we can't. Instead of banging your head on a brick wall trying to pretend it's not there, go find a ladder. Even though you can change your body and might want to, your body today still deserves some love. How can you show love and care to that body? How can you give it pleasure?

AFFIRMATIONS FOR PLEASURE

I know talking about sex and relationships can be challenging for some. So here are some final reminders to hold on to about pleasure, eroticism, sex, and relationships.

You are enough. You are not too much.

There is nothing wrong with your body. Even if you want to change it.

You deserve to feel pleasure in your body. Even if you want to change it.

You are desirable and "desire-able."[13]

You don't have anything to prove.

You deserve to have a partner(s) who sees and respects you for who you are.

You're magic. Don't accept partners who treat you as anything less.

When in doubt, repeat to yourself, "I deserve pleasure equity." Scream it if you have to until you believe it.

Everybody has brakes when it comes to experiencing pleasure, eroticism, and sexuality. Brakes are normal and play a large role in keeping us safe. I recognize there are many more brakes than this book has the space to discuss. Some will be quick fixes and some will take a lifetime to address. But it's possible for everyone—*everyone* (and yes, that includes you!)—to experience pleasure no matter what brakes they have.

Remember, it all starts with working to (1) notice what hits your brakes, (2) slow down before a "curve" so you don't crash, (3) keep your eyes on your why, and (4) hit the accelerator just enough to get you around the curve.

Working with your brakes might be as simple as locking the dog out of the bedroom or might mean a lot of work with a therapist to patiently and lovingly work through old wounds.

But it's possible. And it's worth it. Because you're worthy of pleasure.

BRAKE LIST AND REFLECTION

This exercise is meant to give you some food for thought in considering what your brakes are and how you want to handle them. I encourage you to grab a notebook and a pen, find somewhere quiet and comfortable filled with pleasurable things (good music, good smells, good views if you can), and give yourself at least twenty minutes to think through these questions. Allow your brain to come back to these over and over again as you have more information and start addressing your brakes. Sometimes, addressing certain barriers will create space to address others that feel bigger or more complicated.

- What brakes do you have from the following?
  - your body
  - your brain
  - your previous experiences
- What clues help you realize you might have a "curve" coming up ahead?
- What does "slowing down around a curve" mean to you? What helps you slow down?
- What cultural messages might be informing your brakes? Are the messages you're reacting to in line with what you believe and your values? Why or why not? Who are these messages benefiting?

- Are these cultural messages and expectations realistic and attainable?
- Are these cultural messages rooted in heteronormative and patriarchal models of sexuality, pleasure, and eroticism?
- What do you need to unlearn?
- Where does shame show up in your ability to tap into pleasure, eroticism, and sexuality? How can you practice shame resilience when shame shows up?
- What are some tiny steps you can take to start addressing your brakes? (Pro tip: Start with what feels like the most easeful first.)
- Who's on your team to help you?

CHAPTER 9

Partnered Pleasure

In the last two chapters, we focused on you—how you can unlock your erotic mind and incorporate pleasure, sensuality, and eroticism in your life. But focusing on ourselves is only part of the equation. Partnered sex (if that's something you want) can be a vital and affirming source of pleasure.

In this chapter, I'm going to broaden the focus to talk about experiencing pleasure with partners in safe and supportive ways. I'll discuss how to feel safe physically and emotionally, how to detach gender from bodies and sex, and how to map out your sexual interests and orientation. Lastly, I'll address how to find affirming partners—whether that's in a long-term relationship, on a date, or even in casual contexts.

Designing Pleasurable Sex and Relationships

"You restored my faith in threesomes," an onlooker said after watching me and two other non-binary individuals at a play party. The three of us looked at each other and laughed in joy. Something felt different about this experience than many others I'd had. It flowed perfectly. Feeling sexy and seen for all of who we were and none of who we weren't wasn't entirely unfamiliar, but it was special.

We all had body parts in various configurations, but nothing we did with them felt gendered. By talking about what we each wanted, the three of us found pleasure in each other's body in ways we were all delighted to experience (and some things that made me say, "I dunno if that's going to work logistically, but let's try!"). I felt connected and attuned to my partners and, most of all, sublimely seen and safe.

Maybe you've had a group sex experience like this or maybe you are just dipping your toes into sexuality with one person. The number of partners and whether you're alone in your bedroom or at an orgy are unimportant.

What *is* important is this: I know what it looks like to thrive in sex and relationships, both personally and through the experiences of numerous clients. I want that for you, and I believe it's 100 percent possible.

You deserve it.

Exploring sex and relationships, whether new or old, is an adventure. This is especially true when you are also navigating, exploring, or transitioning your gender.

Bodies are changing, identities are shifting, and suddenly everything you think you know about sex and relationships can be called into question. It often feels like going through puberty again as an adult, with the awkwardness and will-anyone-come-to-my-birthday-party insecurities.

Designing fulfilling sexual and romantic relationships takes work regardless of gender identity. After all, relationships are complex—full of joy and wonder and new discoveries and connection and misadventures and loneliness and disappointments.

It's all part of the process.

Showing up authentically takes effort, vulnerability, openness to risk, and a lot of hard work, but I can say I've never had a client regret the choice to be more authentic in their sexual and romantic relationships, even if those relationships end. Feeling seen, safe, and joyful with a partner or partners is an irreplaceable feeling. It's one you deserve, and it's one we can create.

Fears about Partnered Sex

You might feel disconnected from your body and sexuality as your gender or sexual identity shifts or as your body changes due to medical transition. Things that used to feel okay can feel intolerable as you tap into your "Yes!" and become more aware of your nos. Additionally, knowing you want to undergo gender-affirming surgery but not having access to it yet can increase dysphoria as you become more aware of incongruence between how your body is and how you want it to be.[1]

There might be new concerns about safety or fear of fetishization, transphobia, and transmisogyny. You might be concerned about losing long-term relationships or fear your transgender or non-binary identity makes you undesirable or, on a deeper level, unlovable.

These fears aren't coming from nowhere. And there's also a world of partnered pleasure, eroticism, and sexuality that is available to you. Right now. No matter where you are in your journey.

The word I hear most from the transgender/non-binary folks I work with about navigating sex, sexuality, current relationships, and dating while exploring or transitioning their gender is "lost." But being lost isn't always something we need to fix. Sometimes it gives us the most freedom to explore without an agenda, say, "Yes!" to new things, and be present in a new way. It creates opportunities for surprise and openness that often don't happen when we're sure of where we are going.

I often hear from clients a version of "I'll date / get into a relationship / have sex when I reach a certain physical-appearance goal."

It's valid to take time to focus on yourself and your gender journey without adding complications of dating or relationships. However, the core belief often underlying this is feeling not good enough or attractive enough to be seen and respected for who you are right now.

This is 100 percent false.

You don't have to have everything figured out, look exactly the way you want to look, or meet any certain transition milestones (including medical transition) to have pleasurable and satisfying sexual and romantic relationships with people who think you're sexy as hell.[2]

It's true there will be people who don't want to date you because of your gender identity. It's also true that, no matter what your gender identity or expression, there will be people in the world who are not attracted to you. I say this to ground you in the fact that, as my friend Elmo says,

"No one is everyone's favorite flavor, and everyone is someone's favorite flavor."

The reason you might feel unlovable and undesirable is the result of a transphobic and transmisogynistic culture, not because there is anything wrong with you. You are worthy, deserving, lovable, and desirable. You're magic. Full stop.

Gender Freedom in Partnered Pleasure

Tearing down our assumptions about what is possible and what we "should" do or like, regardless of gender identity, sexual orientation, or body parts, creates more freedom and possibility within our partnerships. This doesn't mean we have to like all the things. No one does. But often, we limit ourselves based on the boxes that society has put us in and the boxes we put ourselves in.

De-gender Bodies

As discussed in chapter 1, the meaning we make out of differences between bodies is culturally constructed, and this is especially true when it comes to pleasure and sexuality. Our culture thinks whether individuals are assigned male or female at birth makes them as different as apples and oranges when it's more like comparing Honeycrisps to Galas. There is a great deal of diversity between bodies, but bodies, like different varieties of apples, are more alike than different.

For example, genitals are made of analogous tissues, meaning the tissue that creates a penis and a scrotum and the tissue that creates a clitoris and a vagina are exactly the same in the womb, just organized in different ways. They both have a similar number of nerve endings, concentrated at different intensities, and experience arousal and pleasure in parallel ways.[3]

Yet we assume that because our body parts look or function in a particular way, it must mean something about our gender. It doesn't. We often assume we must partake in certain kinds of sexual activities, relate to our bodies in culturally prescribed ways, and show up in a particular way in the bedroom to be valid in our gender identity or sexual orientation. None of these things are true.

On the flip side, it can feel deeply affirming of your gender identity to partake in certain kinds of sexual activities, relate to your body in ways you weren't "allowed to" in your sex assigned at birth, and show up in a particular way in the bedroom. Gendering bodies and culturally enforcing gender roles and presentation on the basis of appearance are nonsense. Yet having our bodies reflect our gender identity and relating to them in gendered ways can be lifesaving and are often a core piece of our identity. We can hold both of these things as true.

De-gendering bodies isn't about erasing gender, ignoring differences between bodies, or saying our body's appearance doesn't impact how we feel about our gender. It's about choosing how we want to relate to our bodies. It gives us room to intentionally play with gender in erotic and sexual ways.

It can also feel great to gender the hell out of bodies during a sexual experience. The trick is to gender your body however you like, regardless of what it looks like. Having a lover call your bits exactly what you want them to be called, getting a blow job on a clitoris, or feeling delicious swirls on a hard or soft penis* can sometimes take a sexual encounter from a dysphoric minefield to an experience of gender euphoria (instead of or alongside the dysphoric feelings) with just a few words or licks.

MYSTIFY YOURSELF

"Mystification" is a term coined by my friend Lucie Fielding to describe relating to our bodies and sexuality with new eyes.[4] I like to think of mystification as imagining you're an alien who has just gotten transplanted into a human body. Your advanced alien race has no conception of gender. I invite you to explore your body from this frame.

Explore your body with your hands like you've never seen it before and have no meaning attached to it, my little alien friend.

How would this change how you touch it, how you use it, and the ways you experience pleasure?

---

* For clarity, I use traditional medical terms here, but the point is to call your body parts whatever feels good. Language is made up. Play with it.

What would you be curious about?

(Don't be afraid to get silly. I just told you to pretend you were an alien…)

What sort of cultural meanings put on bodies do you want to let go of?

De-gender Sexual Roles and Energy

Exploring partnered sexuality also includes exploring different sexual roles and energies. Our culture usually portrays "masculinity" as a dominant energy and the "top" in sex, while "femininity" is often portrayed as a more submissive, receptive energy and the "bottom" in sex. Referring to energy as masculine or feminine puts those energies into gendered boxes, and I find it to be limiting and lazy language. When we say "masculine" when we mean dominant, top, or rough and "feminine" when we mean submissive, bottom, or sensual, we are taking away our agency, and this erodes the potential for play and imagination. How would you describe the energy if you took away the gendered language? Instead of gendering these concepts, let's say what we mean.

What brings more pleasure and affirmation during partnered sex is not bringing more "masculine" or "feminine" energy. It's showing up confidently with whatever the hell energy you want. Maybe this matches up with traditional ideas of masculinity or femininity. Or your version of masculinity might be soft and nurturing and your version of femininity might be fierce and in charge. We get to determine what sort of energy feels authentic to us without placing ourselves right back into a gendered box.

The energy of being a top or a bottom is also different than a sexual position. You can bring top or bottom energy to an encounter whether you're a penetrating or receptive partner (if that's your thing) or physically in a more dominant or submissive position. You can top from the bottom or bottom from the top. There is a difference between saying, "Put your mouth on me—now," and "Please, Daddy, I need your mouth on me." Same action, very different vibe.

For some, leaning into a new gender identity might come with gendered expectations that don't resonate with you, even within the queer community. There can sometimes be pressure for transmasculine folks to be more dominant and transfeminine folks to be more submissive. As a non-binary person who leans toward a more masculine presentation frequently, it's often assumed I bring more dominant, toppy energy simply because of my appearance (and the fact that I have six placements in Capricorn in my chart). Spoiler alert: I make mad decisions all day long and it feels great not to do that as much during sex. This CEO is tired.

Being clear about what you are hoping for in a sexual situation and experimenting with different types of roles, energies, and interests are playful ways to marry gender exploration and erotic pleasure.

The energy we bring to sex, the roles we play, and even who we are attracted to often change with context, different partners, and over our lifetime.

Sexual Maps

Sexual orientation is a concept that helps us name and understand ourselves better in relation to who we are attracted to and is different but connected to our gender identity. It's also limiting, often assumed to be binary and fixed, and falls apart quickly with any sort of critical eye.

Once again, society has constructed a system of categorizing humans based on binary categories that don't make much sense. Sexual orientation is centered around bodies and gender, assuming these two things are aligned. This in and of itself is fraught as we move away from binary understandings of both bodies and gender.

Additionally, there are many aspects of attraction and sexuality that are both related and unrelated to what bits we have and our genders. For example, if you say you're attracted to men, do you mean men regardless of the presence of a penis, folks whose gender is male, folks with muscular shoulders and frame, bears, twinks, or a specific type of energy? Suppose you're attracted to other transgender/non-binary people. Are you attracted to a shared experience and understanding, a particular presentation, folks who have the same gender as you, certain bodies, specific energies, shared sexual interests, or the sexiness that is gender fuckery?

Beyond bodies and gender, our sexual maps include number of partners, ranges of interest in romance or sex, age, race, ethnicity, cultural fit, relationship type and intensity, mutual interest in kink or BDSM, intellectual stimulation, creativity, and playfulness, to name a few.

For these reasons, I prefer the term "sexual map"[5] as a term that integrates all the aspects of romantic and sexual interest instead of only focusing on body and gender factors. By putting gender and bodies on a pedestal when defining our sexuality, we reduce our nuanced sexual "maps" to a checkbox that ultimately says very little about partner choice.

Our sexual maps are both fixed and fluid. It's well researched that sexual interest and attraction to different types of partners can and do change for many people over their lifetime.[6] It is culturally understood and normalized for changes in interest to happen as someone grows related to desired age, physical and emotional characteristics, shared values and lifestyle, and shared experience. Yet changes in sexual and romantic attractions over the lifetime regarding anything in the realms of sex/gender are often considered identity redefining and a Big Deal.

I sometimes see transgender clients clinging for dear life to the label of "straight." To be clear, there's nothing wrong with being straight. However, some folks insist on this label from a place of anxiety and rigidity, believing that being with a straight person, in a straight relationship, will validate their binary gender identity.

I invite you to consider that your partner's gender and sexual orientation say nothing about the validity of your gender identity and sexual map. Even if you continue to identify as straight, there is only freedom if this label feels authentic to you, not just something you need for your self-worth.

Integrating romantic and sexual interest into a larger sexual map that includes, but doesn't centralize, bodies and gender identity gives us more space to authentically explore our sexuality without getting so caught up on labels. This isn't to say that attraction to certain types of bodies or genders isn't an important or defining aspect of our romantic and sexual identities. But it isn't the only factor and may not be the most important when considering who you want to be with.

As folks explore or transition their gender, it's common to experience shifting and expanding attraction. It takes guts to be authentically you in a world that is determined to make you smaller and more digestible. Feeling more comfortable in your own skin often leads to feeling more free and open to new experiences. Refusing to be boxed into an assigned gender creates new possibilities for connection beyond binary and rigid sexual orientation labels.

For me, the term "queer" encompasses my sexuality, since the word at its core is about disrupting binaries and forced boxes. Trying to map my sexuality and attractions onto anything else would require a longer explanation than anyone wants. My sexual map includes gender queerness in some way, a powerful yet nurturing and curious energy, polyamory, kink, and the ability to keep a house clean. The type of body someone has and their gender identity are pretty inconsequential to me. Their values and how they show up in the world are much more important factors in my attraction.

For trans folks, sexual "orientation" can get downright confusing, albeit usually more so for cisgender folks talking about or to transgender and non-binary people. As a transgender diversity and inclusion educator, I frequently get asked a version of "If X is transgender and Y is their partner, what sexual orientation do X and Y have?" My answer to this math problem is always the same: Whatever X and Y choose to call themselves is their sexual identity.

Language is limited. Remember that labels are only helpful when we apply them to ourselves, and we get to determine what those labels mean to us.

Here's a wild thought: You can simply be in a relationship with someone you like, regardless of their gender identity or your typical sexual map. Mind-boggling, I know. I've met many people who are in relationships that are an exception to their typical attractions. The important thing is whether both partners feel seen, respected, and affirmed in who they are.

TWO IMPORTANT CAVEATS

First, you can't force sexual identity and interests to change. Research shows that forcing a transgender/non-binary or queer person's sexual and romantic attractions to change is damaging and ineffective, often resulting in depression, PTSD, and suicide.[7] Researcher Sari van Anders uses the analogy of changing with age. People change with age, but you cannot control or force aging.[8]

Second, often, sexual attractions to things like certain types of bodies and body size, gender identities, race, ethnicity, ability level, etc., are based on internalized cultural bias. There is a big difference between a transgender/non-binary person being attracted to other transgender/non-binary folks or a BIPOC person preferring to be with other BIPOC folks and someone with a more privileged identity showing bias against someone because of body type, gender identity, or race.

Navigating a New Sexual Landscape

Exploring and transitioning your gender creates an entirely new sexual landscape to explore. This is both an exciting and nerve-racking time, as you step into the unknown. A "scare-cited" time, you might say.

Whether you decide to have gender-affirming surgeries, take hormone therapy, or not change a thing about your body, the general principles of pleasure and affirming partnered sex are the same.

Get Out of Your Head

It's easy to get stuck in your head during partnered sex as you navigate your own feelings about your body and how your partner might be perceiving you. Some transgender/non-binary folks dissociate from their own bodies and focus entirely on their partner's pleasure. This is an understandable reaction and also a form of avoidant coping.[9]

To move into more facilitative coping, a mindful focus on your own pleasure is the way through. Whether or not pleasure includes every part of your body, focusing on the pleasurable sensations on your skin helps you stay present and engaged with both yourself and your partner. It's sexy to feel like a partner is having fun and is as into touching your body as you are into receiving touch.

Communicating any boundaries, known gender dysphoria triggers, affirming language, or sexual roles or activities that do or don't feel good for you is helpful before engaging in sexual contact. I find this helps folks feel safer in a sexual environment and stay out of their head a little easier. Knowing the person you're with has your back and is willing to go through the hard stuff *with* you creates more trust, ease, and pleasure.

It can also help to bring nuance and range to what does and doesn't feel good during sex. Often folks get stuck with the story that "sex feels bad." However, after digging in with clients, I often find it's only *certain* ways of touching, roles, positions, or activities that don't feel good. Tiny adjustments often make a big difference in sex feeling affirming.

Embrace Your Desire Template

Your natural desire template might shift over gender exploration or transition, especially if it includes medical transition. Gender-affirming bottom surgeries that affect nerves, sensation, and functioning of genitals also shift how arousal is experienced in your body and how your body functions when it's aroused.

The *feeling* of being aroused and having your genitals respond with blood flow, swelling, hardness, and lubrication don't always match up. This is also known as arousal non-concordance and is a common experience for many people, cisgender and transgender alike.[10] The essential thing is to notice the changes and work with them instead of fighting them.

There is no desire template or way of being aroused that is better or worse than another. It's simply finding what works for you and your unique body.

It's important to note that subjective arousal is more important than genital arousal. It doesn't matter what is happening in your genitals if you don't want to have sex; however, the reverse is also true. Sometimes we are 100 percent aroused and ready for sex, but our bodies aren't cooperating in the way we would like because of medical transition, stress, chronic illness, etc. In these cases, using lube or toys like dildos and cock rings can help us engage in sexual activity in a way that feels good. Additionally, go slow and give your body a chance to catch up with your brain.

THE JOY OF SEX TOYS

Sex toys are wonderful things. In addition to adding delicious sensations and options for sexual activities, they are just plain fun. I find it helpful to think of sex toys as adaptive devices for transgender and non-binary folks. Far from a consolation prize, things like dildos, harnesses, vibrators, and strokers can play a central part in gender-affirming sex.

If you've ever watched someone give a blow job to a dildo, you know that it's just hot as hell. For transfemme folks who want to be a penetrating partner but don't want to use their genitalia, some harnesses accommodate larger genitalia. Similarly, a product like Lorals, a single-use latex underwear, is an excellent option for receiving oral sex while tucking.

While not explicitly sex toys, binders, lingerie meant for tucking, breast forms, and packers can also be powerful tools for increasing gender euphoria during sex. If you aren't sure where to start, check out your local feminist sex toy store or find one online. Early to Bed is a Chicago-based, queer-centered shop I highly recommend.

Give Yourself Permission

Give yourself permission to take your time as you learn what you like and want and figure out how to communicate that clearly to partners. Asking a partner to experiment and explore your new sexual landscape with you is a fun and intimate way to connect.

It's also essential to give yourself permission to change what you're doing, pause, or stop sex at any time if you're noticing dysphoria coming up. To revisit our motorcycle metaphor from chapter 8, if you know gender dysphoria is a "curve" for you, you might want to slow down before the curve by letting your partner know what words you want them to use to describe you, and hit the gas (go, pleasure, go!) just enough to get around the curve safely by, for example, wearing a packer during sex that brings you gender euphoria.

It's not always possible to know everything that will cause you to hit your brakes, so creating space for ongoing consent and a shared understanding that you can stop whatever you're doing at any point during partnered sex is important and grounding.

When you notice gender dysphoria in a sexual situation, the tendency is to shut down all sexual activity. Yet taking a pause or a water break, spending some time cuddling, or refocusing on non-genital touch is regulating and can help you ground enough to resume sexual activity, if that's what you'd like to do.

My last permission slip for you (not that you actually need it from me!) is permission to receive. You don't have to "make up" for your transgender or non-binary identity by overgiving. You deserve to receive pleasure and to ask for what you need to make that happen.

Experiment and Play

Creating space to experiment and play with romantic and sexual pleasure takes pressure off everyone to have it all figured out. And it is a lot more fun.

I introduced the "this or that" game in chapter 7 as a way to play with different sensations with a partner while exploring your body. Here are a few more possible ways to explore pleasure and sensation in your body. This is by no means a full list or even a long list. The world is your oyster when it comes to exploring the breadth and depth of sexual pleasure, and there are people who spend their whole lives learning about themselves and their partners and discovering new ways to experience pleasure and connection. Ask any sex educator or sex geek. I've been in the sex therapy and educator field for many years and I still get "Oh, what's that?!" energy at all the new things there are to explore and learn.

Explore new ways of stimulating erotic nerves: The body is full of nerve-endings waiting to be teased, touched, and tortured in the best ways. Muffing, a term coined by Mira Bellwether in the now-famous zine *Fucking Trans Women*,[11] or prostate play are two examples of ways to stimulate erotic nerves, but these are only the beginning.

Kink/BDSM: Kink is not just for folks who like to get consensually beaten up (or consensually do the beating), though this is definitely a fun part of BDSM. Kink and BDSM extend beyond giving and receiving pain to exploring a variety of sensations, playing with power in psychological ways, living out fantasies and role-playing, as well as providing a medium for trauma recovery if that's the intention.[12] Kink and BDSM have the added bonus of focusing on the entire erotic experience and not fixating on genitals and orgasm as the main event of sex, or even a necessary part of an erotic experience.

Tantra: My tantric friends might kill me for saying this, but I think of tantra as the shawl-wearing cousin of kink/BDSM. If kink/BDSM is getting lost in the music of your favorite band for hours at an EDM festival, tantra is a meditation retreat on a mountaintop. Both practices are impactful, are mindfulness based, decentralize genitals and orgasm, drop you into a different state of mind, and focus on the connection to self and a partner. There are different types of energy being exchanged and different vibes to the practices, but both are equally helpful, depending on your and your partner's preferences.

Gender play: Explicitly playing with gender during sex is a powerful way to have a space in your life where everything you want to be true about you is. We often think of fantasy or role-playing, especially during sex, as a version of the games of make-believe we played as kids. However, it can be so much more than that. You are speaking into existence the world you hope for in a tiny microcosm of a way. A world where you are fully seen for who you are. It acknowledges and affirms all the parts of you. The words you and your partner(s) use to describe you, your body, your gender, your genitals, your chest, and your sexual activities hold power.

Ultimately, the only questions that matter during sex are "Do I like this and want this?" and "Does my partner like this and want this?"

Finding an Affirming Partner

Dating while exploring or transitioning your gender can be exciting and affirming. Some individuals I've worked with, ranging from their twenties to their fifties, swan-dive into dating and are pleasantly surprised at how much interest there is in them, the quality of connections they develop, and, of course, the great sex.

I've also had clients who tiptoed into dating (or avoided it altogether) with their anxiety screaming what it thinks are helpful and protective things like the following:

No one wants to date you.

You need to get X medical procedure done before anyone will see you for who you are.

Just accept you'll be alone forever.

You're not sexy.

The only guys who want to date you are guys who have a fetish for transwomen.

You get the gist. It's true that dating can come with challenges for transgender and non-binary folks. There is still a lot of hatefulness in the world, and depending on where you live, the pool of potential dates might be smaller and you might deal with issues of safety. You will likely experience rejection (everyone who dates does), and it will hurt. Dating can be hard and frustrating at times. But the aforementioned messages your anxiety is giving you? Those aren't true.

Let me be clear.

You are lovable as you are.

You are desire-able and desirable just as you are.

You are datable just as you are.

Folks often approach dating from a mindset of "Who will want to date me? What's the best I can get?" These are the wrong questions. The more empowering questions are "Who do *I* want to date? What sort of person would be romantically and sexually fulfilling for me?"

Having an affirming partner(s) is essential to designing a romantic and sexual life that feels good to you.[13] Don't settle for non-affirming partners or partners who make you feel like a fetish. They aren't the best that you can get. I promise. You deserve more.

You're a catch. Trust me.

#T4T

Transgender people are magic, and I highly recommend dating them. As a non-binary person who has been in many relationships of varying types and intensities with folks of different genders, I can say there's a unique understanding, affirmation, and a particular type of joy from being intimately and sexually connected with other transgender/non-binary partners.

Similarly, many queer and trans BIPOC folks I know prefer to date other queer and trans BIPOC folks because there is a unique understanding and affirmation about what it means to be a person of color in our world today.

That isn't to say that there's no joy, affirmation, and understanding available from cisgender partners (or white partners). There is! However, there is a shared experience between transgender folks that can't be replicated, in the same way there is a shared experience between people of color.

Meeting Partners

It's hard to avoid being on dating apps these days, and this is both wonderful and terrible. Dating apps allow you to meet new people you might not otherwise meet, match with folks who want the same thing out of a partnership or sexual relationship, and create montages of men with fish.

Dating apps can also be a dumpster fire of unsolicited dick pics, a nightmare to navigate as a transgender/non-binary person with any sort of nuance to their gender identity or sexual map, and just plain frustrating.

On dating profiles, I encourage you to do an audacious thing: Say exactly who you are and what you want. This means saying what you (really) want in a partner, including monogamy/polyamory, serious/casual, and non-negotiables. Depending on the vibe of the app, this might or might not include explicit sexual interests.

When I say "who you are," I mean both related and unrelated to a transgender/non-binary identity. I find folks have the most luck on dating apps when they share their transgender/non-binary identity up front. Here's an important mindset shift: This is not for the potential date. This is for *you* to weed out transphobic folks and TERFs.* Because you don't have time for that shit and they aren't worth your energy.

Remember that your gender identity is not the most interesting thing about you. On dating apps, share who you are outside of your gender identity. What lights you up? What could you talk about for hours?

Staying grounded while using dating apps helps control the roller-coaster cycle of quick dopamine hits to your brain when you get a like and the despair and frustration when you aren't getting the response you want. Tinder is basically *Candy Crush* with the potential of getting laid when you "win." It's exhausting in a weird way. Take breaks! You can set a timer on your phone or turn off notifications and commit to only checking at whatever pace works for you.

It's easy to "mind read" why you might not be getting many responses or why a potential date stopped talking to you. While it's possible that someone isn't interested in you because of a transgender/non-binary identity, there are also other possibilities.

When I'm on dating apps, I swipe left on folks for all sorts of reasons beyond gender identity and how someone looks—including politics, sexual role preferences, if they want kids, if it seems like our interests are not aligned, etc. I've also stopped talking to folks after exchanging a few messages for reasons having nothing to do with them—like being busy with work, forgetting to check the app, or being at capacity with polyamorous relationships.

Your brain might be telling you a story that rejection is about your transgender identity, and your brain might be right. But it also might be wrong. Since we can't read strangers' minds, we can't know for sure

* Trans-exclusionary radical feminists. They believe in the transmisogynistic idea that womanhood is defined by biological essentialism and specific gendered oppression directed at those assigned female at birth. This ignores biological diversity and the fact that gendered oppression is not homogenous and interacts with race, class, ability, etc. It also ignores the gendered oppression and misogyny that transfemme people experience based on gender nonconformity and transphobia. See also assholes reinforcing gendered oppression.

why someone isn't responding to us. When you believe rejection could be about a million different things, with gender identity being one potential, it can keep your brain from running away to the circus with negative thoughts.

Remember there are other places besides dating apps to meet potential partners. I've had clients meet new sweeties at the gym, playing Dungeons & Dragons, at work, at their bowling league, at an open mic, or at a book club. If you feel stuck when it comes to your dating pool, try leaning into more of the nerdy, sporty, and creative things you love in a social setting. Beyond meeting new people, you get the added bonus of meeting folks who share your hobbies and interests.

Now, I live and work in Chicago and am lucky to be in a city where there are lots of queer folks and people whose values and interests align with mine or my clients'. But I grew up in Louisiana, so I get it if you're about ready to chuck this book across the room because you live in a rural area and the dating pool is legitimately tiny.

If you have the ability to do so, it's okay to venture somewhere outside of your geographic area. There are significant life changes like moving, but there are also opportunities to go to events and conferences where you might meet more of your people. These include transgender-specific events, like the Philadelphia Trans Wellness Conference, and conventions for every interest under the sun—kink, anime/gaming, wellness, polyamory, political activism, outdoorsy things, etc. Whether you end up with a date or not, sometimes a change in environment reminds you that the world is full of interesting, affirming, and hot humans.

Avoiding Fetishization

There is often a valid and understandable fear of being fetishized while dating. Prior experiences of being fetishized and fear of being fetishized can cause folks to avoid dating or relationships altogether.[14] There is a long history of cisgender men treating transgender women and nonbinary folks assigned male at birth as a novelty or a fetish. For many, this intersects with fetishization based on race or ethnicity.

The reality is that fetishization happens. Instead of giving up on dating and relationships altogether, you can learn how to spot red flags. For example, the easiest way to spot someone viewing you as a fetish and not an entire person is to look at the rest of their life. What engagement do they have in the transgender community outside of you? How are they an advocate? Are there other transgender/non-binary folks in their social circle? Are you a secret, or are you integrated into their life? Are they curious about you as a whole person, or do they think your transgender identity is the most exciting thing about you?

You can be desired without being fetishized.

Assessing Safety

For transgender/non-binary folks, especially transgender women of color, partnered sex can be dangerous and result in violence. This fact's individual and cultural impact is an understandable hyperawareness of safety in sexual situations. Keeping yourself safe is the number one priority, as it should be. Building trust with someone slowly and at a pace that feels comfortable to you is okay.

As you learn to be more connected to your body, you're also learning how to tap into your intuition. Our bodies are brilliant and will often tell us if something feels off or weird if we pay attention to them. Taking the time to exchange messages about who you are as people and/or having a FaceTime date can help you tap into your intuition about a person before you meet up in real life. Looking for red flags related to fetishizing is also critical for safety.

When you do meet up with someone, especially for the first time, it can be helpful to follow a few basic safety checks—like meeting up in a public place and sharing your phone location with a friend and letting them know who you are with and where you are. It can also be helpful to drop intentional comments to your date about telling so-and-so you are meeting up with someone, as well as personal details to humanize yourself.

I've also seen clients engage in behavior that is risky, knowing what we know about rates of violence against transgender communities. Often, this risk-taking behavior is a direct result of not feeling like they deserve better.

So, let me say it again for the people in the back: You don't have to settle. You don't have to put yourself in a dangerous situation because you think this is the best you can get. It isn't. I promise. You deserve more.

WHEN PLEASURE BRINGS PANIC

When I experience pure joy or pleasure, it feels like my heart is outside my chest. It's a delicious feeling, full of awe and vulnerability. And vulnerability can be scary, especially when it includes other people. It requires us to open ourselves up in ways that put our hearts at risk. It can feel tempting to mentally rehearse all of the bad things that could happen to take away our joy, preparing for the other shoe to drop. However, all mental rehearsing does is rob us of priceless moments in our lives, the moments we live for if we are lucky enough to experience them.

If you find yourself anxious when you experience joy or pleasure, it's helpful to name that anxiety as vulnerability. Just accurately naming the feeling can take away power from the negative thoughts and give us space to decide how to respond to our worries.

Intentionally expressing gratitude also helps to ground you in the moment. Indeed, these experiences of intense joy or pleasure don't last forever, like a spectacular sunset, but this makes them so much more precious. Savor them.[15]

You can also check the evidence as a way to address your anxious thoughts. For example, the thought "I'm so happy with my partner right now, but my partner is going to eventually break up with me because of the difficulties that come with being transgender/non-binary in the world" can be replaced with something like "I can't know if my partner and I will stay together forever, but I do know they've shown love and commitment to me. They affirm me, I feel safe with them, and they express care and affection regularly. We've gone through hard moments before and come out on the other side closer. Our communication is good, and if there are any concerns, I trust that we can talk it through together."

Or simply "If my partner breaks up with me because I'm transgender/non-binary, that's about them, not me."

Navigating Existing Relationships

I've seen many existing relationships thrive when someone comes out as transgender/non-binary. While it's a transition period and every transition in a relationship creates challenges, there can also be a unique and special deepening and transforming of existing relationships.

There's often a legitimate fear of losing long-term relationships when exploring or transitioning your gender. It's true that not all relationships make it through a partner's personal growth, which can be hard and painful.

Mindset significantly affects which relationships make it and which ones don't. It's easy to stay stuck in fear when there's a big change in a relationship. When we are scared, we often try to control it in an effort to feel safe again. Bringing curiosity and openness to the experience of change in a relationship can move the energy from "AHH—change!" to "What could this be? What could this look like?"

It's also helpful to stay curious when something feels off in your relationship. It's an easy jump to assume feeling disconnected sexually or romantically is about your evolving gender identity. While this might be true in some cases, it's often not the whole story. Intentionally moving from "They must hate being with me because of X thing related to gender identity and expression" to "I wonder why it felt off with them today. What do they need to feel safe and sexy?" is a powerful and grounding energy shift.

As with all relationships, managing expectations, boundaries, and communication is vital.

Expectations, Boundaries, and Communication

There is likely to be an adjustment period as a partner gets used to things like new names, pronouns, and identities and navigating changing family terms (like "mom" or "dad") and changing bodies. This is normal, and there's room for feelings and mistakes as everyone gets used to a new dynamic. It's a process and it's never perfect.

However, this is not an excuse for a partner to continually make the same mistakes without accountability or an effort to correct them. Setting clear boundaries for yourself about using affirming names, pronouns, and language is asking for basic respect, regardless of what other feelings a partner may be working through.

In order to feel safe, we have to know that a partner has our back. Communicating expectations related to if and how you'd like a partner to correct others on your name, pronoun, and identity is an important part of developing secure attachment with a partner. This might look like correcting someone in the moment, pulling them aside, or simply commiserating with you.

If you're in a relationship where your partner is disrespectful, not affirming, and not supportive of you and your changing gender identity, you have to decide what you're willing to tolerate and what your boundaries are. It's always your choice to stay, and only you know what you need, but I invite you to consider at what cost.

Remember that having a supportive and affirming partner is one of the primary factors that leads to satisfying sexual and romantic relationships and positively impacts general self-esteem.[16] And that marginalized folks tend to believe they deserve and imagine less-satisfying sexual and romantic relationships.

What if more was possible for you?

A NOTE TO CISGENDER PARTNERS

You have an opportunity to help the person you love feel amazing and affirmed for being authentically themselves in the world. What a gift! Research shows that having partners who proactively validate and respect their partner's gender identity creates more gender euphoria.[17] Trust me—you want a partner who feels amazing about themselves. And you have a big role in that.

When a partner comes out as transgender/non-binary, it's an adjustment for everyone in the relationship. Transition is a form of personal growth, and growth of any kind will *always* disrupt existing relationships as old patterns and assumptions are tested.

Any relationship shift will bring up feelings. That's normal and expected.

Being able to honestly communicate with your transgender/non-binary partner about how those changes impact you is important, and there's room for that. Your feelings, like theirs, are valid. However, getting outside support, preferably from a transgender-affirming therapist, for any initial negative reactions and working through any internalized transphobia are essential to creating a safe and affirming home base for your partner.

When it comes to sex, be proactive about asking what words your partner would like you to use or not use for their body. Initiating conversations and experiments with different sexual activities, roles, and desires can help take some pressure off your partner (who is probably already stuck in their head a bit) and facilitate both of you moving into a more playful, relaxed, and pleasurable sex life.

If a partner expresses dysphoria during sex, you have an opportunity to provide some co-regulation. Affirm their feelings, don't make it personal, and ask them what they need to feel safe and sexy again and if any adjustments in activities or words might feel better. They might not want to resume sex, but by creating space for the difficult feelings, it's more likely that everyone can move through them and still connect, strengthening your relationship overall.

Tiny Steps

Sometimes achieving new levels of sexual and romantic satisfaction isn't about massive changes in your life. Sometimes the tiny steps open up a world of new possibilities, like using a new sex toy or adaptive device, or asking a partner to use new words for your bits.

A non-binary client plopped down on my office couch and immediately teared up. "I wore a strap-on last night for the first time and didn't think it was possible to feel that much pleasure during sex."

I want that moment for you. And I want you to know the connected, sexy, seen, and safe romantic and sexual relationship(s) you crave is (are) not only possible but achievable. If you aren't there yet, it's okay. Take your time and enjoy every yummy tiny step you take.

FIFTY-FIFTY ATTENTION

Try this: Have a goal of fifty-fifty attention during a sexual experience. Put 50 percent of your attention on your partner's body (not what they are thinking of you, but on their pleasure) and 50 percent on your own pleasure. This experiment can be challenging for folks who are used to putting all of their attention on their partner's reaction to their body and what they might be doing with it.

Imagine sharing a delicious ice-cream cone. You might be so focused on wondering if your partner likes the flavor that you forget to taste it yourself. If this is the case, you're robbing yourself of the moment where you look at each other with wide eyes and say, "OMG, that was so good." Alternatively, you might love the flavor and your partner might think it's meh. Or vice versa. By trying to hold fifty-fifty attention, you also have the opportunity to enjoy what's good while also creating space for upgrades to make it even better for both of you.

As with everything to do with sexuality, the prerequisite here is that you are in a safe and sexy context, whatever that means to you.

CHAPTER 10

Queer It Up

I met a girl and I want to marry her."

I sat in front of the therapist I saw every week and made my proclamation with nervous excitement.

Most people who know Brook are a little in love with her.

She's a bright, shining star of a human—a tiny spitfire with a mane of jet-black curls, vivid red lipstick for all occasions, sparkling blue eyes, and a warm smile—and once you enter her orbit, it's almost impossible to leave. As a professional jazz and blues singer, Brook has a mesmerizing voice. She's also genuinely nice and makes anyone talking with her feel they are the most important person in the room. I once witnessed her share various facts about bees to an enraptured crowd of people.

Brook and I took classes at the same burlesque studio. At first, I was too busy focusing on attempting to shimmy while also moving my feet to pay much attention to her. I did, however, note her mentions of an ex-girlfriend. When I finally got up the courage to ask Brook "out," I forgot to mention it was a date.

But she said yes, so after our next class we went to a cocktail bar close to the studio, where the conversation flowed over two overpriced drinks.

I was in love. Completely. But Brook still didn't know it was a date.

About halfway through our second drink, Brook informed me she had a lover. And used that word—"lover." My stomach plummeted. She told me all about her lover, glowing, and my heart sank lower and lower with every sentence.

Her lover was a photographer. Uh-oh.

She met her at a nude photoshoot. This was not good.

Her lover was French—no, worse: *Parisian.*

And she was going to visit her in Paris in a few weeks.

I was doomed.

But I was also persistent.

She was the woman of my dreams. I would not give up without a fight. I pursued Brook shamelessly, and pretty soon she realized I was interested in more than just "hanging out." I asked her out on another date. And then another.

After a few dates, Brook invited me into her tiny Chicago apartment where she put a red scarf over a lamp for ambiance. We sat on the couch, listening to a record. I tried to pretend I didn't notice the music was in French. Our hands inched closer, touching and intertwining slightly sweaty fingers. This was it. With all the grace of a baby queer, I kissed her. She kissed me back. I drove home from her apartment floating on air. All was well in the world.

She ended my daydreams of our wedding day a week later.

Brook let me down easy and, with an awkward smile, told me she was smitten with her Parisian photographer lover and wanted us to be friends. I was devastated but holding it together because I was not about to let this French vixen steal my dignity as well as my dream girl.

But Brook had unlocked a piece of me I didn't know existed. I fell in love with a woman. It was terrifying, and it was painful, and it was a revelation. I was queer. It was real. This was not a small part of me I could hide from my conservative, evangelical parents forever with straight-passing relationships. I was Queer with a capital Q. It was freeing and disorienting and exciting as I began exploring my queerness in fresh ways, fumbling my way through a new world of unfamiliar words, sexual and gender identities, and culture.

Brook and I remained friends. To this day, we have a bat-signal text of "Fried chicken?" whenever one of us needs the comfort of a listening ear and greasy food. She introduced me to the woman who is the mother of my godchild. I've spent holidays with her and her family.

By the time Brook's French photographer fiancée moved to Chicago, we were all more than friends. We were family. A family I desperately needed when my own did not react well to my newfound queer identity. And when she asked me to officiate her wedding to that same French vixen, I said yes with tears in my eyes. At the ceremony, I quoted Jeanette Winterson, Brook's favorite author: "It is a big surprise falling in love . . . away you go, falling into someone else's orbit and after a while, you might decide to pull your two planets together and call it home."

So, in a way, I was right when I told my therapist that day, "I met a girl and I want to marry her." I just wasn't the one who got a wife out of it. Instead, I got a home.

The point of this story isn't that all of your intimate relationships will end up with you officiating a wedding or becoming a chosen family. The point is that intimacy of all types—platonic, romantic, sexual, short-term, long-term—is a nourishing source of joy that we can often limit unnecessarily.

If you're feeling lonely and disconnected on your gender-exploration journey, or simply want more connection in your life, embracing intimacy in all of its forms is life-giving. Intimacy is a cornerstone of being able to take care of ourselves and others whatever may come our way. Finding the people who will tell you you are loved and valid (and hot!) makes everything feel more possible.

The queer community often excels in designing friendships that are intimate in deep and meaningful ways regardless of how those friendships began. This is often out of necessity, as many members of the queer community—me included—have fraught or no relationships with their families of origin. My friends are my family, the ones who have my back, and the ones I would bury a body for (metaphorically, of course).

There's often a narrative that the only "successful" friendships are the ones who have been around you forever and are in close proximity to you. But I disagree. What about those friends you only see once every few years but pick right back up where you left off every time? Or the ones you talk to infrequently who fill your heart up with joy as you chat late into the night? Or the ones who hold the truth of that horrible year when you went through a bad breakup, your cat died, your spleen was swollen from mono, and you had to move unexpectedly because your landlord jacked your rent? These friendships are just as valid and intimate as someone who has been your best friend since third grade.

Likewise, we are largely given one paradigm of what a "successful" romantic and sexual relationship looks like that includes staying together in a monogamous relationship with the same relationship structure and agreements we started with, forever and ever. It's much more common in the queer community than the heteronormative community for sexual and romantic relationships to change with time, or be non-monogamous from the start, while still maintaining intimate and familial connections. Your partner calling an ex and a friend that you used to sleep with to offer company and treats on a hard day? Totally normal. And honestly, so nice. While Disney would have us reserve this kind of intimacy for our "one true love" (and maybe a talking animal), it's available to us in more relationships than you might think, and in less-restricted quantities.

We often think of intimacy like a pie—a limited resource where if someone gets a slice, it means someone else goes without. I prefer to think of intimacy like mycelium, a powerful and extensive network of fungal threads creating balance and symbiotic relationships in the natural world.* Mycelium networks are abundant, deep, and wide, creating conditions for life to thrive. They communicate and work together to share resources and defend and adapt against threats to their survival. As your mycelium relationships become more vast, interwoven, and intimate, they give more and receive more—they're endlessly generative and supportive. While there *are* limits to our time and energy, there's no limit to the love and intimacy available to us if we take a broader perspective about what intimate relationships can look like.

---

* Speaking of mycelium networks, this metaphor was fact-checked by Alex Kuhn, a mycologist and previous Tinder date and travel buddy. You never know where your connections will lead.

Intimacy comes from both deep relationships and moments of connection (platonic, sexual, and romantic) where you can be vulnerable, seen, and supported. This is crucial as our networks of intimacy create the interdependence we need to thrive. Shame and systemic oppression are winning when we feel isolated, disconnected, and depleted, making it even more important to embrace complexity, stay adaptive, and remain connected to one another.

In previous chapters, I've talked about being physically intimate as a way to explore pleasure, sensuality, and eroticism and a bit about how our support networks are one of our biggest strengths during gender exploration and transition. In this chapter, I'll talk about "queering" intimacy in friendships as well as romantic and sexual relationships.

WHAT DOES QUEER MEAN?

"That person is a little *queer*," my Louisiana-born grandma said to me in a whisper as a child. Many of us grew up with the term "queer" being an insult, insinuating that someone was part of the LGBTQ+ population and not normal or acceptable. A quick history lesson: This term was reclaimed in the early nineties by the LGBTQ+ community in much the same way we use the term "feminist." You can identify as a feminist and go study feminist scholars. Queer is similarly used as both an identity (I identify as queer) and a field of study. You can read books by queer theorists such as Butler, Sedgwick, and Foucault and take classes on queer theory.

To reduce an entire field of study to a couple of sentences, "queer" emphasizes flexibility and fluidity of identity and identity categories and is a giant "Fuck you!" to the idea that any of us should strive to be "normal." In short, queer theory asserts that putting complex humans into tiny, assumed binary boxes of gender, sexual orientation, relational structures, and "normalcy" is...well...nonsense. And boring.

"Queering" is also a verb, meaning to critically look at the ways society has constructed ideas about what is "normal" and deconstruct traditional assumptions and power structures to add more nuance, flexibility, and freedom for us all.

Platonic Intimacy

I sat naked in a large Jacuzzi tub with a couple of hot blondes. We sipped wine as we soaked, warm and wet, for hours. But unlike what you might think, this wasn't a threesome. One of the blondes was having a hard time in her relationship and the other two of us were there for emotional support.

We talked, we listened, we laughed, we cried.

We held hands and said, "I love you, I got you, and it's going to be okay."

All while naked in a tub together. The moment was nourishing, intimate, sensual, erotic, and pleasurable, but it wasn't sexual. A move across the country later, one of my favorite rituals with this friend is a monthly bath date, FaceTiming while we take a bath "together."

When we put pleasure, eroticism, intimacy, and sensuality in a tiny box reserved for romantic and sexual relationships, we cut ourselves off from the beautiful world of platonic intimacy and the nourishment and connection it can provide. Now, this doesn't mean everyone is gonna jump naked into a tub with friends (though I highly recommend it), but intentionally designing a network of intimate connections is one of the most worthwhile endeavors you can undertake.

We live in a world where The Couple often reigns supreme as the main source of love and getting our needs for affection, intimacy, and attachment met. Friends can be close but are always secondary to romantic relationships. How limiting!

Prioritizing friendships as a core part of our "mycelium network" takes the pressure off romantic or sexual partners (or lack thereof) to be our only source of intimacy and is an equally valid source of attachment and care.

Queering intimacy includes questioning who benefits from the status quo of reserving deep connection and commitment for romantic and sexual partnerships over friendships. Writer and organizer Dean Spade says, "Redefining the way we view relationships is to try to treat the people I date more like I treat my friends—to be respectful and thoughtful and have boundaries and reasonable expectations—and to try to treat my friends more like my dates—to give them special attention, honor my commitments to them, be consistent, and invest deeply in our future together."[1]

I love to date my friends and do romantic things, like a fancy dinner at a restaurant with velvet corner booths typically reserved for people trying to get laid. Your commitment to doing life with your friends is just as important as your commitment to a future with a romantic or sexual partner and just as vulnerable.

Designing Platonic Intimacy

While many of the folks I work with are hungry for more connection and affection, the level of vulnerability required to be deeply intimate with friends makes them want to run for the hills. Building intimate connections outside of our cultural construct for friendship takes guts and willingness to risk hurt, rejection, or seeming "weird." Platonic intimacy requires addressing the brain trash saying we are a burden to our friends when we need care, while also mindfully and consistently showing up for others when they ask for the same.

If you've never experienced this type of deep intimacy with your friends, you might be wondering where to start. First, bring them in on the experiment. You can use this book as a starting point: "I read *Gender Magic* and it had a section on platonic intimacy that I found mind-blowing, life-changing, and thought-provoking. Want to hear about it? Maybe I should buy you a copy. I'm going to do that right now." (Oh, you're too kind, reader.) If they're open to it, you can then talk about what types of intimacy you might be interested in with them.

Second, share expectations and boundaries, especially around touch. It's best practice to ask for consent frequently and be mindful to not take a "no" personally. For example, asking if someone wants to cuddle or hold hands and not overthinking it if that's not the vibe for the day.

Third, commit to checking in and renegotiating if something doesn't feel good for either party. Awkwardness or discomfort doesn't necessarily mean something is wrong. It's okay for what intimacy looks like to shift and change over time. The overarching intimacy and friendship are the priority, not one particular expression of them.

SHORT-TERM INTIMACY

We've learned from mainstream culture that true intimacy is only available in long-term, romantic relationships. However, I've had many moments of true intimacy with new acquaintances, short-term lovers, and even strangers that have been deeply meaningful and connecting to me, if not long-lasting. If you've ever been to a summer camp, you know the magic of meeting strangers at the beginning of the week and crying your eyes out as you leave them by the end of the week. It takes courage to open yourself up to connecting with others without the certainty of a long-term relationship, but it can also be a beautiful thing.

The Galaxy of Intimacy

There are many types of intimacy beyond just emotional and sexual intimacy.* Intimacy isn't any one thing or action so much as it's a state of mind. When you are intimate with someone, you are *familiar* with them.

I love this word because it has "family" at its root and because one dictionary defines "familiarity" as "knowledge or mastery of a . . . subject."[2] In this case, the subject is each other. Intimacy means you are free to be you without masks, at ease and with affection and warmth.

When designing your intimate relationships, it's important to consider what types of intimacy you most value as well as how you're interested in expressing intimacy with different people.

* This list is adapted from a blog post entitled, "Twelve Types of Intimacy," by Alan Rutherford, which was adapted from *The Intimate Marriage* by Howard and Charlotte Clinebell. I find both versions quite dated, cis-/heteronormative, and steeped in strange connections to religion.

Emotional intimacy: sharing deep feelings, thoughts, and letting others into our innermost lives. This looks like sharing the hard parts of life honestly, as well as the great parts. We often overlook the vulnerability of joy and can make our excitement and wins smaller out of a fear of judgment. Emotional intimacy means sharing the full spectrum of our emotions.

Intellectual intimacy: exploring ideas and passions together. Bring on all the nerdery!

Aesthetic intimacy: sharing a love of beautiful and awe-inspiring things. This could look like art, music, design, nature, or whatever the two of you find uniquely beautiful.

Erotic intimacy: finding joy in affirming each other's bodies, erotic material, and sharing erotic experiences. Remember that eroticism doesn't need to be sexual.

Recreational and creative intimacy: doing hobbies, fun things, sports, or creative pursuits together. This also includes "shoulder time," or things like reading or working on separate creative projects in the same room.

Logistical intimacy: sharing the everyday responsibilities of life like a home, yard, children or pets, or other logistical tasks.

Mundane intimacy: pleasure in the simple, everyday parts of life like drinking coffee on the porch, taking the dog for a walk, or cooking dinner together. A Sunday-morning kind of love.

Crisis intimacy: showing up for each other in individual or shared crises, such as a flat tire, natural disaster, or a death.

Values-based intimacy: a shared commitment to a common cause or values. This might look like going to protests together or political organizing.

Sexual intimacy: This includes intensity and type of sexual intimacy. For example, having a kink scene with someone at a play party might feel great but having one-on-one sex might not. Or vice versa.

The galaxy of intimacy is a starting point to think about what types of intimacy you want to cultivate in your life. It might feel the most authentic to connect with folks in different ways or to pinpoint types of intimacy you want to integrate into all of your closest relationships.

FRIENDS AND BODIES

I've seen most of my friends naked. Between burlesque, skinny-dipping, previous sexual relationships, kink events, baths, naked bike rides (it's a thing in Chicago), gay beaches, and thirst traps, I'm familiar with their bodies.

One of my best friends, an aesthetician, once waxed my butthole.

Talk about intimacy.

Our culture likes to sexualize and create a taboo out of the naked body. This is why some chests are considered "obscene" when not wearing a shirt while others of similar size are perfectly acceptable and breastfeeding in public is still a divisive issue. The more we can normalize the fact that we all have bodies and none of them are indecent or inherently sexual, the more comfortable we can get just existing in each other's presence.*

At the same time, it's not always a bad thing to eroticize or sexualize a friend's body if there is consent to do so. Your friends are sexy! You know it's true. We are often scared to even dip a toe into any interaction that acknowledges this fact out of fear of crossing a line. What a shame! I'm not suggesting you start coming on to your friends without consent, do sexually suggestive things that make anyone uncomfortable, or cross any preexisting relationship boundaries. Yet comments about our bodies typically come with an expectation or hope of a sexual interaction. Asking, "Can I give you a compliment about your body?" is a magic phrase that goes a long way.

Once, a social media thread in a queer group exploded with dozens of transgender/non-binary folks posting thirst traps. I watched with joy as people felt sexy and reacted to others' affirmations of their delicious bodies. I made a personal rule that day to not save my best nudes and thirst traps for lovers if I can help it. It can feel amazing to have our bodies and sexiness complimented by a friend who wants nothing from us other than to make us feel good about ourselves.

---

* This does not include nakedness that is sexualized in an aggressive and non-consensual manner.

Similarly, if it's in line with the boundaries of your relationships, romantic and physical affection that feels erotic but has no expectation of becoming sexual can be intimate in an entirely different way. In some of my friendships, it's common for us to cuddle, kiss, and give each other massages. There's no weirdness or expectations. Simply two people who enjoy showing each other affection and love.

Evolving Existing Romantic and Sexual Relationships

While I was writing this book, my partner of five years and I broke up. I wouldn't recommend this particular confluence of events to any writer. Yet it did offer a unique perspective from which to write about the complexity of human relationships and, in particular, evolving relationships.

The short story is that some core needs weren't met for either of us after years of work and therapy. As we made this heartrending decision, our conversations settled into... gratitude. Gratitude for the ways our relationship continued to work, the love and care we felt for each other, how we still supported each other, and the home we had built together.

We were curious if the typical narrative of a breakup, where the partners go their separate ways, break the attachment bond they have, and move on while harboring animosity for each other, was the only option. What if we could design something different?

So we did something that many folks might consider a terrible, horrible idea. We decided to keep living together. This means, at the time of writing this, we continue to share a home and responsibilities, emotional intimacy, and spend time together. We have separate bedrooms and other partners (which is not a post-breakup development), and our attachment looks different. But it's still loving, and we share a large part of our lives. We want to remain connected, even though I imagine what that looks like will change significantly over time as we both grow (and eventually don't live under the same roof).

Dominant culture taught me that once a relationship was over, that was it. Bam. Nada. Nothing.

The queer community taught me different. One of the most beautiful things about the queer community is how folks often prioritize maintaining and transforming relationships instead of cutting former sexual or romantic partners out of their lives when something is no longer working in their relationship. It's one of the greatest gifts of my life to be able to evolve many relationships with folks that I put a great deal of time, energy, and love into cultivating.

I don't mean to put relationship evolution (or non-monogamy) on a pedestal or imply that it's the morally right or best way to do relationships. Evolving a relationship instead of ending it completely is not for the faint of heart. I mention it simply to give you more choices for connection and intimacy outside of the very limited "instruction book" we are typically given for straight and strictly monogamous relationships. If you take nothing else away from this chapter, I hope that you know you get to choose how you want to design your relationships, not that any choice is better than another. Sometimes the best choice for everyone involved is to let a relationship end; sometimes it can shift.* Only you can know what works for you.

Gender Transition and Evolving Relationships

Like any significant personal growth or change, exploring or transitioning your gender while in a long-term relationship can shake the foundations of that partnership. This is true for both straight-appearing relationships with a cisgender person and queer relationships with someone of any gender. It may feel scary, but shaking things up isn't an inherently negative thing. I've often seen relationships become stronger as the partner who is transitioning leans more into their authentic self, and their partner builds skills in communication, boundaries, and emotional intelligence.

The foundation of a healthy relationship is a desire for everyone in the relationship to thrive. It's hard to thrive when you're hiding or shutting

* Please note severing relationships where abuse is present is usually the right decision for one's mental health and safety.

down a part of yourself. Whether or not your relationship continues with the same structure or intensity, the genuine desire to see each other happy, authentic, and flourishing is the foundation on which relationship evolutions are built.

You and your partner might come to the conclusion that your relationship structure needs to shift to allow each other to grow. As you have these difficult conversations, it's important to co-create a relationship structure that supports both of you. A relationship that only works for one person doesn't work.

For transgender and non-binary folks, relationship evolutions are not about settling for a partner who misgenders you all the time, is unable or unwilling to work through internalized transphobia, or shames you for transitioning your gender because of the impact on them. Regardless of whether or not your relationship continues, you deserve to be treated well by a partner or ex-partner and have your identity respected. Remember, your identity is not a burden.

Queering your current partnership means coming to the table as teammates, with curiosity and care, to figure out what type of relationship and intimacy feel good to you. In order to do this effectively, you'll need skills like understanding and communicating your feelings, understanding your attachment needs, creating and maintaining boundaries, prioritizing self-care, and letting go of the need for certainty. Let's walk through these one by one.

Understanding and Communicating Your Emotions

People need time and space to heal from the hurt of a relationship dynamic changing. Creating space for grief without trying to fix it is an important part of the process. Any large change in life is stressful, with both marriage and divorce being among the ten most stressful life events.[3] Evolving a relationship doesn't mean ignoring the stressful and difficult feelings that come up but rather moving through them with self-love and compassion.

It's not sustainable to have the person you're evolving a relationship with be your sole source of support, and I highly recommend having the professional support of a therapist and friends. I've also found sharing *some* parts of the hard feelings coming up within your existing relationship to be a connecting experience. Simply naming what we are feeling is powerful. When we shut down grief or sadness, we also shut down joy and intimacy. We contain multitudes. We can hold it all.

Navigating a relationship's evolution well requires emotional intelligence. And no, stoically naming everything you're feeling with laser-sharp accuracy and communicating it without emotion is not emotional intelligence. Real emotional intelligence is about understanding and integrating what you're feeling in all its messiness into your communication.

When your emotions are too big and intense to kindly communicate with your partner, emotional intelligence means taking a break to feel your big feels elsewhere before coming back to your partner more grounded. This might look like doing something physically such as running, biking, or lifting. Or processing your feelings in another way with a friend, therapist, or journal.[4]

It can also look like naming sensations in your body as a guide when you don't have words for the feelings, like "a tightness in my chest" or "light" or "heavy." Getting it perfect isn't a requirement, but mindfully centering emotions in this process helps you respond instead of react when things get hard. To keep feelings from building up and spilling over in frustration, it's helpful to have a regularly scheduled check-in time for both feelings and any logistics in the midst of a relationship transition.

Understanding Your Attachment Needs

Everyone's attachment systems and needs are different. As infants, we rely completely on our caregivers to survive. It's literally life or death. For the lucky folks with attentive and emotionally mature caregivers, it's reinforced that we are safe and our needs will get met the majority of the time.

For others, early experiences of inattentive or inconsistent care create feelings of anxiety and a mistrust that our loved ones will stick around and our needs will be met. Some folks react to feeling unsafe in relationships by avoiding connection, and others react by seeking constant reassurance they won't be abandoned, or some combination of the two.

When we feel like we have a secure base in a relationship, we feel safer to explore ourselves and others from a grounded place.[5] We are able to tolerate discomfort and self-soothe when our needs can't be met 100 percent of the time by a partner, because we trust they still have our back. We are able to enjoy both autonomy and closeness without fear.

In most conversations about attachment systems, secure attachment is considered the only "good" type of attachment, characterizing anything except a secure attachment style as wrong and something to be fixed instead of something to accept and work with. However, all attachment styles come with strengths and weaknesses.

When we are not in a reactive place, both anxious and avoidant attachment styles can be legitimate expressions of needs and desires in a partnership. It's normal for different folks to have different needs related to closeness and autonomy.

While feeling safe and secure in a relationship is the goal, some folks thrive with more autonomy and some folks thrive with more closeness. There is nothing wrong with either. Being honest about what your unique needs are in an intimate relationship can create more opportunity for connection or more clarity about why a relationship might not be working for you.

Establishing Boundaries

Contrary to the idea that boundaries create limitations, boundaries can be immensely freeing. When you're evolving relationships, clear boundaries create a feeling of safety instead of confusion. A study on landscape architecture and playgrounds compared children's reactions to a playground with no fence versus a playground with a fence. Contrary to what you might think, the kids felt freer to explore when they felt safe within the boundaries of the fence.[6] Knowing our limits allows us to play without fear.

Types of boundaries to discuss include what types of intimacy you're interested in, what adjustments to both time spent together and time spent apart are needed to recalibrate your relationship, and capacity for emotional support. If you're exploring non-monogamy, boundaries will include disclosures, relationship agreements, and a vision for what you want your relationship to look like.

Prioritizing Self-Care

Successfully navigating a relationship's evolution means taking excellent care of yourself. Change and managing the emotions that come with it can be hard and exhausting. Treat yourself the way you would treat a friend going through the same circumstances.

The basics go a long way: Get enough rest, eat food that nourishes you, move your body in ways that feel good, go to therapy or talk with a trusted friend, connect with your loved ones. Additionally, take time for pleasure and joy—treat yourself to a solo date and do your favorite things, get a massage, go on a walk in nature. Whatever excellent self-care looks like to you.

Letting Go

As folks explore gender, it's common for sexual needs and desires to shift as well. Likewise, a partner's sexual needs and desires might shift and change as a transgender/non-binary partner leans into a new gender identity or expression. As we've discussed in previous chapters, this can be an exciting time full of new possibilities to explore and immense pleasure.

It can also be a time to honestly question if sexual and romantic needs and desires are still compatible for both partners. For some folks (like me), romantic and sexual intimacy is at the core of attachment needs in a primary relationship. Different types of intimacy might be equally or more important for other folks.

If it's aligned for you and your partner, this could be an opportunity to consider changing the intensity and structure of your romantic and sexual relationship. Focusing on different types of intimacy may take some pressure off. Exploring ethical non-monogamy and polyamory can be an excellent way to get needs met while maintaining an intimate connection with a current partner. While it's outside the scope of this book to dig into polyamory, there are many great resources out there to help you navigate non-monogamy, and I'd encourage you to check out *Polysecure* or *Opening Up*.

ON BUILDING TRUST

Creating and maintaining intimacy require building trust, which takes time and intention.

A person worthy of your trust is someone who non-judgmentally supports and accepts you for who you are. They want you to be the most authentic version of yourself, whatever that looks like.

Trust is also built through boundaries and consent. Trusting someone's enthusiastic "Yes!" and ability to express a no and accept yours are fundamental to intimacy.

A trustworthy partner, platonic or romantic, can admit mistakes, move through conflict, and connect again on the other side. When you make mistakes, there is still an assumption of best intent and you aren't "disposable." In any intimate relationship, people will likely unintentionally hurt each other at some point. In a relationship you're committed to, this can be an opportunity to deepen and grow your relationship rather than signal the end of it, with exceptions for things like abuse or hurt that comes from core incompatibilities.

Lastly, building trust includes knowing that someone will keep your conversations private if they need to. We often get clues to this by listening to how they talk about conversations they've had with others.[7]

We have an opportunity to design our "mycelium networks" of deeply intimate connections in whatever way works for us, regardless of what society says our relationships "should" look like. Platonic or romantic, intimacy is creative fuel.

It gives us the energy we need to boldly lean into our most authentic self, turning down the volume on shame while inspiring us to disrupt the oppressive systems we live in from a place of abundance and love.

You deserve a life full of people who think you're magic, who will answer the call when you say, "Fried chicken?" on a hard day, and who are committed to your relationship. You deserve moments of intimacy with the people who cross your path in life.

If you're willing to take the risk to be vulnerable and authentic and to go deep with people, I guarantee those relationships—platonic, sexual, and romantic—and the love within them are available for you.

You deserve pleasure. And more than that, you deserve a life full of possibilities that make you happy cry.

QUESTIONS TO CONSIDER WHEN QUEERING UP RELATIONSHIPS

- What boxes do you have in your friendships and romantic/sexual relationships that feel confining to you?
- What types of intimacy do you crave more of?
- What relationships do you currently have that give you energy and make you feel intimately connected and why?
- What do you know about your attachment system and needs? What does this tell you about what you need to thrive in an intimate relationship of any kind?
- What does relationship "success" mean to you?
- What types of intimacy are most important to you in a primary partner? What types of intimacy can be met elsewhere?
- What does it mean to you to treat your friends like lovers and your lovers like friends?
- What sorts of outside support do you need to evolve a current romantic or sexual relationship?
- What boundaries do you need to set up for yourself in an intimate or evolving relationship?
- Do you need a regularly scheduled check-in conversation with a friend or partner?
- What does self-care look like for you if you are evolving a long-term relationship?
- How do you know that you can trust someone enough to be vulnerable with them?
- What relationship structures are you interested in exploring?
- What's one tiny step you can take to queer up your relationships?

PART III

POSSIBILITY

CHAPTER 11

Create Space

Gender doesn't exist in a vacuum.

Transitioning one area of your life, like gender, often sheds light on the other areas of your life that don't feel congruent with the person you want to be and what you value. I've had many clients who, once they start transitioning their gender, can't ignore the other areas of their life that don't feel great for them—and that's a good thing. After all, you haven't been doing all this hard work to experiment, to discover and share your magic, to seek pleasure, and to build intimacy with yourself and others just to say, "Nah, that shitty [roommate / job / relationship / lack of fulfillment] I've been putting up with? That can stay."

Part 3 of this book is about bringing more possibility into your life both within and beyond gender exploration. It's about envisioning a life worth living and then making it happen. This chapter digs into your life as a whole, and the following chapters will discuss building your chosen family—your kinship network—and, finally, how to live with pride (as a verb).

Just like with gender, bringing an attitude of play, experimentation, and possibility to our life as a whole helps us move toward the things we desire with more ease and flow. When we attach our worth to "success" and insist that "success" looks a particular way, it's easy to put pressure on ourselves to "achieve" that exact idea of "success" and see everything else as failure. So, let's not. Let's just play and say, "Wouldn't it be cool if..." and see what happens.

Maybe you'd make a leap like the following:

- going for the promotion
- getting into and out of relationships
- moving or changing roommates
- moving your body in new ways you love
- learning new hobbies
- starting a business
- finding a new passion, cause, or career
- exploring BDSM or polyamory
- traveling

This chapter is about learning how to bring intentionality and possibility to *all* the areas of your life, no matter what barriers you're facing.

I want you to reconsider what's possible.

Remember Your Strengths

My Spidey sense tells me I see major life changes in the folks I work with for a reason. Transgender and non-binary folks develop sneaky life skills along their journey—like assertiveness, setting boundaries, self-trust, and self-efficacy—and those skills spill over naturally into other areas of their lives. As folks cultivate more self-love and compassion, they also tend to have higher standards for how they expect to be treated and set firmer boundaries for themselves. Once you believe you deserve to be treated with respect and care, you're much less willing to accept anything else.

Doing the work to know who you are, what you need, what matters to you, and how to support yourself through anything gives you immense strength. I know those superpowers can be hard to see when you're just trying to get through the day, so let me help you. Let's remember together some of the things you've learned throughout this book that are now strengths you can apply to any part of your life.

Tapping into Pleasure

As you lean into your authentic self, you naturally experience more pleasure, whether through gender euphoria or just plain ol' eroticism. Learning what "Yes!" and "No!" feel like in your body becomes a powerful clue to intuition. Over time, those gut feelings expand beyond just sexuality and relationships, and you can tap into your "Yes!" and "No!" in *all* the areas of your life. And the more you know what your yes feels like, the more you can take steps toward the things that light you up.

Doing Hard Things

Many of my clients have already done the scariest thing they can imagine: transitioning. But even if you're just beginning to explore or want to transition in the future, you've also done hard things—like making it through Trump's presidency and a global pandemic while showing up for social justice protests after George Floyd's murder, gun violence, and the loss of many reproductive rights.

That sentence makes me tired just reading it.

Or maybe for you the hard thing is getting out of bed in the morning day after day and remembering to drink water. This isn't the hard-things Olympics. It doesn't matter what the hard thing is. What I want you to remember is that you did it, and you survived. You're magic, and don't let anyone tell you differently. Proving to yourself that you can do hard things builds the confidence and self-efficacy that help move you from "I can't" to "I wonder how..."

Breaking the "Rules"

Gender explorers are already breaking one societal taboo, so it's not as big of a deal to break another. Or two. Or a hundred. Once you've had the experience of doing something society says is bad, improper, impossible, too hard, and not allowed, you begin to wonder what other "rules" and self- or societally imposed limits are complete bullshit. (Hint: There are a lot of them.)

Wondering what would happen if you didn't follow the rules at all gives you space to design a life that feels authentic and works for you. You start doing more things that once felt impossible.

A Bias to Action

Learning to do tiny experiments in order to figure out what you want and what you might be interested in exploring works in all the areas of your life. The impulse to try, to test, to move and get more information will keep us growing and stretching into our authentic selves both within and beyond gender exploration.

Jump-Start Your Imagination

Throughout this book, you've been doing the work to move out of survival mode. When we're focused on just surviving, our imagination (understandably) shuts down, and we are less able to envision an audacious future for ourselves. This is where a lot of my clients are when I first meet them and where you might have been when you opened this book. Most of us aren't used to thinking bigger about what we want our lives to look and feel like. As we begin to explore who we are, we get to practice thinking bigger, setting boundaries that protect and support us, and treating ourselves with self-love and compassion.

We get to jump-start our imaginations.

This can feel uncomfortable and challenging if you've been in survival mode for a while, but in my experience, all it takes is a single question:

What Would You Do if You Weren't Afraid?

The uninhibited answer, the one that pops into your brain instantly, is usually something you're longing for on a deep level but that you have told yourself is impossible. Our challenge is to shift from pushing that answer down to honoring it—moving from "I can't" to "How could I?"

My client January, a Black, non-binary individual assigned male at birth, is a great example. When I first met them, they struggled with imposter syndrome around their non-binary identity. They lived with their conservative parents and were reliant on them financially as they struggled to find a job that provided a consistent income. Feeling limited in what types of gender expression they could experiment with while still living with their family frustrated January. Their circumstances were such that it felt impossible to be financially independent enough to move out of their parents' house and be able to relax into who they were.

When I asked them this question, January's answer was instant: They wanted to make a living from writing, move out of their parents' house, and be able to dress however they wanted in their day-to-day life.

Bingo.

Remember how our brains can't move away from something and toward something at the same time? By engaging their imagination, January shifted out of survival and started moving toward a goal—one that lit them up like a comet every time they said it out loud.

This question doesn't only apply to gender exploration but also to the rest of your life. I find it helpful to ask myself this question when I'm as relaxed and inspired as possible—after moving my body, having a deep conversation with a friend, or doing something I love. Or while in the middle of a great journaling session. Maybe something pops into your head like moving to a new home or finding a career and a workplace that celebrate who you are.

For me, answers to the question "What would you do if you weren't afraid?" over time have included the following:

- coming out as queer to my super-conservative family
- moving to Chicago, where I knew a total of three humans
- quitting a job I no longer liked
- starting my own business
- changing my name to Rae
- changing my pronouns to they/them
- publicly identifying as non-binary

- wearing whatever the hell I want without feeling the need to "prove" my gender identity with androgyny
- getting a neck tattoo
- buying a home
- learning to drive a motorcycle
- getting top surgery
- writing a book

At one point or another, these desires all made me want to puke, at least a little bit. I wanted them so badly that even saying I wanted them felt risky and vulnerable, as though I were opening myself up to hurt and disappointment if they didn't work out. Staying where I was at the time felt, at least, familiar and predictable. These audacious goals? Total unknown. Terrifying. And exciting.

I'll keep my current unmet desires to myself, but they feel equally puke-worthy. I've learned, however, to view my wide-eyed, pukey feeling as an intuition clue that I desire something so important to me that the risk of failing makes me want to throw up. That usually means I should do it.

I recognize that it's a great privilege to follow so many of my dreams over the past years, and I see you if what you dream about isn't possible for you right now. But here's what I can tell you about being on the other side of these big, terrifying decisions full of uncertainty: My life is better because I made the choice to go for what I really wanted, even though it was scary.

I've had other desires I went for that didn't work out—relationships, business ventures, speaking gigs, connections, and, hell, even vacations—but not getting what I wanted doesn't mean I shouldn't have tried. Every "failure" teaches me great lessons that only help me achieve my goal eventually or point toward other, sometimes more important goals.

It takes guts to name who you are and what you want when you strip away all the pretenses and the making-yourself-smaller and the fear. As my friend and author Jen Pastiloff says, "May I have the courage to be who I say I am."[1]

So, let me ask you: *What would you do if you weren't afraid?*

WHAT WOULD YOU DO IF YOU WEREN'T AFRAID?

Take a second to write down the answer that popped into your head, no matter how crazy or impossible it might seem right now. Now put that paper where you can see it every day.

Remember that "letter from your future self" you wrote in chapter 2? I want you to revisit it. No, really. Go grab it.

I want you to put reality on hold for a second to read this letter (out loud if you can) like it's *actually* a message from your future self, not an exercise in a self-help book. This multiverse version of you has crossed the space-time continuum to give you an essential message.

They want you to know who you are and remember what you want. Listen to them and, while you're at it, tune in to your body.

The tickle in your gut, the breath you may be holding, the thing you want so badly it gets caught in your throat because to say it out loud means you might "fail" at it—that's it. The thing you want. Who you are. Stay with it.

Write it down. Say it out loud.

Now, imagine you *are* your multiverse future self and see if you can embody them. Maybe have some fun with it. Will the future contain space-age glitter and a lot of postapocalyptic leather? Find some glitter and leather and make an outfit. Make a multiverse-future-you throwback playlist and put it on. Come on—be weird with me.

Read the letter (again, out loud if you can) as if you are reading it to the you of today. And notice: How does your posture change? How do you feel as you step into their life (your life) ten years from today? What body sensations do you have? Write it down.

Follow those feelings. What creates them for you now? What feelings do you want more of? What feelings do you want less of? These are clues.

When Your Goals Feel Far Away

Maybe what you wrote down in the previous exercise isn't anywhere close to your reality. If you're frustrated or talking down to yourself about how you feel far from your goals or you don't have the resources right now to go for them in the way you want, you're not alone.

We know the system is rigged, and many of us have multiple oppressed identities impacting our ability to move toward our goals.

I recognize my ability to do many of the big, scary things I desire comes from a place of privilege as a white person with a graduate degree and professional licensure.

I don't rely on my family for financial support and haven't since I was nineteen, and I have a wonderful network of chosen family.

I work in an industry that is largely accepting of non-binary folks.

I can make a sustainable living as a business owner, therapist, coach, and speaker.

I have health insurance.

AND. I also know that there are inner resources, and often outside resources and relationships too, available to every person that can and will support your journey. I've said it before and I'll say it again: You are magic. You are strong in ways that you might only just be realizing, and I know that you can design a life for yourself that is fulfilling, joyful, and full of love.

Instead of beating yourself up, I invite you to have some self-compassion for where you are in this moment. Life isn't a race. Everyone's pace and path will be different and are influenced by both micro and macro factors outside of our control. I want you to feel pleasure and as much ease as possible every step of the way. Which means being loving to yourself and focusing on the tiny steps you can control.

Gravity Problems

The tiny steps I'm talking about are realistic changes, meaning changes that are achievable with the resources you have (or can get) and have full control over. Often, we find ourselves trying to solve "gravity problems"—challenges as unsolvable and outside our control as, well, trying to fight gravity. For example, goals like "I want my family to accept me" or "I want to be a doctor tomorrow even though I didn't go to medical school" are gravity problems. There is no amount of wanting or hoping or doing that will "fix" them.

That may sound bleak, but accepting reality helps us change, not stay stuck. Once we accept how things are, we can brainstorm how to work around those limitations. We can transform these goals into things like "I want to be loved and accepted by my kinship network" and "I want to go to medical school." Those are goals we can influence. Obstacles be damned.

Just be careful not to limit yourself here! Don't put yourself in a box based on your past experiences or the limits of your imagination in this moment. Don't assume gravity is in full effect until you've dropped a few apples. The me of ten years ago could not imagine the person I am today. I invite you to consider that the you of today can't visualize the you of ten years from now.

There are possibilities you haven't yet begun to imagine.

Doing the Thing

While I was exploring my own non-binary gender identity and expression, I adopted what might seem like an odd routine: Most mornings, I stood in front of the mirror and put a binder on over my chest. I immediately panicked. I peeled the binder off and then put it back on. This cycle repeated two or three times every day for about six months.

Over time, my panic—which was caused by fear of being a fraud—lessened.

I slowly gained more confidence by adding a simple question to my mornings:

What do I want?

Each day was a new chance to decide whether I wanted to wear a binder, based on my answer to that question.

It took me years to decide if top surgery was the right decision for me, and like many parts of my gender-transition journey, it was something I kept largely private.

I didn't want a big fuss, and I definitely didn't want to be called "brave." I only told a few people before my surgery date. But my decision to schedule that surgery—on my thirty-second birthday—was based on another powerful question:

What would I want *if I weren't afraid?*

When we're experiencing fear, our world gets smaller. Our brain, in fight/flight/freeze/fawn, has one goal: Don't die. When faced with the unknown, fear whispers, "Stay small; stay safe." But when we take fear out of the equation, we bring ourselves back to curiosity and possibility instead of focusing on making the "right" decision; it helps us reorient toward thriving. As I took my binder on and off, my brain told me I was being silly and a fraud for wanting to wear a binder. I doubted myself and felt confused. But when I slowed down and asked myself, "What would I want if I weren't afraid?" the answer was clear. And that clarity helped me find the courage I needed to wear the binder out of the house.

I don't know where my gender journey will take me over my lifetime, but I can tell you I've never been happier in my body. And as testosterone and top surgery cause my body to change in ways that feel aligned with my gender identity, I don't think so hard about my decisions about my gender presentation and identity. I even feel more interest in expressing some more feminine sides of myself. These days, I just ask myself, "Will this make my life bigger and better? Will this bring me one step closer to being able to relax into my own skin?"

If the answer is "Pretty sure it will," I do it.

Because that's enough. Desire is enough.

You don't have to wait to "decide" what gender identity "fits" you; it's enough to want something different and live in that direction. In the rest of the chapter, we're going to talk about strategies to start doing exactly that.

The only way to bring our goals from our imagination to reality is to take steps toward them. Once again, I want to ground you in the power of tiny steps. While I can't promise you will be able to fulfill all of your desires, I know for sure you won't if you don't try.

And wouldn't it be fun if it worked?

For the folks I work with, major life changes can feel impossible because of the bigness of gender transition, leaving them frozen in indecision and overwhelm. It becomes a circular mind game of "If this, then that" or "I can't do X because I have to do Y first, and I can't do Y first because X." Breaking down seemingly giant problems into smaller problems helps you solve them one tiny step at a time. We've seen this already with our tiny-step experiments.

Some of these big, hairy, audacious goals might feel larger than life, but the process to reach them is the same as how we've been talking about gender exploration and transition. Follow your curiosities and your desires and take it one tiny step at a time or, as we'll talk about later in this chapter, take a small leap into the unknown.

"I'm happy. I can't believe it. I'm happy." Wrapping up my work with Lennox, a fortysomething Greek transmasculine individual, these words made my heart grow two sizes.

When we started working together, Lennox was terrified of taking any steps forward. He felt frozen because he couldn't see any way out of his current situation and had a hard time imagining a positive future for himself.

Lennox was just beginning his gender-transition journey and wasn't out to his family. He worked in the family business and feared what being out as queer and transgender would mean for both his relationship with his family and his job, which he had worked in some capacity since he was young and was a vital source of financial security, stability, and community. He felt like he couldn't start medical transition because he had no career backup plans.

As part of our work together, we broke down this seemingly impossible conundrum into tiny steps to get Lennox moving forward right away, in line with his goals for himself. He couldn't envision what the end result would look like, but he didn't need to at this point. He just needed to take the first tiny step.

Lennox started exploring other career options to see what he might be interested in and created a resumé and LinkedIn profile. While he wasn't sure exactly what he wanted to do, he was able to recognize patterns in what he enjoyed doing in his current role, transferable skills, and natural strengths.

When he was ready to start coming out to his family, we started by identifying potential allies. Lennox came out to his sister first. She was surprised and fumbled with language but ultimately expressed support. When Lennox came out to his parents, it didn't go well. They were fearful and uninformed about transgender identities and this came out as anger, hurt, and disappointment. They asked Lennox to continue going by his old name and feminine pronouns at work, especially for any client-facing interactions, and said many hurtful things to him.

While Lennox felt grief and disappointment at his parents' reaction, it simply wasn't worth it to him to hide who he was anymore, even though the future was uncertain. While he felt grounded in his decision to resign, it was also a difficult one and a Big Deal, as most people in his family worked at the company for their whole lives.

It was important to Lennox that his next workplace be supportive of his transgender identity, so he researched the companies before applying and spoke about his identity in his cover letter. Armed with his new resume and greater understanding of his natural strengths, skills, and interests, Lennox surprised himself with how quickly he found a new job doing work he enjoyed.

Growing more confident as he felt more like himself, Lennox started learning to play guitar by taking classes at the local arts center and soon had a thriving community of affirming musicians and artists around him. After that, he joined a band.

While Lennox's grief over his estranged family didn't go away, it decreased in intensity, and he has skills to navigate it. Lennox and his sister got closer over the years, and his kinship network relationships are strong. He always has somewhere to go for the holidays.

At the end of our work together, Lennox was enjoying a new job and was part of the LGBTQ-affinity group, advocating for more inclusive policies. This quickly expanded to a variety of speaking and consulting gigs around transgender-affirming practices in business. Lennox reflected on the past few years in our last session. "It wasn't always easy, but I don't regret anything. I'm happier now than I've ever been in my life."

Stretch Your Asking Muscle

Sometimes having big dreams and goals come to fruition is about believing we can take up space and ask for what we want. Many people never bother to ask because they *assume* they'll get a no. As with any request, the trick is being okay with a no. Nobody gets everything they want, and holding the outcome of requests loosely feels way better in the long run.

As part of imagining more, it can be helpful to stretch your asking muscle in a low-stakes environment. This is a silly example, but I recently needed a late, late checkout at a hotel. I went to the front-desk person early in the morning and said, "I know this might make your life difficult, but are you opposed to letting me check out at three p.m. today instead of eleven a.m.?" I explained my late flight and daytime plans, and the employee was able to accommodate my request.

Would I have been heartbroken if she had said no? No.

But it was a good opportunity for me to practice asking confidently for something that would make my life better and easier. Something doesn't have to be life or death to ask for it. You can just want it. Other examples are asking for something extra at a restaurant or asking for a new dish instead of picking things out if they mistakenly give you a meal with something you're allergic to, asking for another color or size of clothing in a dressing room, or asking someone to move over if they are crowding you.

Replacing "I Can't" with "I Wonder How..."

Replacing our immediate thought of "I can't do ______" with "I wonder how I could do ______" is a helpful exercise to get our brains into a more curious and playful place.

Remember January from earlier? We gathered facts to see what it would take to make the audacious goal of moving out of their family's house happen. After running the numbers and looking at options, like moving to a more affordable part of town and finding a trans-friendly roommate to share costs, the goal began to hold a hint of possibility.

Another example that might feel silly but is deeply meaningful to me: I don't cook. Like, categorically. That's a wild thing to say, but it's true. I realized a long time ago that (a) I don't enjoy cooking; (b) I was bad at it since, as a kid who grew up in a motor home on the road, there wasn't much of a kitchen; and (c) standing even twenty to thirty minutes a day to cook made my arthritis hurt so much that I couldn't enjoy the food I cooked anyway. Cooking decreased my ability to do anything else I wanted to do afterwards, including socializing with friends.

Rather than judging myself, I started to wonder: *What are some ways I can live my life and not cook?*

I ran the numbers on how much I spent on groceries and eating out (hint: I spent way more on eating out back then because I hated cooking) and how much more I could afford to add to my budget. By cutting back on eating out and a couple of other items, I had a reasonable but non-extravagant budget for food for little more than my current grocery budget.

I thought of getting the prepackaged meal kits (still too much standing and too many dishes) or batch cooking myself (took too much time on my day off and *way* too much standing), and I looked up personal chefs in Chicago (too expensive). I tried cooking and chopping from a stool (not great logistically) and only eating things I didn't have to cook (turns out you can't live off hummus alone).

So finally, I did what, in retrospect, feels obvious but at the time was like an epiphany. Ready for my wild, ingenious idea? I put out a Craigslist ad. I said exactly what I was looking for and how much I had to spend. The result was a mom who loved cooking and wanted to start a catering company. She started delivering eight fully cooked meals a week to me in bulk. And she was excited to do it! When a partner moved in with me, we negotiated a lower rent split for them in exchange for taking over batch cooking and saving us both money.

Would I starve if none of these were an option anymore? No; I'd figure it out. But it sure is an upgrade in my life that I love and never would have gotten if I hadn't imagined beyond "Deciding I don't want to cook anymore is ridiculous and too expensive." I also wouldn't be the king of cheese boards in my social circle, since that's literally my only contribution to parties. Which, trust me, would be a loss for everyone involved.

TWENTY WAYS TO SKIN A CAT

Getting creative takes practice, so as you get used to replacing "I can't" with "I wonder how...," I invite you to try on one (or all) of these three prompts for practice. Brainstorming ways to meet a goal that include both wild, outrageous options and practical things, with no self-censoring, helps you see possibilities you might not otherwise consider. Push yourself to get all the way to twenty, and enjoy the playfulness of your answers. (Oh, and if anyone has a real way to meet Cate Blanchett, please call me!)

What are twenty ways I could do the following?

- meet my celebrity crush
- throw a house party without needing to put in more than an hour of work
- make my life puppy ready

Play with Goals

Setting and writing down goals is a useful strategy for getting the ball moving in your life—says every self-help book ever. Not rocket science, I know, but for better or worse, it's true. Too often, working toward our dreams sounds something like this:

Let's say Devon has a giant ambition, like having a solo show at an art gallery. They think about it. Daydream about it. Forever. Maybe they paint a few pieces here and there, but they're never satisfied, because the paintings aren't perfect. They decide that getting money to rent a professional art studio is the only way to make the perfect art, and they need to save up (an absurd amount of money) first. They are precious with their dream, knowing this will be their breakout show, so it has to be the best.

Unsurprisingly, Devon's solo show never got off the ground. It languished in dreamland, because there was never a *plan*. Goals, at their best, aren't just hopes—they're a road map toward what we want. The good news is that there are lots of different approaches to goal setting, so you get to figure out what works for you.

The classic is a concrete goal or habit, like a New Year's resolution, but personally, I'm drawn to more project-based goals that activate just the right amount of adrenaline and challenge. Something like "Sign up for a paid burlesque class" instead of "Go to the gym" works for me since it accomplishes moving my body but also feels juuuust out of reach and slightly "scare-citing." Which, again, is a clue for me that I should do it. It's also something I'm likely to do since I've paid money for it and people expect to see me there.

I frequently utilize and also share with clients an adaptation of author and leadership coach Tara Mohr's concept of "leap goals."[2] Leap goals use a tiny jump to get you moving right away, can be finished in a short amount of time (preferably about a couple of weeks but can be up to a couple of months), involve other people, and come from a place of curiosity and not pressure. Leap goals are an experiment. They also typically make you want to puke just a little bit, often bringing up feelings of vulnerability. Think back to your list of things you want. Which of them makes you excited but also maybe throw up a little bit in your mouth? That's probably the one. Remember our example of the art show? A leap goal for Devon might look like one of these:

- painting a piece and putting it in a group show
- sending a piece to an artist friend for feedback
- creating an Instagram artist profile and posting one painting and some videos of them painting
- talking to art friends to see who has access to a cheap gallery space at an off hour (or the upstairs of an antique store with white walls)
- creating a temporary mini studio in the one closet in the house you can fit in with your painting gear

A leap goal pushes you because you are trying something new or sharing something with the world that isn't perfect or super polished. It takes the pressure off of a giant goal by designing a series of experiments to test it out. The goal isn't "success"; it's to learn something new. It's all just spaghetti on the wall.

For January, whom we met earlier in the chapter, leap goals included researching ways to use their writing and editing skills in different careers (some of which paid more than they had imagined), updating their resume and LinkedIn profile, and applying to several positions within a couple of weeks. After a couple of false starts, they found a job that resonated with them and met their financial needs. It wasn't long before they saved enough money, found a queer-affirming roommate, and moved into a new apartment.

While January's life isn't perfect, and they still have challenges, they move with a newfound confidence in who they are and in their ability to do hard things and use their resources to move in the direction of what they desire.

Like January found, self-compassion and a bias to action are essential to successful leap goals. We often hesitate reaching for what we want because we get stuck in our heads. Our brains start spouting off all sorts of trash about why we can't do the thing we want to do. The root of these thoughts often includes feeling unworthy of happiness, thinking we don't have what it takes, and fear of failure.

This voice is our bodyguard. It's a younger part of us trying to protect us from getting hurt again. That's a nice thing for our brains to do in theory, but these protective thoughts are often holding us back instead of protecting us from pain. Remember that discomfort isn't harm, and these goals will ABSOLUTELY make you uncomfortable. But you (very likely) won't die or suffer such dire consequences that you'll never recover.

Turning down the volume on these thoughts is less about vanquishing the evil, mean person in our heads and more about having self-compassion for the younger part of ourselves that is scared and hurt and just wants to keep us safe. We can show love and compassion for that voice while still not letting it drive the bus. Leap goals not only give you practice in showing yourself self-compassion; they also remind you that you can do hard things.

The magic of leap goals is that, often, there is a rush of adrenaline and joy as you move closer to what you desire. It's a taste of what it would be like to live your life really going for what you want. And this feeling is hard to ignore and even harder to shut down once you've felt it. Leap goals help you tap into your yes, as well as your no. Both are excellent outcomes.

Get in Flow

Once you have a goal in mind, the next step is to act, and how we move toward what we want is as important as the action itself. Instead of buying into the idea that we need to hustle, strive, and grind to achieve . . . we can flow.

Flow describes a state of being where the prefrontal cortex, our thinking brain, goes offline a bit.[3] This means your fraudy feelings, self-doubt, and anxiety fade as you immerse yourself in an activity that lights you up. Time seems to lose its meaning, and you experience euphoria, pleasure, alignment, and ease combined with just the right amount of effort. It's a challenge you're choosing.

Now, I know I've been advocating for you to get into your thinking brain for most of this book, and now I'm telling you to get out of it. As with most things, there's nuance here. To oversimplify a complex cognitive and physiological process, flow states synchronize the neuron activity in your brain. That alignment decreases levels of cortisol, the stress hormone, even if you're experiencing things in your body that feel like stress, such as an increased heart rate and breathing more deeply or quicker, and dopamine, the happy hormone, increasing.

In other words, cultivating more flow in your life teaches your brain and body that it's safe and possible to feel simultaneously activated and grounded. It builds your capacity to take on new challenges without overwhelming yourself. As we access more states of flow in any area of our life, whether it be gender, our career, or simply for fun, we are building important neural pathways and body memories that support living with more ease, pleasure, and alignment in a more integrated and sustainable way.

As Mihalyi Csikszentmihalyi, the psychologist who recognized and named "flow," notes, "The best moments in our lives are not the passive, receptive, relaxing times... The best moments usually occur if a person's body or mind is stretched to its limits in a voluntary effort to accomplish something difficult and worthwhile."[4]

What makes up a "limit" in this case is a challenge that requires concentration and attention but is not so difficult that it overwhelms us. It brings to mind the montages of the '80s inspirational movies of the story's hero learning to dance, do karate, or ice-skate. It's lots of shots of them waking up early, falling down, messing up, and then getting up to do it all over again until you see them finally master whatever challenge they're faced with (and nail the triple lutz or run-and-catch dance move).

I was curious about the nuances of applying principles of flow with transgender and non-binary folks, both in the context of goals outside of gender exploration and how gender exploration and transition impacted someone's ability to access flow. So I called up my friend Dr. Julia Colangelo, who has studied and taught flow extensively (and has been pivotal in helping me deepen my understanding of it personally).[5] Julia and I got nerdy about applying these concepts to gender freedom. What we know is that there are two truths:

First, flow is often blocked by gender dysphoria. As Julia told me, "If you're experiencing self-doubt that leads to misalignment with any aspect of your true identity, it will be more challenging to enter a flow state because you'll be spending excessive time and energy focused outside of your flow, and more in fear." But, hopefully and paradoxically, we can also decrease gender dysphoria by being in flow. As we spoke about this second truth, Julia explained to me that when we're ready to embrace our authentic self, intentionally "activating a flow state positions you to enjoy the exploration and process, therefore leading to a decrease in inhibition and fear responses. Not only will you honor yourself throughout the process, but flow will allow you to radically trust yourself because you're IN the process not just moving through the motions."

I've seen this moment of magic happen for my clients when they activate flow in an area of their life not related to gender—like surfing or making art. January, whom we've been following throughout this chapter, created space for themselves to consistently write science fiction. Writing lit January up, helping them feel more confident, calm, present, accomplished, and creatively fulfilled.

These flow states and the positive feelings attached to them tend to overflow into other areas of their life, decreasing mental health symptoms and fear while increasing euphoria, curiosity, and self-trust.

Applied directly to gender exploration and transition itself, experiences of flow while actively exploring gender can feel wildly good. For example, dressing in gender-affirming clothes and going dancing with some friends or going surfing while presenting how you like could activate flow because (1) it's challenging if you haven't done it much or before, and (2) it brings you enjoyment you can get lost in. When you notice yourself able to get lost in something you love *while also* being more authentically you, it creates magic.

This might leave you with questions about where to start in this classic chicken-and-egg scenario. But the good news is that it doesn't matter where you start as long as you start somewhere. This is what you're creating space for: flow, ease, pleasure, alignment. Practicing being in flow with activities that are fun or pleasurable is a great way to build that muscle. Likewise, finding flow outside of your exploration of gender will make you hungry for more flow in the rest of your life. It reminds you of why you are going to the trouble of exploring or transitioning your gender in the first place—to live your life! Like we've talked about, gender can take up a ton of brain space. My goal for you is to not think about gender so much *so that* you have brain space for all the other amazing things in your life that make you, you.

I often hear transgender/non-binary folks express they are scared to take up space in their own lives. They feel like simply asking others to respect their identity is a burden and they can't possibly expect or ask for more. This is a load of crap.

It's okay to take up space, create room for growth and change, and have a life that leaves you feeling lit up and alive. This is your invitation for a bigger, bolder, more joy-filled, self-actualized version of you to keep taking tiny steps forward, until one day you look up and you're somewhere you never could have imagined. And loving it.

You deserve it.

Imagine more. Put passion and energy into the things you care about, regardless of the outcome. Dare to do things that scare you. Live. Put one dirty foot in front of the other.

Let's do the thing.

MAKING A BIG GOAL LESS SCARY THROUGH FLOW

Julia walked me through simple steps to help you activate a flow state while working toward big goals. I invite you to pull an idea from your letter from your future self and try this exercise with me. I've modeled my answers here to give you an idea, but adapt this and make it your own.

- *Identify one activity you enjoy or believe you would enjoy.* For me, I had a dream of learning to ride a motorcycle.
- *Identify a challenge within that activity.* Real obvious in this example—I had never driven anything beyond a 50 cc moped and needed to take a safety class to learn how to safely drive a motorcycle.
- *Devote time to the activity and enhancing skill.* Dr. Colangelo recommends from thirty to ninety minutes up to three hours. Schedule this into your calendar as an appointment and take it seriously. For me, this meant committing several days to motorcycle classes and prep for the DMV motorcycle test.
- *Set yourself up for success.* This might look like setting a timer and making sure your environment is as calm and conducive to the task at hand as possible. In this example, it meant making sure I had coffee (lots of coffee), water, snacks, and hand warmers.
- *Enjoy it!* This seems obvious, but make efforts to be present and engaged in whatever you're doing. Turn off distractions and notice what it feels like to be doing this activity that you love. For me, this looked like talking back to my brain trash that said I looked

silly. Because who cares? I'm driving a fucking motorcycle, which automatically makes me a badass.

- *Don't force it.* Look, we all have off days. If you struggle to enter a flow state, be kind to yourself. Take a break or take care of what's distracting you and come back. You can also choose to move on and try again on a different day.
- *Track it.* Get curious about what worked and what didn't in your flow experiment. Notice what was distracting and what you might need to more easily get to a flow state next time.
- *Repeat and refine.* Do the thing again. Just keep swimming. Fall off your bike? Cool. Pick it up and get back on it.

CHAPTER 12

Curate Kinship

The closest I come to church these days is walking through a redwood forest. These mammoth, ancient trees hold more sacred presence for me than any guru. Like standing beside an ocean or staring up at the Milky Way, I find the only logical response is quiet reverence and marveling at the miracle of their colossal size. Or scream-crying. Knowing the cathedral of impossibly tall trees is big enough to hold it all.

Giant sequoias have widespread, shallow roots that intertwine and fuse together with the roots of the trees around them, clustering around a mother tree in a "fairy circle." This network is the source of their colossal strength and resiliency against nature and time. Humans, like redwood trees, intertwine our roots to create the networks of immense strength that allow us to thrive, and the fairy circles we build around ourselves are called kinship.

Kinship is line and lineage, blood and bond, clan and community, ancestor and ancestry, family and folks, house and home. A kinship network is interdependence at its finest, creating grounded, practical, and intimate connections that are nourishing to everyone.

In chapter 10, I invited you to think about intimacy as a mycelium network—vast, deeply nourishing, and a resource that gets stronger and more abundant as we allow ourselves to go deep with others. Those moments of connection, both short-term and long-term, fill our cups, but intimacy and care, given over time, are how we build our kinship network. In other words, the difference between intimacy and kinship is that kinship includes *commitment*—commitment to interweave your lives in some way, to be steady, to be consistent, to show care and love, and to have each other's back in both practical and emotional ways.

Kinship is claiming someone as your family.

It's the people who show up with food when you're sick or sad, who buy a bottle of champagne when you pass the big test (or get a divorce), who hold your hand when you get nervous the first time you leave the house in clothing that feels like magic to you.

It's a sense of belonging with and to a constellation of others.

No one person will have the capacity to meet your needs 100 percent of the time. But knowing your loved one will show up reliably to the best of their ability and prioritize their commitments to you makes you feel more secure in the natural ebbs and flows of relationships. The beauty of a deep and wide kinship network is that you can spread out support among many people.

Too often, when we think about kinship, we think of the roots we share with our biological family. However, many cultures organize their primary source of interconnectedness and support around networks other than biological family members, and so I'm going to invite you to think bigger.[1]

As an adopted kid (and for most of my adult life), I didn't have any blood relatives, only legal ones. With blood taken out of the equation, "family" meant something different to me from a young age. I had no deep roots, so for me, family was always about choice: Their choice to adopt me and offer me a home. And my choice to not rely on my adoptive family after I realized they weren't able to provide the intimacy, nurturing, and shared lives that true kinship requires. While we have no control over who our given family is, whether through blood or adoption, we do have control over who we choose to do life with.

This is the vision of family I have for you—a family of choice, of deep love, and of mutual commitment—and it's what this chapter is all about.

In this chapter, we're going to talk about finding your kin, a (likely small) group of people who are your family—whether they are blood related to you or not. You might have kin in your life already you haven't named as such. Or maybe you're just beginning to plant seeds of kinship. Wherever you are in your journey, I want you to know that you are right on time. It's never too late.

Finding and cultivating a kinship network that has your back, where you are welcomed and celebrated for who you are, creates resiliency and a soft place to land when the world is not always kind. You deserve that, and intertwining your roots with the people in your life who truly see you will keep you upright for the long haul, come what may.

KINSHIP AND MENTAL HEALTH: THE NERDY STUFF

One reason curating a kinship network is vital is because it provides social support—something public health nerds call a "social determinant of health" for transgender/non-binary folks. Social determinants of health are the environmental, social, and cultural conditions that affect our physical and mental health and quality of life, both positively and negatively.[2] When folks don't have social support, they tend to use avoidant, bury-your-head-in-the-sand coping strategies. But when they do, folks tend to use more active coping strategies and, as a result, feel less anxious and depressed.[3]

A playful, pleasurable gender exploration is more possible when you have a kinship network because it provides significant support for your general mental health. Social support even helps you tap into the thinking part of your brain you need to thrive even when faced with challenges. So go find your people—doctor's orders.

Community and Connection

Often when we think about community in the context of our identities as queer or transgender, we think of the transgender community or the LGBTQ+ community as our de facto family.

And as you probably already know, being in a large group of queer and trans people *can* feel pretty magical. From dyke marches to sweaty, packed dance floors, to the mythical lesbian bar, to the Philadelphia Trans Wellness Conference, the freedom and joy we experience in these settings is often palpable. And hot damn are we cute! As a newly out queer person, and later as a newly out non-binary person, the idea of automatically having a community of queer and trans people who accepted and loved me for me felt healing. I love being in these spaces, and they are frequently deeply nourishing to me.

Which is why it shook me when I realized the LGBTQ+ community is made up of humans and not all of them are my people or my kin. And far from being a utopia of love, some folks are just as abusive and toxic as the fundamentalist Christian community I grew up in.

In short, I learned there is no such thing as "the transgender community."

Let me explain what I mean before you throw this book against the wall.

While the transgender community is useful as an organizing principle to talk about a large group of humans who do not currently have equal protections and rights and access to life-saving mental and medical healthcare, it's not always helpful to think of the transgender community as a monolith.

There is no transgender community, because transgender and non-binary folks are diverse, holding different intersectional identities, life experiences, values, beliefs, and norms. Like any large group of people who share a common identity, there will be spaces and people whom you resonate with and those with whom you don't. There will be people who see you for who you are and love it and those who don't. If you're struggling to feel connected to the transgender community, you're not alone.

Here's why this is important: If your sense of belonging and worth is based on any one defined community giving you a stamp of approval, or being liked by everyone in it all the time, you've set yourself up to have your worth determined by an amorphous group of people, often strangers or acquaintances.

In the same way your validity as a transgender or non-binary person is not determined by being gendered correctly by a grocery store clerk, your lovability and belonging are not determined by being universally adored by the transgender community.

Now, obviously, our brains know it's unreasonable to want to be liked by everyone all the time. But when our brains go into anxiety and self-doubt mode, it's a quick spiral into no-one/everyone/always/never thoughts territory. Especially when you're coming from a family that isn't supportive and you're in a vulnerable place of gender exploration or transition, feeling rejected or unseen by the community that is supposed to welcome you with open arms can feel like death, a threat to your very survival.

Our need to belong is hardwired into us. Ultimately, it's a good thing. The deep longing to belong is what motivates us to cultivate our roots and kinship network. However, we often look for belonging without recognizing what community actually is.

I believe there is no community without kinship—by which I mean real intimacy, connection, and commitment. The people who are *your* people don't blow smoke up your ass while still being your biggest fan. They hold you accountable when you (inevitably) make mistakes, but they do so with compassion and care, knowing who you are and what you value. They tell you the truth while not treating you as disposable or being abusive. There is a commitment to repair after conflict, knowing that this is what creates trust, intimacy, and secure attachment. They are able to hold nuance while compassionately challenging you to grow.

In short, they love you.

ON ACCOUNTABILITY AND DISPOSABILITY

It's outside the scope of this book to dig deep into the nuanced topics of accountability and disposability, nor do I think I'm the right person to lead that conversation. As I've developed my own understanding, integrity, and values around these topics, a few resources have been invaluable to me.

I recommend picking up *We Will Not Cancel Us* by adrienne maree brown, *I Hope We Choose Love* by Kai Cheng Thom, and *Care Work: Dreaming Disability Justice* by Leah Lakshmi Piepzna-Samarasinha, in particular the chapter "Protect Your Heart," if you'd like to explore these topics further.

Navigating Given Family Relationships

When you begin to assess who you want to include in your kinship network, a starting point for lots of folks is figuring out how to navigate less-than-perfect given family connections. There are many families out there who wholeheartedly accept and love their transgender/non-binary family members, use new pronouns and names consistently, and celebrate the changes. Yet for many transgender/non-binary folks, given family can be a painful topic. If members of the family you grew up with aren't providing you with the roots you need to thrive, you're not alone. Navigating relationships with given family is rarely straightforward.

In chapter 6, I talked about coming out to family, authenticity, expectations, and boundaries. Now it's time to talk about boundaries for the long haul. For many who are exploring our gender, there can sometimes be a quick cry of "Cut them off!" when given family members are not immediately supportive of an evolving gender identity or expression.

If this is the right choice for your mental health and safety, I fully support it.

But if, like me, you don't have the desire to cut off all family members completely, or you're not able to due to other factors like children, financial ties, or overlapping lives, there are a few questions you'll need to ask yourself.

The first questions in navigating complex family relationships are "What do I want out of this relationship?" and "Are they willing and able to meet my needs most of the time?" Be honest. Acknowledging what sort of connection and support you would ideally like from your family can break your heart open, especially if your answer to the second question is no. Sometimes you have to acknowledge that wanting to feel seen and supported by your given family is a gravity problem. If you're looking for validation where it's not possible to get it, you're setting yourself up for disappointment. It's like trying to buy eggs at a hardware store: Look all you want, but you're in the wrong place for what you need.

Give yourself space for all the feels that come up. Cry, rage, scream, be sad. Feel the loss and let it move through you. Because that's the way to freedom.

The next question is "What types of connection do I want that I can reasonably expect from this relationship?" I've accepted that the majority of my given family will never be able to truly know me or connect with me in the way I would like. While that reality hurts, it also creates space for me to make different choices about boundaries and honestly assess what sorts of interactions I have capacity for.

When answering this question about unsupportive family members, consider what types of connection are still available to you that feel good, or at least okay.

For example, I can still connect with my mother about her garden, her woodworking, and updates on other family members. She will still express care if I'm sick. This is tempered by a lack of curiosity or questions about my life, yet these small points of connection can be meaningful.

TRYING OR TRANSPHOBIC?

While no one is perfect, there is a tangible difference between a family member who is trying to support you and fumbling over language and a family member who is being blatantly transphobic.

For family members who are doing their best to support you but making hurtful mistakes along the way, your boundaries are likely going to look different than for a family member who is intentionally rejecting your transgender/non-binary identity.

For supportive-but-fumbling family members, connection that feels possible might be talking to them about what is hurtful and asking them to do better. Or it could be using strategic gender expression from chapter 6 to share about some aspects of your gender identity and expression, but not others. It might look like not talking much at all but doing things together that feel affirming and connecting. You get to figure out what feels the best to you.

The final question is "What do you need to feel *good enough* in a space with your family?" Maybe it's not being belittled or yelled at and engaging in only small talk. Maybe it's a sincere apology and behavior change if they call you by the wrong name and pronouns. Maybe it's a time limit on visits or calls. Maybe it's knowing you have an escape route if you need it.

You have permission to leave any situation that feels painful or emotionally unsafe to you. You don't have to engage in a conversation that's hurtful. You don't owe anyone an explanation. And your boundaries and capacity to engage can shift and change over time.

You get to just live. As you. Unapologetically.

Sometimes You Just Have to Laugh about It

My family has said some ridiculous shit to me over the years about my queer identity (and beyond). Things that were horrendous and hurtful, but also... what?! At some point, you just have to laugh at the absurdity of it. As I accepted they would continue to do and say homophobic and transphobic and wild right-wing things, I discovered a dark humor as a coping skill.

When my aunt sent my newly out cousin a letter with the phrase "The world belongs to Satan," I made a T-shirt out of the phrase with a triumphant (and very queer) Satan.

Eventually, I made a bingo card for all the strange and fucked-up things typically said or done when I visit my family. When I hit a bingo, I buy myself a treat. Some squares have included these:

- no one asking me a question about my life all day
- mentioning my tattoos
- "Global Warming? Look how cold it is!"
- monologuing about the "end times" (this one's the freebie)

These little secret pleasures add elements of gamification and make challenging interactions just a little more fun.

The Joy of Being a Disappointment

When I embraced being a disappointment to my parents and other family members, I found a lot of freedom. The things I love most about myself are the things they disdain—my curious mind and critical thinking, my education, my queer and trans identity, my work, my choice to end my marriage, my embrace of living outside the lines, my cultivation of many kinds of pleasure, and my refusal to live a life that feels small for the sake of others. I'm proud of myself for clawing my way out of my upbringing and designing a life that makes me feel free and authentic. They aren't. They never will be. And they don't have to. Regardless of what they think, I'm still free. Letting go of the need for my given family to celebrate who I am gives me more space to cultivate a kinship network that does. And loudly.

Identifying Your Kin

The people that make up my kin have changed over the years, but I can say with confidence I have folks I've intertwined roots with. For me, it's not the people who watched me grow up but the people who've watched me grow into myself and have consistently had my back whom I consider my family.

Building that kind of trust and commitment with people can take a long time—sometimes years or decades. Sometimes the initial gut "You!" happens very quickly, but even then, trust takes time. Building a kinship network is about playing the long game and investing your time, energy, and attention into curating the life, and kin, you want for yourself.

I can't tell you who to choose as your kin, because each person is unique in their kinship needs. However, anyone worth having will share some common characteristics:

- They see and validate you for who you are.
- They want you to live your best, freest, most pleasurable life.
- They're trustworthy.
- They're consistent (this doesn't mean available 100 percent of the time, but reasonably consistent).
- They express care and nurturing for you.
- They have your back.

Your chosen family relationships are also intimate relationships, though (like we talked about in chapter 10) there are many ways that people build, express, and prioritize intimacy. The great thing about building your kinship network thoughtfully and intentionally is that you get to design it for what you need and want. What kinds of intimacy are the most important to you? For example, emotional intimacy is essential in my kinship network, but recreational and creative intimacy might be essential in yours. I love to spend long hours talking about... everything. Whereas you might want to go rock climbing for hours and not talk about your feelings a ton.

Keep in mind that all of these characteristics go both ways. Being kin is a mutual relationship. So, get ready to show up for your people.

Embrace the Imperfect

Support might come in unexpected places if you give people a chance to build trust with you. There are really wonderful people who may not get the lingo perfectly but are still supportive of you to the best of their ability. It's about progress, not perfection.

I once stood in a circle of Sicilians loudly singing "Going to the chapel and we're gonna get maaarriiied" as we celebrated one of my best friend's engagement to her girlfriend with her family. It was midnight and the celebration was going strong. I've spent many holidays with this family and have never felt less than wholeheartedly welcome. Running into the kitchen for a refill of (the abundant) champagne, I overheard my friend's dad ask something about me, referring to me as "she." He immediately got popped in the arm by my friend's mom: "Them!" He gave a huge shrug and said, "I didn't know!" She said, "Well, now you do!" My friend's dad immediately came around and gave me a big hug and said he was so happy I was there and I was family. I believed him.

An older Sicilian man who plays bocce ball on the weekends with friends named Vinny and Luigi was not at the top of my list of potential supports. But he had my back. He treated me like family. And I felt cared for by him, even if he struggled to get my pronouns right sometimes. He was part of my kinship network.

Don't Forget Multigenerational Relationships

We often get caught in a rut of only having friends roughly the same age as us. Yet multigenerational relationships are often rich and beautiful things. Some of my close friends are ten to twenty years older than me or at least a few years younger. When we restrict our kinship networks to those in the same generation, we cut off a well of potential connections. Our given families don't include just one generation, and neither should our chosen ones.

Look Right in Front of You

Sometimes we have people who are potential kin right in front of us if we let them in. My first roommate after my divorce was a transfemme person named Dylan. At the time, she was exploring her identity and I was a baby queer who said many well-intentioned but cringeworthy things in an effort to be supportive. She was brilliantly creative and a true friend while I was fumbling through tremendous personal change and growth. We lived together for years in our tiny place in a hipster neighborhood of Chicago, and it was never boring. I'd come home to things like a sign taped to our bathroom door that said, "Cat inside. His name's Bubba," or a giant spider trapped under a glass in the living room (why?!).

Dylan set up a cam studio in her bedroom, which made for fun stories over coffee. For Christmas one year, she gave me this tiny little plaque she found at a thrift store. It said, "We need each other." And we did. As roommates and friends, Dylan and I supported each other while we were both flailing our way through figuring out our identities and learning to express them to the world.

Making Moves

Ever meet those people who can make friends at the grocery store? Not all of us are wild extroverts with the ability to talk to a wall, but there are some lessons to be learned here.

Pay attention when your pupils dilate, you feel a pull on your heart, or your brain goes, "Oh, what's that?" Whether you're reacting to a person, art, ideas, activity, or space, these are important clues to who and where your people might be. And pay special attention to people that make you go, "YOU!"

I take friend crushes seriously. Many of my kin today are people I felt viscerally drawn to. Some were friend-love at first sight. And most are kind of random.

The handful of people from my sex therapy cohort that I spotted on the first day and whose brains I fell in love with when they got sassy with a teacher? One of them flew two countries over to see me. The person who walked into an election "party" in 2016 with thick-rimmed glasses and sublime presence? She helped me out when I needed an emergency place to stay. The audience member of a professional seminar with blue eyes that made me wet? They contributed to this book. The Sicilian at a friend's house who makes perfect homemade pasta and can talk ad nauseam about our favorite books? I'm her baby's godparent. The friend of a friend who made my brain come alive on a Chicago rooftop during a house party? They send me texts of symphonies saying that's how I make them feel after we talk for hours over breakfast. The Southerner who likes the same bluegrass bands as me? We live together. Or the tiny human that I hated for a while because we were too alike and dated all the same people? Gives me emergency pizza and expertly mixed cocktails and always shows up with champagne to celebrate me.

I have clients who find their people at gyms, at school, in a forum of a niche sci-fi TV show, while playing D&D, in support groups, in art classes, and at shows. You never know where you might find someone who will later become kin. No one is everyone's flavor, but everyone is someone's flavor. Still at a loss? Here are a few more places you can look for potential kinship relationships:

Meet friends of friends. It's cliché, sure, but they're genuinely a great place to start. If you have a friend or acquaintance you think is magic, chances are they also have good taste in friends. Meet them. It becomes a snowball as you expand your network organically from the people you already consider to be kin.

Play the long game. When I notice folks who have great things to say in various online groups, I message them. That fairy witch healer I found online? I popped into their inbox for *years* before we started spending Thanksgiving dinners together. The artists with work that speaks to me? I keep showing up at their shows. The ones who dance with their whole soul? I keep dancing with them. Building strong and connected friendships takes patience, consistency, and a genuine interest in a mutually supportive relationship.

Take time to build trust. Trust is built, and it takes time. We don't usually start out a trusting relationship with a stranger, even if we are drawn to them. We may not be 100 percent certain that someone will support us, and that can feel scary and dangerous (and it sometimes is), but we also have the ability to look for context clues about someone's values and disclose small amounts of information to see how they respond (e.g., "I was watching *Pose* the other day and..."). It's a gift for you to share more of yourself with someone. Make sure they're worthy of it.

NO, RAE, SERIOUSLY—I LIVE IN A RURAL AREA...

I get it. Living in a rural area with few in-person resources available and a general lack of affirming people and spaces is challenging to say the least. First, queers and trans folks are everywhere, so the assumption that there's no one else around who shares your experience is likely not as much of a given as you imagine. That said, it can be hard to find folks. I encourage my clients in rural areas to check out online support options and explore things like conferences and conventions around their interests or transgender- or non-binary-specific spaces if they have the ability to travel.

I recognize this is a privileged statement, but one of the best decisions I made in my life was moving from Texas to Chicago. While there are queer and transgender folks in Texas (obviously), I chose to design a life in a city where I feel comfortable existing the majority of the time. That choice isn't for everyone, but if you have the ability to explore living somewhere dramatically different, it's always an option.

Use the Interwebs

The internet is a horrible, magical place. For all the issues with our current social media platforms, they remain a resource to meet and connect with new people. For example, Facebook has many groups for transgender and non-binary folks to connect with each other, and Instagram can lead you down a rabbit hole of both influencers that fill your feed with affirming content and "everyday" users who might be available to connect.

If you're craving a more structured way to get to know new friends, there are many support groups being offered online that are available for folks across state lines. Additionally, dating apps can be a great way to meet new friends! Simply put what you're looking for on your profile. Many people on the apps are open to connecting in a variety of ways beyond sexual and romantic, and some apps even have filters for those looking for friends.

Use Your Resources

LGBTQ+ centers often have support groups and social events. Art centers run classes. Comic book shops host games. Local coffee shops have events posted. Have friends that are always doing cool things? Ask them where they find the events. Or better yet, ask to go with them next time. Have a car? Drive to another city. Figure out what resources you do have at your disposal and make the most of them.

Ask for What You Want

Figuring out how to make the first move when you want to develop or deepen a relationship can feel daunting and vulnerable.

Here's a wild concept: Ask for what you want and state your intentions clearly. Be honest. Say what you want. People aren't used to others being so up-front, but it's often welcome and refreshing. After you have a chance to get to know someone a little, saying something like, "I've really enjoyed talking to you. I'm trying to build my friend network and

I think you're great and would love to hang out sometime. Would you be into that?" can be a great and easy way to start a friendship.

I can't tell you how many wonderful connections and relationships I have from simply sending a message saying, "Hi, I think the work you're doing is really cool. [Here's what resonates with me and how it's connected to my experience.] Also, I'd love to have a quick coffee date if you ever have time and would like to connect. No worries either way. Keep it up and let me know if there's ever any way I can support you."

Compliments go a long way. Complimenting someone's style, book choice, dancing, art, music, or personality from a place of genuine admiration for someone feels really great and can open the door for more conversation. At worst, it might make someone's day.*

When Your Brain Gets in the Way

Finding and cultivating a strong kinship network is difficult for some transgender/non-binary folks, depending on what resources are available.

When you live in a geographic area that is more conservative or rural or have other challenges (like neurodivergence or a disability or lack of transportation), the pool of potential kin often gets smaller—it's true. Yet sometimes our brain decides something is impossible for us a little too quickly. Okay, a *lot* too quickly.

When I'm working with transgender/non-binary clients, I hear things along these lines:

My transgender/non-binary identity is a burden, and I don't want to bother people with it.

Making friends as an adult is too hard. It's going to be too awkward.

---

* A friendly caution about body-based compliments: For trans folks, this can be fraught. And for others, it might feel inappropriate or off-putting. There are many other things to compliment someone on other than their body. If you do want to compliment someone's body, asking, "Can I give you a compliment about your body?" can be a helpful consent strategy. Above all, don't be creepy.

The queer and transgender community won't accept my non-binary identity because I'm not "trans enough."
I live in a rural town and there is no way that I can ever get social support, and I'm doomed to feel alone forever.
Online friends aren't real friends.
Oh, they wouldn't want to be friends with me.
I don't belong here.

These thoughts, or a version of them, are completely normal and extremely common. Limiting beliefs come from insecurity and wounds we carry with us from previous experiences. They exist to keep us safe. However, they often hold us back from the things we really desire or need out of fear of disappointment.

At the core of these beliefs is often "If I'm not one hundred percent certain this person will accept and love me, I can't take the risk to build trust with them."

Sometimes just naming these thoughts and beliefs and labeling them as limiting can help turn down the volume, but let me help take away some of the pressure. There are some people in the world who think I'm annoying, awkward, too aggressive, too quiet, closed off, boring, too serious, disingenuous, and that I lack empathy, to name a few. And these aren't even the folks who think I'm going to hell! To top it off, I grew up super isolated from pop culture for the '90s and early 2000s and was homeschooled in high school, so my cultural-reference game is abysmal. People start bantering with me and I freeze like a deer in the headlights and respond with brilliant repartee like, "Haha. Yeah..."

Yet the people in my kinship network (and many colleagues and clients) describe me as warm, kind, loving, attuned, present, authentic, compassionate, gentle, caring, badass, and smart. Some even think I'm funny. All of them think I'm magic. And I have a folder on my computer labeled "Nice Things" full of compliments from friends, clients, and colleagues to prove it to myself on days I struggle to believe it.

I've been in rooms with people I assumed were too fancy/popular/

smart/cool/successful to connect with me, where I've felt like a complete imposter for even stepping inside. A lot of those people are now my friends or colleagues. I've also had folks express they thought I was too fancy/popular/smart/cool/successful to want to connect with them. To which I reactively laughed in their face at the utter absurdity of thinking I was cool and popular, much less not interested in connecting.

While it's true that there will be people who dislike you or just don't resonate with you, there are also people out there who will think you're amazing. But a surefire way never to meet them is to let a fear of rejection keep you from putting yourself out there. Like all things in this book, I encourage you to take tiny steps that feel slightly challenging to you but not so challenging that you freeze. As you do this, you'll begin to build your confidence and resiliency, no matter what the outcome of those tiny steps. You're doing a hard thing! And that's pretty amazing.

I'm not going to quote Eleanor Roosevelt or Maya Angelou on belonging, though both have good things to say. I'm just going to say this: Feeling like you don't belong is sometimes about a deep desire to belong. Far from being a signal that you don't belong, it might be an indicator that something about this space or these people is important to you and worth being curious about.

This can sometimes come up for trans and non-binary folks who want to feel a sense of belonging in particular LGBTQ+ spaces. Remember that the LGBTQ+ community isn't a monolith, and neither are identity categories or those within them.

For example, I've had transmasculine clients who felt they didn't belong in spaces predominated by cisgender gay men. The core of this belief is a desire to feel seen in their identity as a gay man and an assumption that cisgender gay men will not view them as a "real" man. They discovered there were, unfortunately, some spaces where they didn't feel welcome and other spaces with cisgender gay men who welcomed them with open arms and saw them for who they are. They belonged in all of those spaces; they only found their kin in one of them. The validity of your identity isn't determined by inclusion in a "scene" of any kind or being universally liked or seen. It comes from you. And your kinship network can help remind you of who you are on the days when it feels hard.

The important question isn't "How do I avoid rejection?" but "How do I want to handle rejection?" Knowing how you will take care of yourself when (yes, *when*) you experience disappointment or hurt while building your kinship network gives you confidence and a feeling of agency for whatever comes your way. Knowing that the world is big and there are people out there who will see, accept, and love you for you helps ground you.

Finding your people is a lifelong journey. But once you have them, those people become a lifelong joy.

You might have kin in your life already or maybe you're just beginning to plant seeds of kinship. Wherever you are in your journey, I want you to know that you are right on time. It's never too late.

Finding and cultivating a kinship network that has your back—where you are seen, welcomed, and celebrated for who you are—and that creates resiliency and a soft place to land when the world is not always kind is what you deserve.

Our kinship roots can provide just as much strength as sequoias. Find your fairy circle, letting your roots go deep in intimacy and wide in kinship, intertwining them with the people in your life who truly see you and can keep you upright for the long haul, whatever may come.

ARE YOU MY PEOPLE?

If you want to find your people, these questions can help.

- When you think about your current kinship relationships or the kinship relationships you want to curate, what thoughts, feelings, and memories come to mind?
- Who are the people you have soundly in your corner already?
- Who are the people that you feel the most like yourself around?

- Who do you already have in your life that thinks you're magic? How can you build a relationship with them more intentionally?
- Who do you think is magic that you've been afraid to approach or go deeper with? Are you holding yourself back from them because of any limiting beliefs?
- Where have you found your people before?
- What art, ideas, activities, or spaces make you light up? How can you build relationships with folks in these spaces?
- Who are your "potentials"? These are people who have some promise for being supportive, but you need to put in the time and effort to build trust.
- What are your resources outside of your geographic area (e.g., online groups, conferences and conventions, friends who live far away, your favorite authors, artists, or musicians), and how can you use these resources more intentionally?

CHAPTER 13

Cultivate Pride

People often think of Pride as a once-a-year celebration with lots of rainbows, glitter, and jockstraps. But real pride isn't a rainbow float or a parade.

Pride is a reflection of how you talk to yourself, how you treat yourself, and the daily actions you take affirming your identity and your boundaries. So many people live their lives on autopilot, never considering that the "manual" we've been given for life is made-up. We can follow it, edit it, or burn it with the vigor of a banned-book bonfire.

We get to choose how we narrate our story.

We get to say who we are.

We get to be proud of who we are.

And personally, I wouldn't trade being outrageously queer and trans and me for anything in the world.

Understanding this deeper meaning of pride is part of building a life of gender freedom and possibility. In this chapter, we'll explore the idea of pride—for ourselves as individuals and as a broader community. We'll discuss pride not only as a feeling, but as taking up space, as a muscle we can build, as owning our story, and as a way to connect to both our own freedom and the liberation of others. After all, in order to fully lean into the most authentic expression of ourselves, we first have to believe in our own dignity and celebrate our right to thrive.

Pride Is Taking up Space

Most transgender/non-binary folks I know are sick and tired of being "resilient."

It's exhausting to feel like you need to be strong all the time.

But the definition of "resilience" is not brute emotional strength in the face of adversity, white-knuckling it through life. It's a natural process of returning to your original state after being compressed, bent, or stretched.

Pride and resilience feed each other, creating a positive feedback loop of making it through hard things and feeling more grounded, steady, and joyful in who you are on the other side of them.

Here's what I want you to know right now: Resilience is not stepping into something new; it's returning. Coming home to the person we are and taking up the space we're meant to take up.

If you take all the stars in our galaxy and compress them, removing all the space between them and shoving them into a tiny box, they would fit into a container roughly the size of the planet Neptune. For scale, this is like taking something the size of a car and squeezing the life out of it until it's the size of a virus in your cells.

You are a galaxy masquerading as a planet.

And you aren't doing yourself or anyone else any favors by not taking up the space you're meant to. Give yourself room to breathe and stretch and exist at the scale of infinity. Pride helps you remember the person you are so you can reflect it back to others. I want your colors to paint the night sky so someone like me can sit on a fence on a Texas ranch, stare up at you awestruck, and know I belong in the world.

DEFINE YOUR SPACE

These small exercises throughout the chapter are meant to be an opening into ways you can connect with both personal and collective pride. Think about them, journal about them, talk about them—whatever feels right to you.

- How have you been compressed, bent, or stretched?
- What is your natural form? (*Hint: Some folks answer this literally, and others create a beautiful metaphor that speaks to them. E.g., If you were a galaxy, what would you look like?*)

Pride Is a Muscle

One dictionary defines "pride" as "a high . . . opinion of one's own dignity, importance . . . whether as cherished in the mind or displayed in bearing, conduct, etc."[1] And while "cherished in the mind" is a strange, Victorian-like phrase, I like it. It feels like a quiet dignity, a deep internal sense of knowing, accepting, and loving who you are.

Feeling pride in yourself and your identity doesn't happen overnight or accidently. Pride is something we cultivate. It's a conscious process of choosing to believe you are important, valid, and worthy just as you are today. It's being you, with intention, and without regard for others' opinions of who you should be. As an ex-Christian, I had to do a lot of unlearning to feel pride in my queer identity. I read and talked to lots of people and sought out alternative voices both within and without religion during parts of my journey. Getting to the place I am now, where I give pretty much zero fucks about what any non-queer- or non-trans-affirming person thinks of me, was the result of years of intentional effort.

Sometimes pride is acting like you are proud of who you are even if you can't quite feel it yet. Like building any muscle, there will be days when you feel on top of the world and powerful and days when you are exhausted, frustrated, and don't feel like your effort is getting you anywhere. You're building muscle on both kinds of days.

Also, it's okay to take rest days and be a lump. Rest is when your muscles alchemize.

PRACTICE PRIDE

- How do you talk to yourself now? How do you want to talk to yourself? What tiny steps can you take to bridge the gap today?
- How would you treat yourself if you believed that you are important, valid, worthy, and lovable? If you struggle to believe those things, what tiny steps can you take to bridge the gap today?

- What tiny steps can you take daily to affirm your identity and boundaries?
- How can you remind yourself each day that you are important, valid, worthy, and lovable?
- How will you rest?

Pride Is Owning Your Story

How we talk to and about ourselves and our story is important. Language constructs our reality, and if you let them, other people will try to construct it for you. At their worst, they will capture a picture of you at your lowest moment and make it all you are. They will take every incredible choice you've made to be your authentic, lit-up self and color it with their own unresolved trauma, fear, ignorance, and worldview. Well-meaning people will sometimes construct a happy story, one where you are the hero—which may seem kind, but even so, it's just not your story.

We often internalize the stories other people tell about us as our own stories. But as author Lidia Yuknavitch says, "I am not the story you make of me."[2]

The story of Cinderella from the stepmother's perspective is about an ungrateful, selfish, lazy stepdaughter who abandoned her family to marry rich. Did I mention Cinderella stole her stepsister's would-be husband? Bitch.

The story of Frankenstein from the villagers' perspective is how local heroes killed an evil, murderous monster.

The story of the Terminator from the robot's perspective is a story of trying to save their species from extinction.

See how quickly perspective shifts everything?

The story of who I am from my family's perspective characterizes me as a selfish, perverted, ungrateful, "worldly" daughter who chooses to not engage with family very much even though all they've ever done is love me. I'm bad. I'm a heathen and going to hell (unless I repent of my wicked ways).

Many folks who cared about me when I was in college had a story about me as a wife in a heterosexual marriage who worked with kids at a church and was going to be a therapist one day. There's nothing wrong with this story. Except I was suffocating to death. It wasn't *my* story.

Perspective is everything. And pride is deciding you are the hero of a story you get to write yourself.

Now, don't take this as blanket permission to go be a tool because Rae McDaniel told you it was just someone's story about you and you're actually a hero. That's not what I'm talking about. If you bad-mouth someone behind their back, or act unkindly, or take advantage of people, no amount of focusing on "being the hero of your own story" lets you off the hook. But sometimes what others call bad, selfish, perverted, or lazy are actually things like having boundaries, leaving a bad relationship, resting, exploring or transitioning your gender, loving who you love how you want to love them, breaking your people-pleasing habit, and (the horror!) letting yourself do things that bring you pleasure and joy unapologetically.

FEEL THE FEELS

My client repeated a refrain I'd heard dozens of times before from many different clients: "I know, I know. I'm worthy and valid just like I am. But I just don't feel it. I still feel shame."

It takes an enormous amount of vulnerability and courage to move toward your most authentic self in a world that isn't always welcoming. It might make you fucking angry. Recognizing this fact helps us show self-compassion when we can't feel pride or love or hope for ourselves or when we feel sad, alone, grief-stricken, or angry.

You may feel like you're in a box with no escape right now. I don't know if that's true for you or not. I invite you to consider that maybe there is a way out you haven't considered yet. But if you're in a place that feels impossible, how do you want to love yourself through it? How do you want to show compassion? How do you want to talk to yourself?

Because you sure as hell didn't put yourself in that box.

This is an invitation to feel the feels. There's space for them. There's space for rest and being held. But don't forget the pleasure and the joy along the way.

How is your heart?
What do you need to make space to feel?
What do you need to feel supported while feeling these feelings?
How can you show yourself compassion and love while experiencing difficult and big feelings?

Choosing to be the author of your own story is a lifelong practice. Sometimes we don't even realize right away when we are living someone else's story of us. Sometimes changing that story takes a whole lot of honesty as you recognize and adjust the way you show up with yourself, with others, and in the world. But from "I remembered to feed my cat" to "I did a thing that scared me" to "I wore a binder out of the house," there are a million reasons to celebrate the person you are right now in this moment and the person you are becoming.

Owning your story isn't about making things up that aren't true. It's about telling the deeper truth. The truth about yourself, like your best friend in the world is writing your biography. A truth where you are deeply seen, held with compassion, and celebrated for all of who you are.

Remember that awe is feeling small in the face of something much greater than you and feeling connected to that greatness. What if you felt awe at the magic of who you are?

Your awe at yourself isn't selfish or like staring at your own reflection until you starve. It's bigger than you. It spills over. Not sharing who you are with the rest of us is as catastrophic as robbing the Milky Way from the sky.

So, my love, what's your story?

TELL YOUR STORY

- What stories are told about you by your family / loved ones / strangers / colleagues?
- What stories are told about you where you are "bad," "selfish," "lazy," "wrong"?
- How would you tell your story differently if you decided you were the hero?

- What stories are told about you that are nice, pleasant, and "approved"? Do these feel like your authentic story?
- How are you awesome?
- Write your story like your best friend is telling it.
- Write your story like your dog is telling it. (Dogs have such unconditional love.)
- How can you make space for self-compassion in your story?
- What story do you *want* to tell? Here's your permission slip: Go tell it.

Pride Is Political

Your personal gender freedom is connected to a much larger movement of collective liberation. When you believe in your own worth and dignity, you can clearly see when someone else is trying to take it from you. You're also better at noticing when people try to take away *anyone's* dignity. We have a long way to go to create true gender freedom across political, medical, cultural, bureaucratic, and mental health systems, yet we are only where we are today because of the advocacy of those who came before us.

It's not physically, emotionally, or financially safe for everyone to stand up for themselves in their personal lives or against larger sociopolitical forces. So, for those of us who can, it's our job to be loud and fight for equal rights and visibility—the visibility we, our community, and future generations deserve.

Pride is actively working to create the world we want to live in.

For some, creating the world we want to live in is about focusing on advocacy that is LGBTQ+ specific. Research shows that getting involved with advocacy and standing up for your rights as a transgender/nonbinary person increase feelings of agency and pride.[3] For others, it might be simply being who you are as you fight against climate change or for racial and disability justice. Whatever your contribution is, it's important. Remember that gender freedom doesn't exist in a vacuum. It's connected to collective freedom. When we are free, the possibilities are endless.

BUILD THE WORLD YOU WANT TO LIVE IN

- What world do you want to live in? How are you contributing to collective freedom?
- In what ways do you want to contribute to creating this world? (*E.g., organizing, legal advocacy, community resource building, finances, writing, speaking, protests, etc.*)
- What tiny steps can you take to contribute to creating this world?
- Who is already doing this work that you can collaborate with?

Pride Is Collective

When you look up "pride" in a dictionary, you'll find the usual suspects about self-respect, satisfaction taken in something, and celebration of a particular group. But there's another bonus definition that may be one of my favorites: "a group of lions."[4] Who doesn't love a built-in metaphor?

See, a pride of lions isn't just a group; it's a family, both biological and chosen. They hunt together, share meals, raise their young together, protect each other, and take lots of naps. Lots. Of. Naps. (Did you know they sleep almost twenty hours a day? We could all learn something about rest from lions.[5]) The slow sway of their gait, near-constant stoned expression on their face, and epic lounging lead me to believe lions aren't brimming with anxiety. They're alert to danger but not consumed by it. They put forth bursts of effort to meet their goals (aka, dinner) and mostly just chill the rest of the time. They know who they are, they take up lots of space, and they seem to give very few fucks. #squadgoals

We often think of pride as a personal trait, and yes, pride is a reflection of our beliefs about ourselves. But pride is also collective. Like our lion friends, we thrive when we feel supported by others in our kinship network.

Beyond our immediate network, feeling connected to others (whether we personally know them or not) who are transgender/non-binary from the past, present, and future is a powerful source of resilience and strength.[6] Collective pride connects your story to the larger thread of gender freedom. It connects you to the transgender and non-binary folks who came before you and will come after you. It connects you to those who are part of your kinship network and the strangers who cause your eyes to light up in recognition as you pass them on the sidewalk.

PRIDE FROM OUR ANCESTORS

Remember Dr. Roger Kuhn, whom we met in chapter 1? While it's important not to appropriate Indigenous culture, he shared that many Indigenous people believe their ancestral knowledge isn't exclusively for Indigenous people.

"The more access that people have to the truth of the land, of the peoples of these lands, the more that we all will move closer toward liberation together. Be willing to open up your own perspectives.... Look to the stewards of this land. Look to the ancestors of this land and learn from them. Learn from our community and then give back to our community. And always, always, always credit. Have a beginner's mind and be willing to promote and center Indigenous peoples and knowledge."[7]

Learning the stories of those who came before us is powerful, and it's important to not limit ourselves to a whitewashed, Westernized history of our gender-diverse ancestors.

It's easy to be in awe of the transgender/non-binary and Indigenous gender explorers that paved the way for us. Picking up a book like Susan Stryker's *Transgender History* and memoirs of other trans folks and consuming queer media is an excellent way to feel more connected to the strength, resiliency, love, eroticism, passion, and magic of all those who came before us.

A connection to our ancestors is also a reminder that feeling pride in who you are, unapologetically, has ripples far beyond what you know. That confidence, that self-love, that freedom are contagious. Strengthening your pride muscle is not just for you but for future generations, as well as the people you don't even know are being impacted. In the musical *Fun Home*, the song "Ring of Keys" describes a pivotal moment in a young queer person's identity development. Alison, a child at the time, notices an old-school butch lesbian making a delivery. Her heart lights up in a way she doesn't quite understand at the time. "I know you. I know you," she sings. Cultivating pride is for the person who "knows" you but doesn't yet know why. Remember, one day you, too, will be an ancestor.

Collective pride is also about letting others' pride carry you when self-doubt and shame creep in. This might look like calling a friend on a bad day and asking for encouragement or having a picnic in the park with a few of your kin and laughing until you cry. It can also look like consuming stories of pride over time—like Marsha P. Johnson and Sylvia Rivera's pivotal role in the Stonewall riots—to remind us of our why and that gender freedom is not just about us.[8]

You don't have to do the thing alone, my friends.

BUILD YOUR "PRIDE" OF LIONS

- Who is in your "pride"? What tiny steps will you take to develop your pride?
- How will you connect with the larger story of gender freedom across time and cultures?
- How can you tap into collective pride on the days you aren't feeling it?
- How can you let others carry you? How do you carry others?

Pride Is Celebration

Lastly, though perhaps most of all, pride is celebration—both of ourselves and each other. Transgender and non-binary joy is revolutionary, and every step you take toward the most authentic version of you is a big fucking deal. To borrow a phrase from Maya Angelou, pride is taking pleasure in belonging to yourself, despite all odds.[9]

Sometimes I look up and have a wave of gratitude for where I am in my life today compared to where I was ten-plus years ago. I couldn't even imagine the life I'm living now back then. It's easy for me to reach a goal and brush past it, onto the next thing, but I'm learning to slow down, notice, and feel gratitude for the tiny steps I take toward living the life I want to live. I'm learning to pop the champagne more often (like when I finally turn in this book). I'm learning to enjoy the process.

I'm learning to celebrate.

The French film *Beats per Minute* will break your heart open a thousand times over. Following the advocacy group ACT UP at the height of the AIDS crisis, it showcases both the gut-wrenching reality of an ignored pandemic and the bittersweet beauty of life despite it. What is striking to me about this film is how it oscillates between scenes of death and grief and scenes of the characters dancing their hearts out, of a hand job at the bedside of a dying man. Raw joy. Hope. Love. Pleasure. In the midst of it all.[10]

Intentionally cultivating celebration—holding space for moments of pleasure and joy—isn't about putting on rose-colored glasses. It reminds us there is hope. It reminds us of why we went on this journey of self-discovery in the first place. After all, why the hell would we be doing any of this if it doesn't bring us pleasure? If it doesn't light us up?

Pride isn't just rainbow floats and parades, but nobody said it can't include a party. Sometimes pride is getting lost in a room full of queers dancing to Lizzo. Sometimes it's marching with hundreds of folks fighting for their rights while also delighting in each other (and how clever our signs are). Sometimes it's the swell of pride when you see someone else killing it and living their best life. Sometimes it's going to a leather party and complimenting the hell out of all the other cuties there.

So, yes, feel your feels deeply. Pursue your needs and wants with unwavering determination. Just be sure you make space to dance, love, pursue pleasure, and get lost in the magic of life along the way.

FINDING PLEASURE IN PRIDE

- How will you celebrate transgender and non-binary folks?
- What makes your heart swell with pride?
- How will you celebrate your own journey of self-growth and discovery?
- What brings you pleasure in your gender-exploration journey?

Pride is a grounded confidence that you deserve to be who you are.

I want you to feel free. Unapologetically you. What I want for you most of all is for you to feel with your whole body that you love being you. Trust me—that feeling is intoxicating.

You are not the story others tell about you.

You are also not the stories you tell yourself about how you aren't valid, worthy, beautiful, handsome, sexy, deserving, "real," or lovable.

You, my love, get to be you in the world. You get to choose that. And you, as your most lit-up and authentic self, are infinitely lovable and worthy. There is nothing sexier or more powerful than someone who knows and owns who they are.

Remember my friend Jen Pastiloff's incredible mantra: "May I have the courage to be who I say I am." I'd like to take it a step further.

My friend,

What would you *want* if you weren't afraid?

What would you *do* if you weren't afraid?

What do you need to have the courage to be who you say you are?

These questions will change your life. I know they changed mine.

And lest we forget to laugh at ourselves in the process, my favorite fact about lions? They're scared of umbrellas, especially if you draw eyes on them.[11]

Conclusion

In the middle of writing this conclusion, a trash bag full of aquarium rocks and a couple of dead fish (honestly, my fault) toppled over in epic fashion, spilling all over the carpet. I put down my laptop and tediously picked up as many of the slimy, putrid, fish-poop-filled rocks as I could before attempting to vacuum up the rest. There's still a giant stain of disgusting aquarium water in my office that I'll likely be trying to clean for months.

Why am I telling you about this? Because as I was down on the floor, cursing gravity and insufficiently tied bags, it struck me that gender was the furthest thing from my mind. I knew, even in a less-than-glamorous moment, that I was authentically me and loved and accepted for who I was. Present. Just me, living my life, fish poop and all. And the ability to be present for both the boring and the gross moments is a gift, my friends. It's freedom.

Life is wild. One minute you'll be weeping with joy, laughing so hard you pee and it feels like your heart will explode. The next you're sobbing in frustration because of how hard and sad and tedious it feels just to get dressed. But you know what? All of those moments—they're yours. Completely. You get to live life as you.

Gender freedom means you are free to _______.

I don't know what your "blank" is, but I'm excited for you to discover it with more pleasure, ease, and connection than you thought possible.

I can share a vision of you as a political candidate, world-renowned speaker, professional athlete, activist, or a celebrated artist. I dream of those things for you, and I believe they're not only possible but inevitable as we collectively move toward more gender freedom. But honestly, the vision that may keep you going is changing your baby's diaper before going out in your garden to play with your dog. And I love that for you.

What I want most is for you to be able to live as the person you know you are, walking around lit up and present in the euphoric moments as well as the mundane and hard ones, because gender doesn't consume your every waking thought. I want you to be able to just *be*.

Traditional gender expectations for how we look, behave, and express ourselves have hurt us all, whether we are transgender, non-binary, or cisgender. But we have the ability to choose a different path. A path where our assigned sex at birth is just a jumping-off point to discover who we are instead of a box we're put in for the rest of our lives. I want gender freedom for you, reader, and a future of cultural freedom, acceptance, and celebration of gender diversity.

As Elisabeth Kübler-Ross, the creator of the five stages of grief, reminds us, "The most beautiful people we have known are those who have known defeat, known suffering, known struggle, known loss, and have found their way out of the depths.... Beautiful people do not just happen."[1]

You are beautiful.

Not despite your gender exploration or transition but because of it.

Wherever you're coming from in journey and wherever you're going, you are valid, you are loved, the world is better for having you in it, and you're not alone.

Don't ever forget that.

Acknowledgments

There is no way to express adequate gratitude to all the people (historically, personally, and professionally) who contributed to the book you hold in your hands.

My work is part of a much larger and much older conversation building on many others that came before me, including many queer and transgender women of color whose names much of history has forgotten—like Marsha P. Johnson, Sir Lady Java, and Miss Major Griffin-Gracy. To the named and unnamed who have contributed to the conversation, the advocacy, and the world-building necessary for a book about gender transition that centers on pleasure, joy, and curiosity to exist—thank you.

This book was ten-plus years in the making for me, a distant dream from the moment I first stepped into a graduate-school classroom hoping to make a difference for the LGBTQ+ community. I can't name each and every one of you, but know that I love you and see you. Thank you.

To my clients—you've taught me so much and I hold each of you in my heart. Thank you for sharing your lives and stories with me.

Thank you to Meghan Stevenson, who was in equal parts a guide, coach, cheerleader, and collaborator. This book wouldn't exist without you.

To my brilliant agent, Steve Troha—you made my dreams come true with an ease I could never have imagined. Thank you.

To my rock star editor, Hannah Robinson—you made an often-scary process into a joyful experience. I couldn't ask for a better editor and collaborator. You saw the vision for this book and championed it all the way through with extreme care and kindness, while also pushing me as a writer. This book was good. You helped make it great.

To GCP Balance—thank you for giving this first-time author a chance.

To my friends and loves—you know who you are. A lot of life

happened while writing this book, and I couldn't have gotten through it without you. You fed me and reminded me of who I was on the days it was hard and toasted with me at every milestone. I love each of you from the bottom of my heart. You're my kin. And I'm the luckiest duck.

To Britt—thanks for supporting me through this (long) process and sending me memes about writers before I was ready to laugh about it. Oops.

To Emily Nagoski—you told me once (a very long time ago) that I would write a great book one day. I've held that comment close to my heart ever since. Thank you for being a great friend and colleague over the years.

To Stephanie Budge, Pidgeon Pagonis, and Sergio Dominguez—your work and insights were invaluable in the development of this book. I'm excited to see where each of your careers goes and will continue to learn from you.

To Roger Kuhn, Lou Lindley, and Lindo Bacon—it was a delight to speak with all of you and include your insights in the book. Getting to dive into our conversations was one of my favorite parts of writing.

Thank you to all my beta readers: Andy Karol, Alex Papale, Alex Kuhn, Lindsay Warner, and Leah Carey, to name a few. Y'all are so smart. Thanks for all your help and insight.

To Lucie Fielding, my brilliant friend. How can one person be so smart and kind (and hot)? Your work makes mine better. Thank you for the long, nerdy talks. I adore you.

To my Practical Audacity team (especially to my admin team: Carolyn, Rysa, Laurel, Krizia, and Roxy)—y'all are magic. I could not have taken the time I needed to write this book without you. I'm lucky to work with such incredible humans.

To Rachel Rodgers—you encouraged me to write a book before I thought I was ready and told me to wait for a better offer. You were right. And I wouldn't have started this process or be where I am today without your unfailing belief in me.

To my Shmillies—you have watched this whole process and cheered me on every step of the way. Now it's your turn. Go change the world.

Thanks to Lidia Yuknavitch and Jen Pastiloff for getting me over the finish line and reminding me of who I am and what I love. And for having my back. I got you.

To my dog, Gizmo, for fulfilling your genetic predisposition to warm my feet under my desk and making me leave the house to walk you. You're responsible for any vitamin D I got this year.

Notes

Introduction: Transition Isn't the Point

1. "BREAKING: 2021 Becomes Record Year for Anti-Transgender Legislation—HRC." Accessed November 23, 2021. https://www.hrc.org/press-releases/breaking-2021-becomes-record-year-for-anti-transgender-legislation. Human Rights Campaign. "The Fight Continues." Accessed October 25, 2022. https://www.hrc.org/magazine/2022-winter/the-fight-continues.
2. Forestiere, Annamarie. "America's War on Black Trans Women." *Harvard Civil Rights–Civil Liberties Law Review*, September 23, 2020. Accessed November 23, 2021. https://harvardcrcl.org/americas-war-on-black-trans-women/.
3. Mock, Janet. "'Redefining Realness' Makes the *New York Times* Bestsellers List." Accessed September 28, 2022. https://janetmock.com/2014/02/13/redefining-realness-new-york-times-bestseller. Bowles, Hamish. "Playtime with Harry Styles." *Vogue*, November 13, 2020. Accessed September 28, 2022. https://www.vogue.com/article/harry-styles-cover-december-2020. Allaire, Christian. "Billy Porter on Why He Wore a Gown, Not a Tuxedo, to the Oscars." *Vogue*, February 24, 2019. Accessed September 28, 2022. https://www.vogue.com/article/billy-porter-oscars-red-carpet-gown-christian-siriano. "Jacob Tobia." *The Daily Show*, season 24, episode 74. Aired March 14, 2019. https://www.imdb.com/title/tt9878576/.
4. Herman, Jody L, Taylor N T Brown, and Ann P Haas. "Suicide Thoughts and 4. Attempts by Transgender Adults: Findings from the 2015 U.S. Transgender Study." The Williams Institute, 2019. https://williamsinstitute.law.ucla.edu/publications/suicidality-transgender-adults/.
5. McDaniel, Rae, and Laurel Meng. "The Gender Freedom Model: A Framework for Helping Transgender, Non-Binary, and Gender Questioning Clients Transition with More Ease." *Journal of Counseling Sexology & Sexual Wellness: Research, Practice, and Education* 3, no. 2 (January 9, 2022): 82–93. https://doi.org/10.34296/03021064.

Chapter 1

1. Piff, Paul K., Pia Dietze, Matthew Feinberg, Daniel M. Stancato, and Dacher Keltner. "Awe, the Small Self, and Prosocial Behavior." *Journal of Personality and Social Psychology* 108, no. 6 (June 1, 2015): 883–99. https://doi.org/10.1037/pspi0000018.
2. Hyde, Janet Shibley, Rebecca S. Bigler, Daphna Joel, Charlotte Chucky Tate, and Sari M. van Anders. "The Future of Sex and Gender in Psychology: Five Challenges to the Gender Binary." *American Psychologist* 74, no. 2 (February 1, 2019): 171–93. https://doi.org/10.1037/amp0000307. DuBois, L. Zachary, and Heather Shattuck-Heidorn. "Challenging the Binary: Gender/Sex and the Bio-Logics of Normalcy." *American Journal of Human Biology* 33, no. 5 (2021): e23623. https://doi.org/10.1002/ajhb.23623. Hull, Carrie L., and Anne Fausto-Sterling. "How Sexually Dimorphic Are We? Review and Synthesis

(Multiple Letters)." *American Journal of Human Biology* 15, no. 1 (2003): 112–16. https://doi.org/10.1002/ajhb.10122.

3. Goldey, Katherine L., and Sari M. van Anders. "Identification with Stimuli Moderates Women's Affective and Testosterone Responses to Self-Chosen Erotica." *Archives of Sexual Behavior* 45, no. 8 (November 2016): 2155–71. https://doi.org/10.1007/s10508-015-0612-3.
4. Hyde, Janet Shibley, Rebecca S. Bigler, Daphna Joel, Charlotte Chucky Tate, and Sari M. van Anders. "The Future of Sex and Gender in Psychology: Five Challenges to the Gender Binary." *American Psychologist* 74, no. 2 (February 1, 2019): 171–93. https://doi.org/10.1037/amp0000307.
5. van Anders, Sari M. "Beyond Masculinity: Testosterone, Gender/Sex, and Human Social Behavior in a Comparative Context." *Frontiers in Neuroendocrinology* 34, no. 3 (August 1, 2013): 198–210. https://doi.org/10.1016/j.yfrne.2013.07.001.
6. Joel, Daphna, Zohar Berman, Ido Tavor, Nadav Wexler, Olga Gaber, Yaniv Stein, Nisan Shefi, et al. "Sex beyond the Genitalia: The Human Brain Mosaic." *Proceedings of the National Academy of Sciences* 112, no. 50 (December 15, 2015): 15468. https://doi.org/10.1073/pnas.1509654112.
7. DuBois, L. Zachary, and Heather Shattuck-Heidorn. "Challenging the Binary: Gender/Sex and the Bio-Logics of Normalcy." *American Journal of Human Biology* 33, no. 5 (2021): e23623. https://doi.org/10.1002/ajhb.23623.
8. Richardson, Sarah S. "Sexing the X: How the X Became the 'Female Chromosome.'" *Signs* 37, no. 4 (2012): 909–33.
9. Richardson, Sarah S. "Sexing the X: How the X Became the 'Female Chromosome.'" *Signs* 37, no. 4 (2012): 909–33.
10. Richardson, Sarah S. *Sex Itself: The Search for Male and Female in the Human Genome*. Chicago and London: University of Chicago Press, 2013.
11. Hull, Carrie L., and Anne Fausto-Sterling. "How Sexually Dimorphic Are We? Review and Synthesis (Multiple Letters)." *American Journal of Human Biology* 15, no. 1 (2003): 112–16. https://doi.org/10.1002/ajhb.10122. BBC News. "How Many Redheads Are There in the World?," October 1, 2013, sec. Magazine. https://www.bbc.com/news/magazine-24331615. "Population of Canada." In Wikipedia, November 9, 2022. https://en.wikipedia.org/w/index.php?title=Population_of_Canada&oldid=1120985933.
12. Hyde, Janet Shibley, Rebecca S. Bigler, Daphna Joel, Charlotte Chucky Tate, and Sari M. van Anders. "The Future of Sex and Gender in Psychology: Five Challenges to the Gender Binary." *American Psychologist* 74, no. 2 (February 1, 2019): 171–93. https://doi.org/10.1037/amp0000307.
13. Keteepe-Arachi, Tracey, and Sanjay Sharma. "Cardiovascular Disease in Women: Understanding Symptoms and Risk Factors." *European Cardiology Review* 12, no. 1 (August 2017): 10–13. https://doi.org/10.15420/ecr.2016:32:1.
14. Mondschein, Emily R., Karen E. Adolph, and Catherine S. Tamis-LeMonda. "Gender Bias in Mothers' Expectations about Infant Crawling." *Journal of Experimental Child Psychology*, December 2000, 304–16.
15. Kuhn, Dr. Roger. Interview with the author. November 2021.
16. *Diagnostic and Statistical Manual of Mental Disorders*. This is used by all mental health practitioners to diagnose clients.
17. Murphy, Em. "Gender Dysphoria and Euphoria." *VSC Blog*. Victim Service Center of Central Florida, November 20, 2020. Accessed October 17, 2021. https://www.victimservicecenter.org/gender-dysphoria-and-euphoria/.
18. "Jacob Tobia—Promoting a 'Gender-Chill' Exploration of Identity with 'Sissy'—*The Daily Show*." YouTube, March 21, 2019. Accessed November 23, 2021. https://www.youtube.com/watch?v=qo3rCzl_JB4.

Chapter 2

1. Crenshaw, Kimberlé. "Mapping the Margins: Intersectionality, Identity Politics, and Violence against Women of Color." *Stanford Law Review* 43, no. 6 (1991): 1241–99. https://doi.org/10.2307/1229039.
2. Maier, Steven F., and Martin E. P. Seligman. "Learned Helplessness at Fifty: Insights from Neuroscience." *Psychological Review* 123, no. 4 (July 2016): 349–67. https://doi.org/10.1037/rev0000033.
3. Nagoski, Emily, and Amelia Nagoski. *Burnout: The Secret to Unlocking the Stress Cycle.* New York: Ballantine Books, 2019.
4. Nagoski, Emily, and Amelia Nagoski. *Burnout: The Secret to Unlocking the Stress Cycle.* New York: Ballantine Books, 2019.
5. Budge, Stephanie L., Mun Yuk Chin, and Laura P. Minero. "Trans Individuals' Facilitative Coping: An Analysis of Internal and External Processes." *Journal of Counseling Psychology* 64, no. 1 (January 1, 2017): 12–25. https://doi.org/10.1037/cou0000178.
6. Ruff, Nadine, Amy B. Smoyer, and Jean Breny. "Hope, Courage, and Resilience in the Lives of Transgender Women of Color." *The Qualitative Report* 24, no. 8 (2019). https://nsuworks.nova.edu/tqr/vol24/iss8/11.
7. Composite adapted from Ruff, Smoyer, and Breny, "Hope, Courage, and Resilience in the Lives of Transgender Women of Color."
8. Frankl, Viktor E. *Man's Search for Meaning.* Boston: Beacon Press, 2006.
9. Nagoski, Emily, and Amelia Nagoski. *Burnout: The Secret to Unlocking the Stress Cycle.* New York: Ballantine Books, 2019.
10. Taylor, Sonya Renee. *The Body Is Not an Apology: The Power of Radical Self-Love.* 2nd ed. Oakland, CA: Berrett-Koehler Publishers, 2021.
11. Neff, Kristin. *Self-Compassion: Stop Beating Yourself Up and Leave Insecurity Behind.* New York: William Morrow, 2011. Germer, Christopher K., and Kristin D. Neff. "Self-Compassion in Clinical Practice: Self-Compassion." *Journal of Clinical Psychology* 69, no. 8 (2013): 856–67. https://doi.org/10.1002/jclp.22021.
12. Miserandino, Christine. "The Spoon Theory." ButYouDontLookSick.com. Accessed October 1, 2022. https://butyoudontlooksick.com/articles/written-by-christine/the-spoon-theory/.
13. Bacon, Lindo. Interview with the author. December 2021.
14. Budge, Stephanie L., Mun Yuk Chin, and Laura P. Minero. "Trans Individuals' Facilitative Coping: An Analysis of Internal and External Processes." *Journal of Counseling Psychology* 64, no. 1 (January 1, 2017): 12–25. https://doi.org/10.1037/cou0000178.
15. Ferriss, Tim. "How to Design a Life—Debbie Millman (#214)." *The Tim Ferriss Show,* January 12, 2017. https://tim.blog/2017/01/12/how-to-design-a-life-debbie-millman/.
16. Ose Askvik, Eva, F. R. (Ruud) van der Weel, and Audrey L. H. van der Meer. "The Importance of Cursive Handwriting over Typewriting for Learning in the Classroom: A High-Density EEG Study of 12-Year-Old Children and Young Adults." *Frontiers in Psychology* 11 (2020). https://www.frontiersin.org/articles/10.3389/fpsyg.2020.01810.

Chapter 3

1. The Interaction Design Foundation. "What Are Wicked Problems?" Accessed November 29, 2021. https://www.interaction-design.org/literature/topics/wicked-problems. Wikipedia, s.v., "Wicked Problem." Accessed February 28, 2021. https://en.wikipedia.org/wiki/Wicked_problem.
2. French, Bryana H., Jioni A. Lewis, Della V. Mosley, Hector Y. Adames, Nayeli Y.

Chavez-Dueñas, Grace A. Chen, and Helen A. Neville. "Toward a Psychological Framework of Radical Healing in Communities of Color." *The Counseling Psychologist* 48, no. 1 (2020): 14–46. https://doi.org/10.1177/0011000019843506.

3. Budge, Stephanie L., Mun Yuk Chin, and Laura P. Minero. "Trans Individuals' Facilitative Coping: An Analysis of Internal and External Processes." *Journal of Counseling Psychology* 64, no. 1 (January 1, 2017): 12–25. https://doi.org/10.1037/cou0000178.
4. *Merriam-Webster*, s.v. "facilitative (*adj.*)." Accessed August 25, 2022. https://www.merriam-webster.com/dictionary/facilitative.
5. Nagoski, Emily, and Amelia Nagoski. *Burnout: The Secret to Unlocking the Stress Cycle*. New York: Ballantine Books, 2019.
6. Budge, Stephanie L., Sabra L. Katz-Wise, Esther N. Tebbe, Kimberly A. S. Howard, Carrie L. Schneider, and Adriana Rodriguez. "Transgender Emotional and Coping Processes: Facilitative and Avoidant Coping throughout Gender Transitioning." *The Counseling Psychologist* 41, no. 4 (2013): 601–47. https://doi.org/10.1177/0011000011432753.
7. Allyson Chiu, "Time to Ditch 'Toxic Positivity,' Experts Say: 'It's Okay Not to Be Okay.'" *Washington Post*, August 19, 2020. Accessed March 5, 2021. https://www.washingtonpost.com/lifestyle/wellness/toxic-positivity-mental-health-covid/2020/08/19/5dff8d16-e0c8-11ea-8181-606e603bb1c4_story.html.
8. "The Nap Ministry | Rest Is Resistance." Accessed January 9, 2022. https://thenapministry.wordpress.com/.
9. "Debbie Millman: Why Does Design Matter?" *TED Radio Hour*. npr.org. September 25, 2020. Accessed November 29, 2021. https://www.npr.org/2020/09/25/916499570/debbie-millman-why-does-design-matter.
10. "Zone of Proximal Development." ScienceDirect. Accessed December 6, 2021. https://www.sciencedirect.com/topics/psychology/zone-of-proximal-development.
11. Budge, Stephanie. Interview with the author. December 2021.
12. Budge, Stephanie L., Mun Yuk Chin, and Laura P. Minero. "Trans Individuals' Facilitative Coping: An Analysis of Internal and External Processes." *Journal of Counseling Psychology* 64, no. 1 (January 1, 2017): 12–25. https://doi.org/10.1037/cou0000178.

Chapter 4

1. Bustos, Valeria P., Samyd S. Bustos, Andres Mascaro, Gabriel Del Corral, Antonio J. Forte, Pedro Ciudad, Esther A. Kim, Howard N. Langstein, and Oscar J. Manrique. "Regret after Gender-Affirmation Surgery: A Systematic Review and Meta-Analysis of Prevalence." *Plastic and Reconstructive Surgery—Global Open* 9, no. 3 (March 19, 2021): e3477. https://doi.org/10.1097/GOX.0000000000003477. Johansson, Annika, Elisabet Sundbom, Torvald Höjerback, and Owe Bodlund. "A Five-Year Follow-Up Study of Swedish Adults with Gender Identity Disorder." *Archives of Sexual Behavior* 39, no. 6 (December 2010): 1429–37. https://doi.org/10.1007/s10508-009-9551-1. Dhejne, Cecilia, Katarina Öberg, Stefan Arver, and Mikael Landén. "An Analysis of All Applications for Sex Reassignment Surgery in Sweden, 1960–2010: Prevalence, Incidence, and Regrets." *Archives of Sexual Behavior* 43, no. 8 (2014): 1535–45. https://doi.org/10.1007/s10508-014-0300-8. Turban, Jack L., Stephanie S. Loo, Anthony N. Almazan, and Alex S. Keuroghlian. "Factors Leading to 'Detransition' Among Transgender and Gender Diverse People in the United States: A Mixed-Methods Analysis." *LGBT Health* 8, no. 4 (June 1, 2021): 273–80. https://doi.org/10.1089/lgbt.2020.0437.
2. Danker, Sara, Sasha K. Narayan, Rachel Bluebond-Langner, Loren S. Schechter, and Jens U. Berli. "Abstract: A Survey Study of Surgeons' Experience with Regret and/or Reversal

of Gender-Confirmation Surgeries." *Plastic and Reconstructive Surgery Global Open* 6, no. 9 Suppl (2018): 189. https://doi.org/10.1097/01.GOX.0000547077.23299.00.

3. Bustos, Valeria P., Samyd S. Bustos, Andres Mascaro, Gabriel Del Corral, Antonio J. Forte, Pedro Ciudad, Esther A. Kim, Howard N. Langstein, and Oscar J. Manrique. "Regret after Gender-Affirmation Surgery: A Systematic Review and Meta-Analysis of Prevalence." *Plastic and Reconstructive Surgery—Global Open* 9, no. 3 (March 19, 2021): e3477. https://doi.org/10.1097/GOX.0000000000003477. Turban, Jack L., Stephanie S. Loo, Anthony N. Almazan, and Alex S. Keuroghlian. "Factors Leading to 'Detransition' Among Transgender and Gender Diverse People in the United States: A Mixed-Methods Analysis." *LGBT Health* 8, no. 4 (June 1, 2021): 273–80. https://doi.org/10.1089/lgbt.2020.0437.
4. Joseph-Williams, Natalie, Adrian Edwards, and Glyn Elwyn. "The Importance and Complexity of Regret in the Measurement of 'Good' Decisions: A Systematic Review and a Content Analysis of Existing Assessment Instruments." *Health Expectations* 14, no. 1 (March 2011): 59–83. https://doi.org/10.1111/j.1369-7625.2010.00621.x.
5. Joseph-Williams, Natalie, Adrian Edwards, and Glyn Elwyn. "The Importance and Complexity of Regret in the Measurement of 'Good' Decisions: A Systematic Review and a Content Analysis of Existing Assessment Instruments." *Health Expectations* 14, no. 1 (March 2011): 59–83. https://doi.org/10.1111/j.1369-7625.2010.00621.x.
6. McQueen, Paddy. "The Role of Regret in Medical Decision-Making." *Ethical Theory and Moral Practice* 20, no. 5 (November 1, 2017): 1051–65. https://doi.org/10.1007/s10677-017-9844-8.
7. Leahy, Robert L. *The Worry Cure: Seven Steps to Stop Worry from Stopping You*. New York: Harmony Books, 2005.
8. Bockting, Walter, Eli Coleman, Madeline B. Deutsch, Antonio Guillamon, Ilan Meyer, Walter Meyer, Sari Reisner, Jae Sevelius, and Randi Ettner. "Adult Development and Quality of Life of Transgender and Gender Nonconforming People." *Current Opinion in Endocrinology, Diabetes and Obesity* 23, no. 2 (2016): 188–97. https://doi.org/10.1097/MED.0000000000000232. Matsuno, Emmie, and Tania Israel. "Psychological Interventions Promoting Resilience among Transgender Individuals: Transgender Resilience Intervention Model (TRIM)." *Counseling Psychologist* 46, no. 5 (July 1, 2018): 632–55. https://doi.org/10.1177/0011000018787261.
9. Johansson, Annika, Elisabet Sundbom, Torvald Höjerback, and Owe Bodlund. "A Five-Year Follow-Up Study of Swedish Adults with Gender Identity Disorder." *Archives of Sexual Behavior* 39, no. 6 (December 2010): 1429–37. https://doi.org/10.1007/s10508-009-9551-1.
10. Murad, Mohammad Hassan, Mohamed B. Elamin, Magaly Zumaeta Garcia, Rebecca J. Mullan, Ayman Murad, Patricia J. Erwin, and Victor M. Montori. "Hormonal Therapy and Sex Reassignment: A Systematic Review and Meta-Analysis of Quality of Life and Psychosocial Outcomes." *Clinical Endocrinology* 72, no. 2 (February 2010): 214–31. https://doi.org/10.1111/j.1365-2265.2009.03625.x.
11. Budge, Stephanie L., Sabra L. Katz-Wise, Esther N. Tebbe, Kimberly A. S. Howard, Carrie L. Schneider, and Adriana Rodriguez. "Transgender Emotional and Coping Processes: Facilitative and Avoidant Coping throughout Gender Transitioning." *The Counseling Psychologist* 41, no. 4 (2013): 601–47. https://doi.org/10.1177/0011000011432753.
12. Brown, C. Brené. *Daring Greatly: How the Courage to Be Vulnerable Transforms the Way We Live, Love, Parent, and Lead*. New York: Gotham Books, 2012.
13. Joseph-Williams, Natalie, Adrian Edwards, and Glyn Elwyn. "The Importance and Complexity of Regret in the Measurement of 'Good' Decisions: A Systematic Review and a

Content Analysis of Existing Assessment Instruments." *Health Expectations* 14, no. 1 (March 2011): 59–83. https://doi.org/10.1111/j.1369-7625.2010.00621.x.

14. Morain, Stephanie R., Susan H. Wootton, and Catherine Eppes. "The Power of Regret." *New England Journal of Medicine* 377, no. 16 (October 19, 2017): 1505–7. https://doi.org/10.1056/nejmp1707273.
15. Morain, Stephanie R., Susan H. Wootton, and Catherine Eppes. "The Power of Regret." *New England Journal of Medicine* 377, no. 16 (October 19, 2017): 1505–7. https://doi.org/10.1056/nejmp1707273. Joseph-Williams, Natalie, Adrian Edwards, and Glyn Elwyn. "The Importance and Complexity of Regret in the Measurement of 'Good' Decisions: A Systematic Review and a Content Analysis of Existing Assessment Instruments." *Health Expectations* 14, no. 1 (March 2011): 59–83. https://doi.org/10.1111/j.1369-7625.2010.00621.x.x.
16. Leahy, Robert L. *The Worry Cure: Seven Steps to Stop Worry from Stopping You*. New York: Harmony Books, 2005.

Chapter 5

1. *Cambridge Dictionary*, s.v., "magic." Accessed August 27, 2022. https://dictionary.cambridge.org/us/dictionary/english/magic.
2. Budge, Stephanie L., Mun Yuk Chin, and Laura P. Minero. "Trans Individuals' Facilitative Coping: An Analysis of Internal and External Processes." *Journal of Counseling Psychology* 64, no. 1 (January 1, 2017): 12–25. https://doi.org/10.1037/cou0000178.
3. Fielding, Lucie. *Trans Sex: Clinical Approaches to Trans Sexualities and Erotic Embodiments*. New York: Routledge, 2021.
4. "Zone of Proximal Development." ScienceDirect. Accessed December 6, 2021. https://www.sciencedirect.com/topics/psychology/zone-of-proximal-development.
5. Fielding, Lucie. *Trans Sex: Clinical Approaches to Trans Sexualities and Erotic Embodiments*. New York: Routledge, 2021.
6. Google Arts & Culture. "The High-Life: A History of Men in Heels." Accessed January 24, 2022. https://artsandculture.google.com/story/the-high-life-a-history-of-men-in-heels/iQ_JCgMgwSKV5Kw.
7. Lindley, Lou. Interview with the author. January 7, 2022.
8. Leahy, Robert L. *The Worry Cure: Seven Steps to Stop Worry from Stopping You*. New York: Harmony Books, 2005.

Chapter 6

1. Lindley, Lou. Interview with the author. January 7, 2022.
2. Miserandino, Christine. "The Spoon Theory." ButYouDontLookSick.com. Accessed October 1, 2022. https://butyoudontlooksick.com/articles/written-by-christine/the-spoon-theory/.
3. Hanson, Heidi. "The 5 Step Self-Holding Exercise." *The Art of Healing Trauma Blog*. September 13, 2014. https://www.new-synapse.com/aps/wordpress/?p=616.
4. "The World Is Not Enough (1999)—Desmond Llewelyn as Q." IMDb. Accessed February 10, 2022. https://www.imdb.com/title/tt0143145/characters/nm0005155.
5. Matsuno, Emmie, and Tania Israel. "Psychological Interventions Promoting Resilience among Transgender Individuals: Transgender Resilience Intervention Model (TRIM)." *Counseling Psychologist* 46, no. 5 (July 1, 2018): 632–55. https://doi.org/10.1177/0011000018787261.

Chapter 7

1. Perel, Esther. "Eroticism." estherperel.com. Accessed April 23, 2022. https://www.estherperel.com/focus-on-categories/eroticism.

2. Nagoski, Emily. *Come as You Are: The Surprising New Science That Will Transform Your Sex Life*. Rev. ed. New York: Simon & Schuster Paperbacks, 2021.
3. TEDx Talks. "Confidence and Joy Are the Keys to a Great Sex Life: Emily Nagoski: TEDxUniversityofNevada." YouTube, February 12, 2016. https://www.youtube.com/watch?v=HILY0wWBlBM.
4. Fielding, Lucie. *Trans Sex: Clinical Approaches to Trans Sexualities and Erotic Embodiments*. New York: Routledge, 2021.
5. Murad, Mohammad Hassan, Mohamed B. Elamin, Magaly Zumaeta Garcia, Rebecca J. Mullan, Ayman Murad, Patricia J. Erwin, and Victor M. Montori. "Hormonal Therapy and Sex Reassignment: A Systematic Review and Meta-Analysis of Quality of Life and Psychosocial Outcomes." *Clinical Endocrinology* 72, no. 2 (February 2010): 214–31. https://doi.org/10.1111/j.1365-2265.2009.03625.x. Johansson, Annika, Elisabet Sundbom, Torvald Höjerback, and Owe Bodlund. "A Five-Year Follow-Up Study of Swedish Adults with Gender Identity Disorder." *Archives of Sexual Behavior* 39, no. 6 (December 2010): 1429–37. https://doi.org/10.1007/s10508-009-9551-1. Rowniak, Stefan, and Catherine Chesla. "Coming Out for a Third Time: Transmen, Sexual Orientation, and Identity." *Archives of Sexual Behavior* 42, no. 3 (2013): 449–61. https://doi.org/10.1007/s10508-012-0036-2.
6. Nagoski, Emily. *Come as You Are: The Surprising New Science That Will Transform Your Sex Life*. Rev. ed. New York: Simon & Schuster Paperbacks, 2021.
7. *Fucking Trans Women*. Accessed May 14, 2022. https://fuckingtranswomen.tumblr.com/.
8. Papale, Alex. Interview with the author. May 12, 2022.
9. Ruff, Nadine, Amy B. Smoyer, and Jean Breny. "Hope, Courage, and Resilience in the Lives of Transgender Women of Color." *The Qualitative Report* 24, no. 8 (2019). https://nsuworks.nova.edu/tqr/vol24/iss8/11.
10. van Anders, Sari M. "Beyond Sexual Orientation: Integrating Gender/Sex and Diverse Sexualities via Sexual Configurations Theory." *Archives of Sexual Behavior* 44, no. 5 (July 2015). https://doi.org/10.1007/s10508-015-0490-8.
11. TEDx Talks. "Confidence and Joy Are the Keys to a Great Sex Life: Emily Nagoski: TEDxUniversityofNevada." YouTube, February 12, 2016. https://www.youtube.com/watch?v=HILY0wWBlBM.
12. Morin, Jack. *The Erotic Mind*. New York: Harper Perennial, 1996.
13. McArthur, Neil. "Ecosexuals Believe Having Sex with the Earth Could Save It." *Vice*, November 2, 2016. Accessed April 27, 2022. https://www.vice.com/en/article/wdbgyq/ecosexuals-believe-having-sex-with-the-earth-could-save-it.

Chapter 8

1. brown, adrienne maree. *Pleasure Activism: The Politics of Feeling Good*. Chico, CA: AK Press, 2019.
2. Lorde, Audre. "Uses of the Erotic." In *Sister Outsider: Essays and Speeches*. Crossing Press Feminist Series. Trumansburg, NY: Crossing Press, 1984.
3. Lorde, Audre. "Uses of the Erotic." In *Sister Outsider: Essays and Speeches*. Crossing Press Feminist Series. Trumansburg, NY: Crossing Press, 1984.
4. Fielding, Lucie. *Trans Sex: Clinical Approaches to Trans Sexualities and Erotic Embodiments*. New York: Routledge, 2021.
5. Fielding, Lucie. *Trans Sex: Clinical Approaches to Trans Sexualities and Erotic Embodiments*. New York: Routledge, 2021.
6. Nagoski, Emily. *Come as You Are: The Surprising New Science That Will Transform Your Sex Life*. Rev. ed. New York: Simon & Schuster Paperbacks, 2021.

7. Nagoski, Emily. *Come as You Are: The Surprising New Science That Will Transform Your Sex Life*. Rev. ed. New York: Simon & Schuster Paperbacks, 2021.
8. Nagoski, Emily, and Amelia Nagoski. *Burnout: The Secret to Unlocking the Stress Cycle*. New York: Ballantine Books, 2019.
9. Brown, C. Brené. *Daring Greatly: How the Courage to Be Vulnerable Transforms the Way We Live, Love, Parent, and Lead*. New York: Gotham Books, 2012.
10. Serano, J. "Autogynephilia: A Scientific Review, Feminist Analysis, and Alternative 'Embodiment Fantasies' Model." *The Sociological Review* 68, no. 4 (2020): 763–78. https://doi.org/10.1177/0038026120934690.
11. Brown, C. Brené. *Daring Greatly: How the Courage to Be Vulnerable Transforms the Way We Live, Love, Parent, and Lead*. New York: Gotham Books, 2012.
12. Taylor, Sonya Renee. *The Body Is Not an Apology: The Power of Radical Self-Love*. 2nd ed. Oakland, CA: Berrett-Koehler Publishers, 2021.
13. Fielding, Lucie. *Trans Sex: Clinical Approaches to Trans Sexualities and Erotic Embodiments*. New York: Routledge, 2021.

Chapter 9

1. Lindley, Louis, Annalisa Anzani, Antonio Prunas, and M. Paz Galupo. "Sexual Satisfaction in Trans Masculine and Nonbinary Individuals: A Qualitative Investigation." *Journal of Sex Research* 58, no. 2 (February 2021): 222–34. https://doi.org/10.1080/00224499.2020.1799317.
2. Goldbach, Chloe, Louis Lindley, Annalisa Anzani, and M. Paz Galupo. "Resisting Trans Medicalization: Body Satisfaction and Social Contextual Factors as Predictors of Sexual Experiences among Trans Feminine and Nonbinary Individuals." *Journal of Sex Research*, January 25, 2022. https://pubmed.ncbi.nlm.nih.gov/35076336/.
3. Nagoski, Emily. *Come as You Are: The Surprising New Science That Will Transform Your Sex Life*. Rev. ed. New York: Simon & Schuster Paperbacks, 2021.
4. Fielding, Lucie. *Trans Sex: Clinical Approaches to Trans Sexualities and Erotic Embodiments*. New York: Routledge, 2021.
5. Van Anders, Sari M., Alex Iantaffi, and Meg-John Barker. *Mapping Your Sexuality*. https://www.queensu.ca/psychology/van-anders-lab/SCTzine.pdf; Van Anders, Sari M. "Beyond Sexual Orientation: Integrating Gender/Sex and Diverse Sexualities via Sexual Configurations Theory." *Archives of Sexual Behavior* 44, no. 5 (July 2015). https://doi.org/10.1007/s10508-015-0490-8.
6. Van Anders, Sari M. "Beyond Sexual Orientation: Integrating Gender/Sex and Diverse Sexualities via Sexual Configurations Theory." *Archives of Sexual Behavior* 44, no. 5 (July 2015). https://doi.org/10.1007/s10508-015-0490-8.
7. Conversion therapy is against the ethical codes of every major mental health association in the United States. "Resolution on Appropriate Affirmative Responses to Sexual Orientation Distress and Change Efforts." American Psychological Association. Accessed May 31, 2022. https://www.apa.org/about/policy/sexual-orientation. Turban, Jack L., Noor Beckwith, Sari L. Reisner, and Alex S. Keuroghlian. "Association between Recalled Exposure to Gender Identity Conversion Efforts and Psychological Distress and Suicide Attempts among Transgender Adults." *JAMA Psychiatry* 77, no. 1 (January 1, 2020): 68–76. https://doi.org/10.1001/jamapsychiatry.2019.2285.
8. van Anders, Sari M. "Beyond Sexual Orientation: Integrating Gender/Sex and Diverse Sexualities via Sexual Configurations Theory." *Archives of Sexual Behavior* 44, no. 5 (July 2015). https://doi.org/10.1007/s10508-015-0490-8.

9. Lindley, Lou. Interview with the author. January 7, 2022.
10. Nagoski, Emily. *Come as You Are: The Surprising New Science That Will Transform Your Sex Life*. Rev. ed. New York: Simon & Schuster Paperbacks, 2021.
11. *Fucking Trans Women*. Accessed May 14, 2022. https://fuckingtranswomen.tumblr.com/.
12. Cascalheira, Cory J., Ellen E. Ijebor, Yelena Salkowitz, Tracie L. Hitter, and Allison Boyce. "Curative Kink: Survivors of Early Abuse Transform Trauma through BDSM." *Sexual and Relationship Therapy*, June 15, 2021. https://www.tandfonline.com/doi/abs/10.1080/14681994.2021.1937599.
13. Lindley, Louis, Annalisa Anzani, Antonio Prunas, and M. Paz Galupo. "Sexual Satisfaction in Trans Masculine and Nonbinary Individuals: A Qualitative Investigation." *Journal of Sex Research* 58, no. 2 (February 2021): 222–34. https://doi.org/10.1080/00224499.2020.1799317.
14. Goldbach, Chloe, Louis Lindley, Annalisa Anzani, and M. Paz Galupo. "Resisting Trans Medicalization: Body Satisfaction and Social Contextual Factors as Predictors of Sexual Experiences among Trans Feminine and Nonbinary Individuals." *Journal of Sex Research*, January 25, 2022. https://pubmed.ncbi.nlm.nih.gov/35076336/.
15. Brown, Brené. "The Fast Track to Genuine Joy." Oprah.com. Accessed May 20, 2022. https://www.oprah.com/omagazine/catastrophizing-how-to-feel-joy-without-fear.
16. Lindley, Louis, Annalisa Anzani, Antonio Prunas, and M. Paz Galupo. "Sexual Satisfaction in Trans Masculine and Nonbinary Individuals: A Qualitative Investigation." *Journal of Sex Research* 58, no. 2 (February 2021): 222–34. https://doi.org/10.1080/00224499.2020.1799317.
17. Lindley, Louis, Annalisa Anzani, Antonio Prunas, and M. Paz Galupo. "Sexual Satisfaction in Trans Masculine and Nonbinary Individuals: A Qualitative Investigation." *Journal of Sex Research* 58, no. 2 (February 2021): 222–34. https://doi.org/10.1080/00224499.2020.1799317.

Chapter 10

1. Spade, Dean. "For Lovers and Fighters." In *We Don't Need Another Wave: Dispatches from the Next Generation of Feminists*, edited by Melody Berger. Emeryville, CA: Seal Press, 2006.
2. Dictionary.com, s.v., "familiarity." Accessed September 2, 2022. https://www.dictionary.com/browse/familiarity.
3. Wikipedia, s.v., "Holmes and Rahe Stress Scale." March 16, 2022. https://en.wikipedia.org/w/index.php?title=Holmes_and_Rahe_stress_scale&oldid=1077447340.
4. Nagoski, Emily, and Amelia Nagoski. *Burnout: The Secret to Unlocking the Stress Cycle*. New York: Ballantine Books, 2019.
5. Fern, Jessica. *Polysecure: Attachment, Trauma and Consensual Nonmonogamy*. Portland, OR: Thorntree Press, 2020.
6. "ASLA 2006 Student Awards." American Society of Landscape Architects. Accessed September 2, 2022. https://www.asla.org/awards/2006/studentawards/282.html.
7. Brown, Brené. *Dare to Lead: Brave Work, Tough Conversations, Whole Hearts*. New York: Random House, 2018.

Chapter 11

1. Pastiloff, Jennifer. *On Being Human: A Memoir of Waking Up, Living Real, and Listening Hard*. New York: Dutton, 2019. Pastiloff, Jennifer. "Writing and the Body." Corporeal Writing. (workshop) August 2022. Hosted by Corporeal Writing (https://www.corporealwriting.com/current-offerings-sign-up?category=Face2Face+Creative+Labs)
2. Mohr, Tara. *Playing Big: Find Your Voice, Your Mission, Your Message*. New York: Avery, 2015.

3. Colangelo, Dr. Julia. Interview with the author. August 10, 2022. Csikszentmihalyi, Mihaly. *Flow: The Psychology of Optimal Experience*. New York: Harper & Row, 1990.
4. Csikszentmihalyi, Mihaly. *Flow: The Psychology of Optimal Experience*. New York: Harper & Row, 1990.
5. Colangelo, Dr. Julia. Interview with the author. August 10, 2022.

Chapter 12

1. Wikipedia, s.v., "Fictive Kinship." Accessed April 28, 2022. https://en.wikipedia.org/w/index.php?title=Fictive_kinship&oldid=1085134993.
2. "Social Determinants of Health at CDC." CDC. Accessed September 30, 2021. https://www.cdc.gov/socialdeterminants/index.htm.
3. Budge, Stephanie L., Jill L. Adelson, and Kimberly A. S. Howard. "Anxiety and Depression in Transgender Individuals: The Roles of Transition Status, Loss, Social Support, and Coping." *Journal of Consulting and Clinical Psychology* 81, no. 3 (2013): 545–57. https://doi.org/10.1037/a0031774.

Chapter 13

1. Dictionary.com, s.v., "pride (*n.*)." Accessed September 5, 2022. https://www.dictionary.com/browse/pride.
2. Yuknavitch, Lidia. *The Misfit's Manifesto*. New York: TED Books, Simon & Schuster, 2017.
3. Budge, Stephanie L., Mun Yuk Chin, and Laura P. Minero. "Trans Individuals' Facilitative Coping: An Analysis of Internal and External Processes." *Journal of Counseling Psychology* 64, no. 1 (January 1, 2017): 12–25. https://doi.org/10.1037/cou0000178.
4. Dictionary.com, s.v., "pride (n.)." Accessed September 5, 2022. https://www.dictionary.com/browse/pride.
5. Tucker, Abigail. "The Truth about Lions." *Smithsonian Magazine*, January 2010. Accessed August 17, 2022. https://www.smithsonianmag.com/science-nature/the-truth-about-lions-11558237/.
6. Budge, Stephanie L., Mun Yuk Chin, and Laura P. Minero. "Trans Individuals' Facilitative Coping: An Analysis of Internal and External Processes." *Journal of Counseling Psychology* 64, no. 1 (January 1, 2017): 12–25. https://doi.org/10.1037/cou0000178.
7. Kuhn, Dr. Roger. Interview with the author. November 2021.
8. Brockell, Gillian. "The Transgender Women at Stonewall Were Pushed out of the Gay Rights Movement. Now They Are Getting a Statue in New York." *Washington Post*, June 12, 2019. Accessed October 10, 2022. https://www.washingtonpost.com/history/2019/06/12/transgender-women-heart-stonewall-riots-are-getting-statue-new-york/.
9. Angelou, Maya. "A Conversation with Maya Angelou." Interview by Bill Moyers. November 21, 1973. Accessed August 19, 2022. https://billmoyers.com/content/conversation-maya-angelou/.
10. Campillo, Robin, dir. *Beats per Minute*. 2017. Memento Films.
11. Tucker, Abigail. "The Truth about Lions." *Smithsonian Magazine*, January 2010. Accessed August 17, 2022. https://www.smithsonianmag.com/science-nature/the-truth-about-lions-11558237/.

Conclusion

1. Elisabeth Kübler-Ross, ed., *Death: The Final Stage of Growth*, Spectrum Book (Englewood Cliffs, N.J.: Prentice-Hall, 1975).

About the Author

Rae McDaniel is a non-binary therapist, certified sex therapist, coach, and transgender diversity and inclusion educator. They are founder and CEO of Practical Audacity, a gender and sex therapy practice in Chicago, and an international speaker on gender freedom. As an expert in sexuality and gender exploration, they have been featured in places such as the *New York Times*, the *Chicago Tribune*, *Time*, *Women's Health*, Well+Good, Refinery29, *Bustle*, Elite Daily, *Entrepreneur*, and the *Independent*. Rae holds degrees from DePaul University and the University of Michigan and is certified by AASECT. They live in Chicago with their dog, Gizmo, who might actually be a gremlin.